# GROUND BEEF COOKBOOK

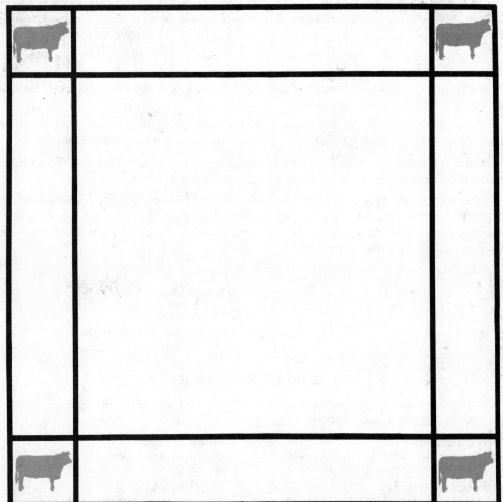

## Favorite Recipes® of Home Economics Teachers

©Favorite Recipes Press, A Division of Great American Opportunities Inc. MCMLXXXIII
P. O. Box 77, Nashville, Tennessee 37202
Library of Congress Cataloging in Publication Data on Page 167.

Cover photograph recipe on page 73.
Page 1 photograph recipe on page 94.
Page 2 photograph recipe on page 34.

# Dear Homemaker:

Home Economics — now more than ever — is vital to the quality of life because never before has the proper management of personal and public resources been so important.

Who do we find on the forefront meeting these modern challenges? The new Home Economics teacher, of course ... more professional than ever before, because today's Home Economics demands it!

In home management, it's the Home Economics teacher who's teaching young people about the dilemmas and complications of the modern home: how to manage a career and home, to keep a family healthy and happy, to develop a realistic budget in a tough economy and to stay on top of all that is new for the home and family.

As a vocational leader, today's Home Economics teacher is serving business and industry by preparing our young people for the highest quality of service in tomorrow's job market.

There is no question about it, today's amazing Home Economics teacher is a practical professional who's dedicated to making our lives easier, better, more enjoyable!

This new *Ground Beef Cookbook* reflects the practical thinking of today's professional Home Economics teacher. It's a basic, versatile cookbook designed for everyday use, featuring recipes that are budget-wise and an inspiration for menu planning. Keep it on a handy kitchen shelf because you will use it over and over!

Sincerely,

*Mary Jane Blount*

Mary Jane Blount
FAVORITE RECIPES PRESS

## BOARD OF ADVISORS

# Contents

Picadillo Peppers recipe on page 102.

# Ground Beef--The Family-Pleasing Favorite

Packed with high quality nutrition and satisfying good taste, ground beef is probably unequaled in its versatility and economy. For that reason, there are very few smart homemakers who enter the grocery store without ground beef on their shopping list. It's a basic element for success in menu planning today!

No matter what your taste for mealtime is, ground beef can fit right in. It can be elegant or casual, creamy or robust, planned in advance or prepared on the spur-of-the-moment. Think of the variations . . . each a family-pleasing favorite! Ground beef can be "basic American" meat-and-potatoes, spicy Mexican, zesty Italian, savory Greek, German, Swedish, or Oriental — you name it!

You can choose ground beef with confidence to be the center of attention in almost any form. Soups, stews, casseroles, sandwiches or on the grill, ground beef is just right! It may even be presented in attractive rings, loaves, and layers for extra-special effects.

## BUYING GROUND BEEF

Ground beef is available year round. It is most often prepared from the least popular cuts of beef and is available in several grades. Select from these according to how you plan to use the ground beef:

*Hamburger:* contains the largest percentage of fat allowed by law, up to 30%.

*Ground Beef:* contains 20%-25% fat.

*Ground Chuck:* contains 15%-25% fat.

*Ground Round:* very lean, contains approximately 11% fat.

Ground chuck is probably the best all-around grade. It will neither shrink too much during broiling or grilling nor become too dry. For a recipe that calls for browning the ground meat and draining the fat before combining with other ingredients, hamburger and ground beef are acceptable. The leaner forms, such as ground round or ground sirloin, are usually fine for hot oil fondue or meatball recipes cooked and served in a sauce to keep them moist. For outdoor grilling, the leaner grinds would need added fat, or to be combined with a fatter meat such as hamburger, ground beef, ground pork or sausage.

## STORING GROUND BEEF

To ensure buying only fresh, top quality ground beef, avoid buying ground beef that has been frozen and thawed. Keep ground beef in the coldest part of your refrigerator after removing the store wrappings and loosely covering with waxed paper. Store in refrigerator no longer than two days before use. Avoid storing in the refrigerator any longer than a few hours before freezing.

For best results in freezing ground beef, remove the store wrappings and rewrap meat snugly in freezer paper. Freeze up to two weeks in freezing compartment of refrigerator; up to 4 months in home freezer unit.

It is very thrifty to buy ground meat in large quantities when it is offered at special prices and then freeze it. Prepare meatballs, casseroles, meat patties, loaves and rings in advance and store in freezer for convenient use later.

## FREEZING GROUND BEEF CASSEROLES

A casserole featuring ground beef is probably one of the most delicious and economical ways imaginable to serve your family a nutritious beef meal. To save extra time and money, prepare enough of the casserole mixture for two meals — one to cook now, the other to freeze for later use. Many of the following freezer tips apply equally to freezing meatballs, meat loaves, meat patties and so forth.

- Salad greens, raw vegetables, and fried foods do not freeze well.
- Add diced potatoes before reheating casseroles, as they become mushy when frozen.
- Fats, which become rancid after two months, should be used sparingly in frozen casseroles.
- Seasonings, except onions, become stronger after freezing, so use sparingly. Onions tend to lose their flavor.
- Toppings for casseroles should be added just before reheating, as should monosodium glutamate, which is used to bring out the flavor of meats and vegetables.
- Undercook casseroles that will be frozen, or the ingredients may overcook during reheating.

## PREPARING AND FREEZING GROUND MEAT PATTIES

One of the great things about ground beef is that it can be a "convenience food" for your menu planning, but with all the homemade goodness and nutrition you demand for your family's meals. Meat patties are ideal to prepare in advance to store in the freezer, ready to thaw and cook on short notice. For best results, use care and forethought.

Use a light touch when shaping patties, meatballs, or any ground meat mixture. If not, the meat may become too compact and toughen during cooking. Go easy on the seasonings before cooking. One teaspoon of salt and 1/8-1/4 teaspoon of pepper per pound of meat is suggested. Add other seasonings and herbs for flavor variety but with a light touch. To avoid overhandling the meat, stir in seasonings with a fork. Wrap the patties singly or in groups of two to four, with waxed paper between each patty to make them easy to separate later. Be sure to label and date the package.

If you're caught on very short notice and must cook meat patties while they're still frozen, take care for best results. Brown each side quickly in the hot skillet, then turn down the heat, cover the patties, and cook them slowly. Turn several times to complete the cooking process to your taste.

Cooked indoors or out, hamburgers are universal family and company favorites. Use your imagination when preparing patties and you may never serve exactly the same patty twice! Here are some suggestions:

On a hot, steaming patty, spread:
- Grated cheese and crumbled, crisp bacon
- Or a mixture of 2 tablespoons melted butter and
  - 1 tablespoon cream cheese, 2 tablespoons chopped chives
  - 1 tablespoon horseradish, 1 teaspoon garlic salt
  - 1 tablespoon lemon juice, dash of nutmeg
  - 1 tablespoon prepared mild or spicy mustard
  - 2 tablespoons blue cheese

*Broiled Patties:* For rare, cook 12-15 minutes or until meat thermometer reads 140°F.

For medium, cook 18-20 minutes or until meat thermometer reads 160°F.

*Grilled Patties:* 1/2 inch patties on medium-hot coals, half the total cooking time per side

For rare, 8-10 minutes total time

For medium, 10-12 minutes total time

To test for medium-hot coals, hold the palms of your hands four inches above the coals. Counting "one thousand one, one thousand two, one thousand three," etc., you should be able to hold your hands above the coals approximately three seconds. For medium coals, approximately four seconds. Add 2-3 minutes total cooking time for medium coals. Note: Meat patties do not respond well to microwave oven cooking.

## MEAT LOAVES AND MEATBALLS

In many homes, meat loaf means "humdrum." But you can change all that with a few imaginative ideas. First, consider different ways to garnish your favorite meat loaf recipe. Frost with mashed potatoes or pipe a fancy rope of mashed potatoes around the upper edge. Add a little color with radish roses, bell pepper rings, carrot curls or parsley. Or, during the last few minutes of cooking, lay process cheese slices over the loaf to melt. You can also invent delicious and varied stuffing ideas for your meat loaf.

Unlike meat loaf, meatballs aren't prepared often enough in day to day menu planning because they seem like "so much trouble." But the use of meatballs can add so much taste variety to mealtime, why not freeze your family's favorites in advance? For best results, place the shaped, uncooked meatballs on a cookie sheet and leave in freezer until frozen. Then transfer desired amounts of the meatballs to plastic bags. You can later remove as many as you need and they'll be ready almost right away! Remember to label and date each freezer package.

As an added note, both meatballs and meat loaves are usually very well suited for the slow cooker and the microwave. For proper cooking methods, consult the cookbooks specifically geared to these appliances.

If you're like most homemakers, you sometimes feel as if you couldn't come up with a new idea for dinner for all the money in the world. Home Economics teachers hope this new *Ground Beef Cookbook* can show you many new ideas for mealtime — very economically, and to the complete delight of your family, friends and yourself!

# Appetizers & Salads

## APPETIZER BEEF PATTIES

2 lb. ground beef
1 egg, beaten
2 tbsp. chopped onion
1 tbsp. Worcestershire sauce
1 1/2 tsp. salt
1/4 tsp. each pepper, nutmeg
1 can cheese soup
3/4 c. cream
2 tsp. mustard

**Combine** .... first 7 ingredients in bowl, mixing well.
**Shape** ...... into bite-sized patties.
**Place** ....... in baking dish.
**Bake** ....... at 400 degrees for 10 to 12 minutes.
**Blend** ...... soup, cream and mustard in saucepan.
**Cook** ....... until heated through, stirring frequently.
**Serve** ....... patties on toothpicks with cheese sauce.
**Yields** ...... 5 dozen.

Sue Lawson
Haworth H. S., Haworth, Oklahoma

## BACON ROLL-UPS

1/2 c. margarine
3 c. herb-seasoned stuffing mix
2 eggs, beaten
1/4 lb. each ground beef, hot sausage, crumbled
1 lb. sliced bacon, cut into thirds

**Melt** ....... margarine in 1 cup water in saucepan.
**Remove** .... from heat.
**Combine** .... with stuffing mix in large bowl, mixing well; chill.
**Add** ....... remaining ingredients except bacon, mixing well.
**Shape** ...... into pecan-shaped balls.
**Wrap** ....... with bacon; secure with toothpicks.
**Place** ....... in baking dish.
**Bake** ....... at 375 degrees for 35 minutes or until bacon is crisp.
**Yields** ...... 6 dozen.

Judy Ender
Stamford H. S., Stamford, Texas

## CHEESY BEEF HORS D'OEUVRES

Tabasco sauce
1/4 c. butter, softened
2/3 c. sifted flour
1   3-oz. package sharp process cheese, crumbled
1/2 lb. ground beef
1/3 c. dry bread crumbs
1 egg
2 tsp. chopped parsley
1/2 tsp. salt
1/8 tsp. dry mustard
Pinch of nutmeg
Sesame seed

**Cream** ...... 1/4 teaspoon Tabasco sauce and butter in bowl.
**Add** ....... flour and cheese, mixing well.
**Chill** ....... for 1 hour.
**Combine** .... next 7 ingredients and 1/8 teaspoon Tabasco sauce in bowl, mixing well.
**Roll** ....... chilled pastry 1/8 inch thick on floured surface.
**Cut** ........ 2/3 of the pastry into 2 1/2-inch squares, 3-inch triangles and 2-inch circles.
**Place** ....... 1/2 to 1 teaspoonful ground beef mixture on each shape.
**Fold** ....... corners of squares to center, pinching to seal.

Roll . . . . . . . triangles as for crescent rolls.
Leave . . . . . . rounds open-faced.
Cut . . . . . . . . remaining pastry into sticks and triangles.
Sprinkle . . . . with sesame seed.
Place . . . . . . . pastries on baking sheet.
Bake . . . . . . . at 350 degrees for 12 minutes.
Yields . . . . . . 2 dozen.

Photograph for this recipe on opposite page.

## CHILEAN EMPANADAS

2 med. onions, chopped
Oil
1 1/2 lb. ground beef
1 tbsp. paprika
1 tsp. salt
1/2 tsp. pepper
2 cans refrigerator biscuits
4 oz. raisins
3 hard-boiled eggs, chopped
1 can ripe olives, chopped (opt.)

Saute . . . . . . onions in a small amount of oil in skillet.
Add . . . . . . . ground beef and seasonings.
Brown . . . . . . ground beef, stirring until crumbly.
Roll . . . . . . . each biscuit into thin circle on floured surface.
Spoon . . . . . . ground beef mixture onto center of each circle.
Add . . . . . . . raisins, eggs and olives.
Fold . . . . . . . to enclose filling, sealing edges.
Fry . . . . . . . . in medium-hot deep oil until golden brown; drain.
Yields . . . . . . 20 servings.

Patricia A. Ervin
Kempsville Jr. H. S., Virginia Beach, Virginia

## COCKTAIL PASTIES

4 slices bacon
1 lb. ground beef
1 can cream of mushroom soup
1/2 med. onion, chopped
1/2 green pepper, chopped
3 c. flour
1 tsp. salt
2 sticks margarine
1 egg, beaten
2 tbsp. vinegar

Cook . . . . . . bacon in skillet until crisp; drain and crumble.
Brown . . . . . . ground beef in 1 tablespoon bacon drippings, stirring until crumbly.
Stir . . . . . . . . in next 3 ingredients.
Cook . . . . . . until thickened; cool.
Add . . . . . . . crumbled bacon.
Mix . . . . . . . . flour and salt in bowl.
Cut . . . . . . . . in margarine until crumbly.
Mix . . . . . . . . egg with 4 tablespoons water and vinegar.
Combine . . . . egg and flour mixtures, stirring until dough leaves side of bowl.
Roll . . . . . . . on floured surface.
Cut . . . . . . . . into 4-inch circles.
Spoon . . . . . . 1 tablespoon beef mixture onto each round.
Fold . . . . . . . to enclose filling, crimping edges to seal.
Place . . . . . . . on baking sheet.
Bake . . . . . . . at 400 degrees for 10 to 15 minutes or until brown.
Yields . . . . . . 40 servings.

Mary French
Alcona H. S., Lincoln, Michigan

## GROUND BEEF PINWHEELS

1 pkg. refrigerator biscuits
1/2 lb. ground beef
1 tbsp. each chopped onion, green pepper
1/2 tsp. salt
1/4 tsp. Worcestershire sauce
1/2 c. peas and carrots, cooked
1 pkg. brown gravy mix, prepared

Shape . . . . . . biscuit dough into ball.
Roll . . . . . . . into 8 x 14-inch rectangle.
Combine . . . . next 5 ingredients in bowl, mixing well.
Spread . . . . . evenly on dough.
Roll . . . . . . . as for jelly roll from long side.
Slice . . . . . . . 1 inch thick.
Place . . . . . . . on lightly greased baking sheet.
Bake . . . . . . . at 400 degrees for 15 minutes or until brown.
Add . . . . . . . peas and carrots to prepared gravy, mixing well.
Pour . . . . . . . over pinwheels.
Yields . . . . . . 12-14 servings.

Roseann Campbell
Warren Harding H. S., Bridgeport, Connecticut

## HANKY PANKIES

1 lb. each ground beef, hot sausage
1 lb. American cheese, cubed
1 tsp. Worcestershire sauce
1 tsp. oregano
1/2 tsp. each salt, garlic salt
Dash of pepper
Party rye bread

**Brown** . . . . . . ground beef and sausage in skillet, stirring until crumbly; drain.
**Add** . . . . . . . cheese.
**Cook** . . . . . . . until cheese is melted, stirring constantly.
**Mix** . . . . . . . . in seasonings.
**Spread** . . . . . on bread.
**Place** . . . . . . . on baking sheet.
**Broil** . . . . . . . for 5 minutes.
**Yields** . . . . . . 75-80 servings.

Melba Sue Hanks
Preble Shawnee H. S., Camden, Ohio

## MARINATED DOLMATHES

1/2 lb. ground beef
1/3 c. chopped onion
Olive oil
1 c. cooked rice
1/2 c. chopped roasted almonds
1 tbsp. dried mint
2 tbsp. beef gravy
1 tbsp. honey
1/2 tsp. salt
1/4 tsp. cinnamon
Pepper to taste
Lemon juice
30 Athena Vine leaves

**Brown** . . . . . . ground beef with onion in 1 tablespoon olive oil in skillet until crumbly.
**Stir** . . . . . . . . in rice, next 7 ingredients and 1 tablespoon lemon juice.
**Cook** . . . . . . . for 5 minutes, stirring constantly; cool.
**Place** . . . . . . . leaves, shiny side down on board.
**Spoon** . . . . . . 1 tablespoon ground beef mixture on center of each leaf, rolling to enclose filling.
**Arrange** . . . . . in shallow dish.

**Pour** . . . . . . . mixture of 1/4 cup olive oil and 2 tablespoons lemon juice over stuffed leaves.
**Chill** . . . . . . . for 3 hours or longer.
**Serve** . . . . . . . cold on toothpicks.
**Yields** . . . . . . 30.

Photograph for this recipe above.

## PICKLE DILLY BURGER CUPS

1   13 3/4-oz. package hot roll mix
1 1/2 lb. ground beef
1/2 c. finely chopped dill pickles
1/3 c. chopped onion
1 clove of garlic, minced
1 tsp. salt
Dash of pepper
1/4 c. catsup
1/2 c. fine dry bread crumbs
4 oz. mozzarella cheese, cut into
    24 strips

**Prepare** . . . . . hot roll mix using package directions.
**Let** . . . . . . . . rise in warm place for 45 to 60 minutes or until doubled in bulk.
**Combine** . . . . next 8 ingredients in bowl, mixing well.
**Shape** . . . . . . into 12 balls.

Place ....... in shallow baking pan.
Bake ....... at 350 degrees for 15 minutes; drain.
Knead ...... dough on floured surface 4 or 5 times; divide into 12 portions.
Press ....... over bottom and side of greased muffin cups.
Place ....... meatballs in prepared cups.
Let ........ rise, covered, in warm place for 20 minutes.
Bake ....... at 350 degrees for 30 to 35 minutes or until edges are golden brown.
Place ....... 2 crossed cheese strips over top.
Bake ....... for 2 to 3 minutes longer or until cheese melts.
Yields ...... 1 dozen.

Photograph for this recipe on page 11.

## CURRIED BEEF WON TONS

*1/2 lb. ground beef*
*1/4 c. finely chopped green onions*
*1/2 tsp. each salt, cornstarch*
*1 1/2 tsp. each soy sauce, Sherry*
*1/8 tsp. freshly ground ginger*
*Oil*
*1 tsp. curry powder*
*1 pkg. won ton skins*
*1 egg white, slightly beaten*

Brown ...... ground beef with next 6 ingredients in 1 tablespoon oil in skillet, stirring until crumbly; drain.
Blend ...... curry powder with 2 teaspoons water in small bowl.
Stir ........ into ground beef mixture; cool.
Place ....... 1/2 teaspoon ground beef mixture in center of each won ton skin.
Moisten ..... edges lightly with egg white.
Fold ....... triangle, enclosing filling.
Fold ....... point of triangle back to long edge.
Cook ....... in 350-degree oil until golden brown; drain on paper towels.
Serve ...... with hot Chinese mustard or sweet-sour sauce.
Yields ...... 5 dozen.

Marilee A. Adams
Hoover Jr. H. S., San Jose, California

## EASY PIZZA APPETIZERS

*1 lb. each ground beef, hot sausage*
*1 lb. Velveeta cheese, diced*
*1 tbsp. oregano*
*1/2 tsp. garlic salt*
*1/2 tsp. Worcestershire sauce*
*1 loaf party rye bread*

Brown ...... ground beef and sausage in skillet, stirring until crumbly; drain.
Add ....... next 4 ingredients, stirring until cheese is melted.
Spread ..... on bread.
Place ....... on baking sheet.
Bake ....... at 400 degrees for 12 minutes or until bubbly.

Gloria Lorenz
Rolling Meadows H. S., Rolling Meadows, Illinois

## HOT CHIP DIP

*1 lb. hamburger*
*1 can Hormel chili without beans*
*1 bunch green onions, chopped*
*1 can green chilies, chopped*
*1 lb. Velveeta cheese, cubed*

Brown ...... hamburger in skillet, stirring until crumbly; drain.
Mix ........ all ingredients in baking dish.
Bake ....... at 275 degrees for 1 hour.
Serve ...... warm with large tortilla chips.

Mary Ellen Hornstra
Yankton Sr. H. S., Yankton, South Dakota

## HOT MEXICAN DIP

*1 lb. hamburger*
*1 onion, chopped*
*1 lb. Velveeta cheese, cubed*
*1 can jalapeno relish*
*2 tbsp. chili powder*
*2 tbsp. Worcestershire sauce*
*Salt to taste*

Brown ...... hamburger with onion in skillet, stirring until crumbly; drain.
Add ....... remaining ingredients, stirring until cheese melts.
Pour ....... into fondue pot.
Serve ...... warm.

Deb Sundem
Sandhills Public Sch., Dunning, Nebraska

## PIZZA DIP

1 lb. ground beef
1/4 c. minced onion
2 cloves of garlic, minced
1  8-oz. can tomato sauce
1/4 c. catsup
1 tsp. sugar
1 tsp. oregano
1/4 c. Parmesan cheese
1  8-oz. package cream cheese,
    cubed, softened

**Saute** ...... ground beef with onion and garlic in skillet until brown; drain.
**Add** ....... next 4 ingredients, mixing well.
**Simmer** ..... for 10 minutes.
**Add** ....... Parmesan cheese, mixing well.
**Mix** ........ in cream cheese.
**Pour** ....... into chafing dish.
**Serve** ....... warm with taco chips.
**Yields** ...... 2 1/2 cups.

Anita Sharp Alford
Madisonville North Hopkins H. S.
Madisonville, Kentucky

## PIZZA FONDUE

1 lb. ground beef
1 med. onion, chopped
1 tbsp. cornstarch
1 1/2 tsp. oregano
1/4 tsp. garlic powder
2  16 1/2-oz. cans pizza sauce
10 oz. Cheddar cheese, shredded
1 c. grated mozzarella cheese

**Brown** ...... ground beef in skillet, stirring until crumbly; drain.
**Add** ....... onion.
**Cook** ....... until tender, stirring occasionally.
**Add** ....... next 3 ingredients, mixing well.
**Mix** ........ in pizza sauce; reduce heat.
**Add** ....... cheeses, 1/3 cup at a time, mixing well after each addition.
**Pour** ....... into fondue pot.
**Serve** ....... warm with bread cubes or tortilla chips for dipping.

Carol Huffstetler
Boca Raton H. S., Boca Raton, Florida
Terry Rakes
Elmwood Jr. H. S., Rogers, Arkansas

## PARTY MEATBALLS

1 lb. lean ground beef
1 tsp. salt
1/2 c. crushed corn flakes
1/4 tsp. pepper
1/4 c. catsup
1/4 c. chopped onion
1/2 c. milk
2 tbsp. Worcestershire sauce
1  8-oz. can tomato sauce
1 tbsp. vinegar
3 tbsp. brown sugar

**Mix** ........ first 7 ingredients and 1 tablespoon Worcestershire sauce in bowl.
**Shape** ...... into 1-inch balls.
**Place** ....... in baking pan.
**Bake** ....... at 400 degrees until slightly brown.
**Mix** ........ remaining 1 tablespoon Worcestershire sauce with remaining ingredients in saucepan.
**Heat** ....... to serving temperature.
**Serve** ....... meatballs with sauce.
**Yields** ...... 3 dozen.

Margaret W. Lyles
Westminster H. S., Toccoa, Georgia

## YUMMY MEATBALLS

2 lb. lean ground beef
1 c. corn flakes, crushed
1/3 c. parsley flakes
2 eggs
2 tbsp. soy sauce
1/4 tsp. pepper
1/2 tsp. garlic powder
1/3 c. catsup
2 tbsp. dried onion
1  16-oz. can jellied cranberry sauce
1  12-oz. bottle of chili sauce
2 tbsp. brown sugar
1 tbsp. lemon juice

**Mix** ........ first 9 ingredients in large bowl.
**Shape** ...... into 1-inch balls.
**Arrange** ..... in rows in casserole.
**Blend** ...... remaining ingredients in bowl.
**Pour** ....... sauce over meatballs.
**Bake** ....... at 350 degrees for 30 minutes.

Colleen Liebhart
Meadville R-IV Sch., Meadville, Missouri

## BARBECUED MEATBALLS

2 lb. hamburger
1/4 c. bread crumbs
2 tbsp. milk
1/2 tsp. each Italian seasoning,
    oregano, parsley
1/4 tsp. salt
1/4 c. Parmesan cheese
4 c. barbecue sauce

**Combine** .... first 8 ingredients in bowl, mix-
    ing well.
**Shape** ...... into 1-inch balls.
**Place** ....... in shallow baking pan.
**Bake** ....... at 325 degrees for 15 minutes.
**Heat** ....... barbecue sauce in chafing dish.
**Add** ....... meatballs.
**Yields** ...... 10 servings.

Cathy S. Ferkes
Niceville H. S., Niceville, Florida

## BEEFY SAUSAGE BALLS

1/2 lb. lean ground beef
1/2 lb. hot sausage
3 c. biscuit mix
1 1/2 c. grated Cheddar cheese

**Mix** ........ all ingredients in large bowl.
**Shape** ...... into small balls.
**Place** ....... on baking sheet.
**Bake** ....... at 375 degrees for 10 minutes or
    until golden brown.
**Yields** ...... 5 dozen.

Kaye Derryberry
Webster Middle Sch, Oklahoma City, Oklahoma

## GOURMET MEATBALLS

2 lb. ground beef
1  12-oz. bottle of chili sauce
1  16-oz. can jellied cranberry sauce
1 can tomato soup

**Shape** ...... ground beef into small balls.
**Brown** ...... meatballs in skillet; drain.
**Place** ....... in baking dish.
**Combine** .... remaining ingredients in bowl,
    mixing well.
**Pour** ....... sauce over meatballs.
**Bake** ....... at 250 degrees for 2 hours.
**Yields** ...... 4 dozen.

Jenell R. Griffith
A. E. Beach H. S., Savannah, Georgia

## CHAFING DISH MEATBALLS

2 lb. ground beef
1 med. onion, grated
1 egg, slightly beaten
2 tsp. salt
1  12-oz. bottle of chili sauce
1 c. grape jelly
Juice of 1 lemon

**Combine** .... first 4 ingredients in bowl, mix-
    ing well.
**Shape** ...... into small balls.
**Mix** ........ remaining ingredients in large
    saucepan.
**Bring** ....... to a boil.
**Add** ....... meatballs.
**Simmer** ..... until cooked through; skim.
**Yields** ...... 60 meatballs.

Joyce Mansfield
St. Martin H. S., Biloxi, Mississippi
Betty P. Lee
Springfield Jr. H. S., Springfield, Georgia

## JUDY'S SWEET AND SOUR MEATBALLS

2 lb. ground beef
1 egg
1/2 c. bread crumbs
1 tsp. seasoned salt
1/2 tsp. seasoned pepper
3/4 tsp. garlic salt
2 tsp. French dressing
1  12-oz. bottle of chili sauce
1  10-oz. jar grape jelly

**Combine** .... first 7 ingredients in bowl, mix-
    ing well.
**Shape** ...... into small balls.
**Mix** ........ chili sauce, jelly and 1 1/2 cups
    water in large saucepan.
**Cook** ....... over low heat until jelly is dis-
    solved.
**Add** ....... meatballs.
**Simmer** ..... for 1 hour.
**Chill** ....... overnight.
**Remove** .... excess grease from top.
**Reheat** ..... to serving temperature.
**Yields** ...... about 40 meatballs

Judy Schwab
Badger H. S., Lake Geneva, Wisconsin

## HOSPITALITY PINEAPPLE MEATBALLS

    1  8 3/4-oz. can pineapple tidbits
    3 slices bread
    1 lb. lean ground beef
    2 eggs
    1 tsp. onion salt
    3 tbsp. butter
    2 tbsp. oil
    3/4 c. beef broth
    2 tbsp. lemon juice
    3 tbsp. catsup
    2 tsp. cornstarch

**Drain** ...... pineapple on paper towels, reserving 1/2 cup syrup.
**Soak** ....... bread in water in bowl; squeeze out excess moisture.
**Combine** .... bread, ground beef, eggs and onion salt in bowl, mixing well.
**Shape** ...... into small balls around pineapple pieces.
**Brown** ...... slowly in butter and oil in skillet; drain.
**Mix** ........ reserved pineapple syrup with remaining 4 ingredients.
**Pour** ....... over meatballs.
**Cook** ....... over moderate heat for 10 minutes or until sauce boils and thickens.
**Yields** ...... 2 1/2 dozen.

Photograph for this recipe on this page.

**Add** ....... remaining ingredients, mixing well.
**Pour** ....... over meatballs.
**Bake** ....... covered, at 350 degrees for 20 minutes.
**Yields** ...... 4 dozen.

Pat Leeser
Montgomery Co. R-II H. S.
Montgomery City, Missouri

## SAUCY COCKTAIL MEATBALLS

    1 lb. ground beef
    2 tbsp. bread crumbs
    1 egg, slightly beaten
    1/2 tsp. salt
    1/3 c. each finely chopped green pepper,
      onion
    2 tbsp. butter
    1 can tomato soup
    2 tbsp. brown sugar
    4 tsp. Worcestershire sauce
    1 tbsp. each prepared mustard, vinegar

**Mix** ........ first 4 ingredients in bowl.
**Shape** ...... into 1-inch balls.
**Place** ....... in 9 x 13-inch baking pan.
**Broil** ....... until brown; drain.
**Saute** ...... green pepper and onion in butter in skillet until tender.

## TINY SWEDISH MEATBALLS

    1 c. fine dried bread crumbs
    3/4 c. milk
    1/4 c. chopped onion
    2 tbsp. oil
    1 lb. each finely ground beef, pork
    3 eggs, slightly beaten
    2 tsp. salt
    1/2 tsp. allspice
    1 tsp. nutmeg
    1 can beef consomme

**Soak** ....... bread crumbs in milk in bowl.
**Saute** ...... onion in a small amount of oil in skillet until tender.
**Combine** .... bread crumbs, onion and next 6 ingredients in bowl, mixing well.
**Shape** ...... into 1-inch balls.
**Brown** ...... in remaining oil in skillet; drain.

**Stir** . . . . . . . . in consomme, mixing well.
**Simmer** . . . . . covered, for 20 minutes, or until consomme has been absorbed.

Dianne Wentzell
St. Martin H. S., Biloxi, Mississippi

## TACO MEATBALLS

*1 lb. lean ground beef*
*1/2 onion, chopped*
*1 egg, slightly beaten*
*1/2 pkg. taco mix*
*Salt, pepper, garlic powder to taste*

**Mix** . . . . . . . . all ingredients in bowl.
**Shape** . . . . . . into 1-inch balls.
**Place** . . . . . . . in baking dish.
**Bake** . . . . . . . at 400 degrees for 15 minutes or until brown.
**Serve** . . . . . . with toothpicks.
**Yields** . . . . . . 35-40 meatballs.

Janelle L. Jones
Spearfish Schools, Spearfish, South Dakota

## AUDREY'S TACO SALAD

*1 lb. ground beef*
*1/2 env. onion soup mix*
*1 head lettuce, torn into bite-sized pieces*
*1 lg. tomato, cut into wedges*
*1 sm. onion, sliced, separated into rings*
*1/4 c. chopped green pepper*
*1 c. shredded Cheddar cheese*
*1   6-oz. package corn chips*

**Brown** . . . . . . ground beef in skillet, stirring until crumbly; drain.
**Sprinkle** . . . . soup mix over top.
**Stir** . . . . . . . . in 3/4 cup water, mixing well.
**Simmer** . . . . . for 10 minutes.
**Combine** . . . . next 5 ingredients in large salad bowl, tossing to mix.
**Pour** . . . . . . . ground beef mixture over salad.
**Top** . . . . . . . . with corn chips.
**Yields** . . . . . . 4-6 servings.

Audrey Hasenbein
Mortimer Jordan H. S., Morris, Alabama

## MYRTLE'S TACO SALAD

*1 lb. lean ground beef*
*1 med. onion, minced*

*1/2 tsp. each salt, cuminseed*
*4 to 5 tbsp. taco sauce*
*1 head lettuce, shredded*
*2 tomatoes, chopped*
*1 cucumber, chopped*
*2 c. shredded Cheddar cheese*
*1 pkg. corn chips*

**Brown** . . . . . . ground beef with onion in skillet, stirring until crumbly.
**Stir** . . . . . . . . in next 3 ingredients and 1 cup water, mixing well.
**Simmer** . . . . . for 10 minutes.
**Combine** . . . . lettuce, tomatoes, cucumber and cheese in bowl, tossing lightly.
**Spoon** . . . . . . ground beef mixture over salad.
**Serve** . . . . . . with corn chips.
**Yields** . . . . . . 4 servings.

Myrtle D. Brookshire
Johnson County H. S., Mountain City, Tennessee

## TACO IN A BOWL

*1 lb. ground beef*
*1 pkg. taco seasoning mix*
*1 sm. can tomato sauce*
*1 can bean with bacon soup*
*1 can tomatoes*
*1/2 tsp. chili powder*
*Chopped green pepper*
*Corn chips*
*Grated cheese*
*Shredded lettuce*
*Chopped tomato*
*Chopped onion*
*Taco sauce*
*Sour cream*

**Brown** . . . . . . ground beef in skillet, stirring until crumbly; drain.
**Add** . . . . . . . next 5 ingredients and 1/4 cup green pepper.
**Simmer** . . . . . for 15 minutes.
**Layer** . . . . . . corn chips, ground beef mixture, cheese, lettuce, tomato, onion and green pepper in individual serving bowls.
**Top** . . . . . . . . with taco sauce and sour cream.
**Yields** . . . . . . 4-6 servings.

Susan Campbell
Independence Sr. H. S., Charlotte, North Carolina

## MEATBALL VEGETABLE SALAD

3/4 lb. ground beef
1/2 tsp. each garlic salt, seasoned pepper
1/4 c. oil
1/2 lb. zucchini, thinly sliced
1/4 c. cider vinegar
1 clove of garlic, minced
6 c. coarsely chopped iceberg lettuce
1 lg. tomato, cut into wedges
3/4 c. onion rings

Combine .... ground beef, garlic salt and seasoned pepper in bowl, mixing
well.
Shape ...... into 24 small balls.
Brown ...... in oil in skillet; remove meatballs.
Cook ....... next 3 ingredients in pan drippings until slightly heated.
Pour ....... over meatballs in bowl.
Chill ....... in refrigerator, stirring occasionally.
Combine .... with lettuce, tomato and onion
rings in salad bowl, tossing
gently.
Yields ...... 10-12 servings.

Photograph for this recipe above.

## MEDITERRANEAN MEATBALL SALAD

1/4 c. corn oil
1 tbsp. lemon juice
1 tsp. dried mint leaves
1 lb. ground round
1/2 c. finely grated onion
1/2 c. soft whole wheat bread crumbs

3 tbsp. chopped parsley
1/2 tsp. salt
1/4 tsp. pepper
1 1/2 c. diagonally sliced carrots,
cooked, drained
1 c. chopped green pepper
3 c. torn salad greens
1 lg. tomato, cut into wedges

Combine .... 2 tablespoons corn oil, 2 tablespoons water, lemon juice and
mint in small covered jar, shak-
ing well.
Chill ....... for 1 hour or longer.
Combine .... ground round with next 5 ingre-
dients in bowl, mixing well.
Shape ...... into 1-inch balls.
Brown ...... in remaining 2 tablespoons corn
oil in skillet; drain on paper
towels.
Combine .... meatballs with carrots and green
pepper in bowl, tossing to mix.
Chill ....... covered, for 1 hour.
Toss ....... with dressing.
Arrange ..... on serving plate with salad
greens and tomato.
Yields ...... 6 servings.

Photograph for this recipe on page 36.

## MEXICAN CHEF SALAD

1 head lettuce, chopped
4 tomatoes, chopped
1 onion, chopped
4 oz. cheese, grated
1 c. Thousand Island or French dressing
1 lb. ground beef
1 15-oz. can kidney beans, drained
Hot sauce to taste
1 lg. avocado, chopped
1 sm. bag tortilla chips, crushed

Combine .... first 5 ingredients in large salad
bowl, tossing to mix.
Brown ...... ground beef in skillet, stirring
until crumbly.
Add ....... kidney beans, mixing well.
Toss ....... with lettuce mixture.
Add ....... remaining 3 ingredients, tossing
well.
Yields ...... 6-8 servings.

Marie Campbell
Texas City H. S., Texas City, Texas

# Soups & Sandwiches

## QUICK AUTUMN SOUP

1/2 lb. ground beef
1/2 c. chopped onion
1/2 c. each chopped carrot, celery, potato
1 tsp. salt
1/4 tsp. pepper
1/2 tsp. meat extract
1 bay leaf, crumbled
Pinch of basil
1  1-lb. can tomatoes

Brown . . . . . . ground beef in soup pot, stirring until crumbly.
Add  . . . . . . . onion, mixing well.
Cook . . . . . . . for 5 minutes longer, stirring occasionally.
Stir . . . . . . . . in chopped vegetables, next 5 seasonings and 2 cups hot water.
Simmer . . . . . covered, for 20 minutes.
Stir . . . . . . . . in tomatoes.
Simmer . . . . . for 10 minutes longer.
Yields . . . . . . 6 servings.

Beth Azevedo
Wilton H. S., Wilton, Connecticut

## BEEF AND BEAN CHOWDER

1 lb. ground beef
1 onion, chopped
3 or 4 sm. potatoes, peeled, chopped
1  1-lb. can stewed tomatoes
1 can kidney beans
Salt and pepper to taste

Brown . . . . . . ground beef in large saucepan, stirring until crumbly.
Add  . . . . . . . onion, mixing well.
Cook . . . . . . . for 5 minutes longer, stirring occasionally.
Stir . . . . . . . . in remaining ingredients and 1 to 1 1/2 cups water.
Simmer . . . . . for 25 minutes.
Yields . . . . . . 6 servings.

Nancy Bledsoe
Fordsville H. S., Fordsville, Kentucky

## BURGER BEEF SOUP

1 lb. ground chuck
3 tbsp. margarine, melted
1/4 c. minced onion
3 c. tomato juice

2 cans cream of celery soup
1/4 tsp. each pepper, garlic salt
1 tsp. sugar
1 bay leaf
2 c. shredded carrot

Brown . . . . . . ground chuck in margarine in soup pot, stirring until crumbly.
Add  . . . . . . . onion.
Cook . . . . . . . until lightly browned, stirring occasionally.
Combine . . . . tomato juice and soup with 1 cup water in bowl, mixing well.
Add  . . . . . . . to ground chuck mixture.
Stir . . . . . . . . in remaining ingredients.
Simmer . . . . . covered, for 15 to 20 minutes or until carrot is tender.
Yields . . . . . . 4 servings.

Cynthia A. Cirelli
Lincoln H. S., Ellwood City, Pennsylvania

## GROUND BEEF-TOMATO SOUP

1 can green beans
1 can mixed vegetables
2 tbsp. each dried onion, vegetables, celery, parsley
1 lb. ground chuck
1 can tomato soup
1/2 tsp. each salt, pepper

Combine . . . . all ingredients with 2 soup cans water in soup pot.
Cook . . . . . . . over medium heat for 2 1/2 hours.
Yields . . . . . . 8 servings.

Mary Grace Ramey
Central H. S., Englewood, Tennessee

## HAMBURGER MINESTRONE SOUP

1 lb. hamburger
1/2 c. chopped onion
3/4 c. chopped celery
Garlic salt to taste
2 cans minestrone soup
1 can pork and beans
1/4 tsp. oregano
1 tbsp. Worcestershire sauce
Parmesan cheese

Brown . . . . . . hamburger in large saucepan, stirring until crumbly.

**Add** . . . . . . . onion.
**Cook** . . . . . . . until lightly browned, stirring occasionally.
**Stir** . . . . . . . . in remaining ingredients except Parmesan cheese with 2 soup cans water.
**Simmer** . . . . . for 1 hour.
**Sprinkle** . . . . with Parmesan cheese before serving.
**Yields** . . . . . . 6-8 servings.

Carolyn F. Chipman
Alta H. S., Sandy, Utah

## CAROLE'S VEGETABLE SOUP

1 1/2 lb. hamburger
3 med. carrots, chopped
2 med. stalks celery, chopped
1 lg. potato, coarsely chopped
2 med. onions, chopped
2 tsp. salt
1 tsp. Kitchen Bouquet
1/4 to 1/2 tsp. pepper
1 bay leaf
1/8 tsp. basil
1 28-oz. can tomatoes, mashed

**Brown** . . . . . . hamburger in soup pot, stirring until crumbly; drain.
**Stir** . . . . . . . . in remaining ingredients and 3 cups water.
**Simmer** . . . . . covered, for 20 minutes or until vegetables are tender.
**Yields** . . . . . . 6 servings.

Carole Fisher
Martinsville H. S., Martinsville, Indiana

## HEARTY HAMBURGER SOUP

1 lb. hamburger
1/8 tsp. each onion salt, garlic salt
2 8-oz. cans tomato sauce
2 lb. frozen mixed vegetables
2 med. potatoes, peeled, chopped
Salt and pepper to taste

**Brown** . . . . . . hamburger in 3-quart saucepan, stirring until crumbly.
**Add** . . . . . . . next 3 ingredients and 2 cups water, mixing well.
**Simmer** . . . . . covered, for 30 minutes.

**Stir** . . . . . . . . in mixed vegetables.
**Simmer** . . . . . covered, for 25 minutes longer.
**Add** . . . . . . . potatoes.
**Cook** . . . . . . . until potatoes are tender.
**Season** . . . . . with salt and pepper.
**Yields** . . . . . . 6-8 servings.

Dorothy M. Ham
Brantley County H. S., Nahunta, Georgia

## MEATBALL SOUP

2 eggs, beaten
1 1/2 c. soft bread crumbs
3 tbsp. grated Parmesan cheese
1 tbsp. each finely chopped onion, parsley
1 clove of garlic, minced
1/2 tsp. salt
3/4 lb. ground beef
6 c. beef broth
3 carrots, chopped
1 10-oz. package frozen peas

**Combine** . . . . first 7 ingredients in bowl, mixing well.
**Stir** . . . . . . . . in ground beef.
**Shape** . . . . . . into 48 meatballs.
**Brown** . . . . . . in skillet, shaking pan frequently; drain.
**Combine** . . . . with remaining ingredients in stock pot, mixing well.
**Simmer** . . . . . covered, for 20 to 30 minutes or until vegetables are tender.
**Yields** . . . . . . 6 servings.

Sandra Bassetto
White Cloud H. S., White Cloud, Michigan

## QUICK BEEF VEGETABLE SOUP

1 lb. ground beef
1 16-oz. package frozen mixed vegetables
2 c. beef bouillon broth
2 c. chopped potatoes
Salt and pepper to taste

**Brown** . . . . . . ground beef in saucepan, stirring until crumbly; drain.
**Stir** . . . . . . . . in remaining ingredients.
**Simmer** . . . . . for 30 minutes.
**Yields** . . . . . . 4-6 servings.

Opal Schubert
Western H. S., Buda, Illinois

## VEGETABLE SOUP WITH SOUP MIX

*1/4 lb. ground beef*
*1 onion, chopped*
*1 med. can okra and tomatoes*
*Salt to taste*
*1 med. can mixed vegetables*
*1 pkg. dry vegetable-beef soup mix*

**Cook** . . . . . . . first 3 ingredients in 3 to 4 quarts boiling salted water in soup pot for 40 to 50 minutes, or until okra is very tender.
**Stir** . . . . . . . . in mixed vegetables and soup mix.
**Simmer** . . . . . for 30 minutes.
**Yields** . . . . . . 6-8 servings.

Jeanne Fleming
Marked Tree H. S., Marked Tree, Arkansas

## AUNT EDRA'S STEW

*1 lb. ground beef*
*1 tbsp. each chopped onion, green pepper (opt.)*
*1   1-lb. can pork and beans*
*1   1-lb. can whole kernel corn*
*Salt and pepper to taste*

**Brown** . . . . . . ground beef with onion and green pepper in skillet, stirring until crumbly.
**Stir** . . . . . . . . in remaining ingredients.
**Simmer** . . . . . for 30 minutes.
**Yields** . . . . . . 4 servings.

Alice R. Carroll
West Hopkins H. S., Nebo, Kentucky

## BROWN HAMBURGER STEW

*1 lb. ground beef*
*1/4 c. flour*
*2 tsp. salt*
*1/4 tsp. pepper*
*2 tbsp. oil*
*3 carrots, sliced*
*3 potatoes, chopped*
*2 onions, sliced*
*2 c. tomato juice*

**Combine** . . . . first 4 ingredients in bowl, mixing well.
**Brown** . . . . . . in oil in skillet, stirring until crumbly; drain.

**Add** . . . . . . . carrots and 1 1/2 cups water, mixing well.
**Simmer** . . . . . covered, for 10 minutes.
**Stir** . . . . . . . . in potatoes and onions.
**Simmer** . . . . . for 10 minutes longer, or until vegetables are tender-crisp.
**Stir** . . . . . . . . in tomato juice.
**Cook** . . . . . . . until heated through.
**Yields** . . . . . . 5-6 servings.

Lynn Holmes
Waubonsie Valley H. S., Aurora, Illinois

## CAMPFIRE STEW

*1/2 lb. ground beef*
*1 sm. onion, chopped*
*1/2 green pepper, chopped*
*Salt and pepper to taste*
*2 cans vegetable soup*

**Brown** . . . . . . ground beef with onion and green pepper in skillet, stirring until crumbly.
**Stir** . . . . . . . . in remaining ingredients.
**Cook** . . . . . . . until heated through, stirring frequently.
**Yields** . . . . . . 4 servings.

Laura M. Studstill
Hawkinsville H. S., Hawkinsville, Georgia

## CHILI STEW WITH DUMPLINGS

*1/2 c. chopped onion*
*1 tbsp. shortening*
*2 lb. ground beef*
*2 tsp. chili powder*
*3 1/2 tsp. salt*
*1   15-oz. can kidney beans*
*2 1/2 c. chopped potatoes*
*1/2 tsp. pepper*
*1 can tomato soup*
*2 c. flour*
*4 tsp. baking powder*
*1 egg, beaten*
*3/4 c. milk*
*1   8-oz. carton sour cream*

**Saute** . . . . . . onion in shortening in skillet.
**Add** . . . . . . . ground beef, chili powder and 1 teaspoon salt.
**Brown** . . . . . . ground beef, stirring until crumbly.

**Combine** . . . . beans, potatoes, pepper, soup, 2 teaspoons salt and 5 cups water in large soup pot.
**Bring** . . . . . . . to a boil.
**Add** . . . . . . . ground beef mixture.
**Simmer** . . . . . for 1 hour.
**Combine** . . . . flour, baking powder, egg, milk and remaining 1/2 teaspoon salt in bowl, mixing well.
**Drop** . . . . . . . by spoonfuls into simmering stew.
**Cook** . . . . . . . covered, for 12 to 15 minutes, or until dumplings are cooked through.
**Stir** . . . . . . . . in sour cream just before serving.
**Yields** . . . . . . 12 large servings.

Ann Callaway
Jal H. S., Jal, New Mexico

# GROUND BEEF AND VEGETABLE STEW

1 lb. lean ground beef
2 med. onions, quartered
2 med. cloves of garlic, chopped (opt.)
1 tsp. basil
1 1/2 tsp. salt
1/4 tsp. pepper
8 med. new potatoes
2 med. green peppers, cut into eighths
1 16-oz. can tomatoes

**Brown** . . . . . . ground beef in soup pot, stirring until crumbly.
**Add** . . . . . . . next 6 ingredients and 1/2 cup hot water, mixing well.
**Simmer** . . . . . for 15 minutes or until potatoes are almost tender.
**Add** . . . . . . . green peppers and tomatoes.
**Simmer** . . . . . for 10 minutes longer or until vegetables are tender.
**Yields** . . . . . . 4-6 servings.

Barbara P. Witten
Richlands Middle Sch., Richlands, Virginia

# GROUND BEEF STEW

1 lb. ground beef
1 lb. small potatoes, peeled, thinly sliced
1 med. onion, chopped
1 1/2 tsp. salt
1/4 tsp. thyme
1/8 tsp. pepper

1 beef bouillon cube
1 10-oz. package frozen peas and carrots, thawed
1/4 c. catsup
2 tbsp. flour

**Brown** . . . . . . ground beef in large skillet, stirring until crumbly; drain.
**Add** . . . . . . . next 5 ingredients and bouillon cube dissolved in 1 1/2 cups boiling water, mixing well.
**Cook** . . . . . . . covered, for 15 minutes.
**Add** . . . . . . . peas and carrots with catsup, mixing well.
**Cook** . . . . . . . covered, for 10 minutes longer.
**Blend** . . . . . . flour with 1/4 cup cold water.
**Stir** . . . . . . . . into stew.
**Cook** . . . . . . . for 5 minutes longer or until thick, stirring constantly.
**Yields** . . . . . . 4 servings.

Photograph for this recipe above.

# TEX-MEX STEW

1 1/2 lb. ground beef
1/4 onion, chopped
1 can corn
1 can ranch-style beans
1 can tomato soup
1 tsp. each mustard, Worcestershire sauce
Salt to taste

**Brown** . . . . . . ground beef with onion in skillet, stirring until crumbly; drain.
**Stir** . . . . . . . . in remaining ingredients.
**Simmer** . . . . . for 20 minutes.

Nan Sulser
Chapel Hill H. S., Tyler, Texas

## ONE-POT SPANISH NOODLES

6 slices bacon, cut into 1-in. pieces
1 lb. ground beef
1 med. onion, chopped
1 green pepper, chopped
1  28-oz. can tomatoes in puree, mashed
1  15-oz. jar Marinara sauce
1 1/2 tsp. salt
Dash of pepper
8 oz. medium noodles
2/3 c. chopped pimento-stuffed olives

**Saute** . . . . . . bacon in soup pot until brown and crisp.
**Drain** . . . . . . reserving half the pan drippings.
**Brown** . . . . . . ground beef with onion and green pepper in pan drippings, stirring until crumbly.
**Add** . . . . . . . bacon and remaining ingredients, mixing well.
**Simmer** . . . . . covered, for 10 minutes or until noodles are tender.
**Garnish** . . . . . with green pepper rings.
**Yields** . . . . . . 6 servings.

Photograph for this recipe on page 21.

## SHIPWRECK STEW

1 lb. ground beef
3/4 c. chopped onion
1/4 c. rice
3 c. chopped potatoes
1  15-oz. can kidney beans
1  8-oz. can tomato paste
1/2 tsp. Worcestershire sauce
1/4 tsp. each chili powder, pepper
1 tsp. salt

**Brown** . . . . . . ground beef with onion in skillet, stirring until crumbly; drain.
**Layer** . . . . . . ground beef mixture, rice, potatoes and beans in large casserole.
**Combine** . . . . remaining ingredients with 1/2 cup water in bowl, mixing well.
**Pour** . . . . . . . over casserole.
**Bake** . . . . . . . covered, at 350 degrees for 1 1/2 hours.
**Yields** . . . . . . 6-8 servings.

Nadine Wiles
Madisonville North Hopkins H. S.
Madisonville, Kentucky

## BERLINER MEATBALL SANDWICHES

1 1/2 lb. ground beef
1/2 c. soft bread crumbs
1 egg, slightly beaten
1/4 c. each natural and golden
    California raisins
Salt and pepper to taste
1  16-oz. can stewed tomatoes
2 tbsp. brown sugar
6 lg. round rolls, split
Butter
German-style mustard
Dill pickle slices

**Combine** . . . . first 3 ingredients with raisins and seasonings in bowl, mixing well.
**Shape** . . . . . . into 6 large balls.
**Layer** . . . . . . meatballs, tomatoes and brown sugar in greased casserole.
**Bake** . . . . . . . at 400 degrees for 45 minutes.
**Scoop** . . . . . . out soft bread from center of rolls.
**Spread** . . . . . rolls with butter and mustard.
**Spoon** . . . . . . meatballs and sauce into cavities.
**Garnish** . . . . . with pickles.
**Yields** . . . . . . 6 servings.

Photograph for this recipe above.

## BUFFALO CHIPS

1 1/2 lb. ground beef
1 lb. sausage
2 tsp. oregano
1 tsp. red pepper
1/2 tsp. each salt, garlic salt

1 lb. Velveeta cheese, cut into chunks
Rye bread

**Brown** . . . . . . ground beef and sausage in skillet, stirring until crumbly; drain.
**Add** . . . . . . . seasonings and cheese, mixing well.
**Cook** . . . . . . . over low heat until cheese melts.
**Serve** . . . . . . . on rye bread.
**Yields** . . . . . . 10 servings.

Marcia Johnson
Prescott H. S., Prescott, Arkansas

## BURRITO OR TACO FILLING

1 lb. ground beef
1/2 onion, chopped
1 tsp. chili powder
1/8 tsp. Tabasco sauce
1 tbsp. flour
3/4 tsp. salt
1/4 tsp. garlic powder
1   16-oz. can whole tomatoes, drained

**Brown** . . . . . . ground beef with onion in skillet, stirring until crumbly; drain well.
**Add** . . . . . . . remaining ingredients, mixing well.
**Cook** . . . . . . . until heated through.
**Serve** . . . . . . . in flour tortillas or taco shells.
**Yields** . . . . . . 6 servings.

Clara Carroll
Des Arc H. S., Des Arc, Arizona

## CRAZY-MIXED-UP-PIZZA SANDWICHES

1/2 lb. hamburger
1/4 tsp. each garlic powder, oregano
Freshly ground pepper to taste
1   8-oz. can tomato sauce
1 c. grated mozzarella cheese
6 hot dog buns

**Brown** . . . . . . hamburger in skillet, stirring until crumbly.
**Mix** . . . . . . . . in seasonings and tomato sauce.
**Add** . . . . . . . 3/4 cup mozzarella cheese, stirring until melted.
**Fill** . . . . . . . . buns with mixture.
**Top** . . . . . . . . with remaining mozzarella cheese.

**Wrap** . . . . . . . each in aluminum foil.
**Bake** . . . . . . . at 400 degrees for 8 to 10 minutes or until heated through.
**Yields** . . . . . . 6 servings.

Joan E. Lowery
Meyersdale Area H. S., Meyersdale, Pennsylvania

## FRENCH HAMBURGERS

1/2 lb. lean ground beef
1 tsp. salt
2 tsp. mustard
1 1/2 tbsp. chili sauce
1 tbsp. each finely chopped onion,
   green pepper
2 1/2 oz. Velveeta cheese, cut into
   1/4-in. cubes
3 hamburger buns, split

**Mix** . . . . . . . . first 7 ingredients in bowl.
**Spread** . . . . . evenly over bun halves, covering completely.
**Place** . . . . . . . on baking sheet.
**Bake** . . . . . . . at 350 degrees for 15 minutes.
**Yields** . . . . . . 6 sandwiches.

Ruth Brasfield
Pelham Jr. H. S., Pelham, New York

## EASY HERO BURGERS

1 1/2 lb. ground beef
1 can tomato soup
4 tsp. dried onion flakes
1 tsp. each mustard, Worcestershire sauce
1 tsp. salt
6 hot dog buns
Cheese slices

**Combine** . . . . first 6 ingredients in bowl, mixing well.
**Spread** . . . . . evenly on hot dog bun halves, covering completely.
**Place** . . . . . . . on baking sheet.
**Broil** . . . . . . . 4 inches from heat source for 10 to 12 minutes.
**Top** . . . . . . . . with cheese.
**Broil** . . . . . . . until cheese is melted.
**Yields** . . . . . . 6 servings.

Mrs. Michael Sweat
West Hardin H. S., Stephensburg, Kentucky

## CHEESEBURGER HEROES

*2 loaves Brown and Serve French bread*
*1/4 c. butter, melted*
*3/4 c. Parmesan cheese*
*1 lb. ground beef*
*1  6-oz. can tomato paste*
*1/2 c. sliced green onions*
*1/4 c. chopped pimento-stuffed olives*
*1/4 c. chopped green pepper*
*1/2 tsp. each oregano, garlic salt*
*1/8 tsp. pepper*
*8 Cheddar cheese triangles*
*3 tomato slices, cut in half*

**Cut** . . . . . . . . bread in half lengthwise and place cut side down on baking sheet.
**Bake** . . . . . . . at 425 degrees for 10 minutes or until brown.
**Brush** . . . . . . butter mixed with 1/4 cup Parmesan cheese over cut sides of bread.
**Bake** . . . . . . . cut side up, for 5 minutes longer; set top halves aside.
**Combine** . . . . remaining 1/2 cup Parmesan cheese, next 5 ingredients and seasonings in bowl, mixing well.
**Spread** . . . . . over bottom halves of loaves.
**Bake** . . . . . . . at 350 degrees for 30 minutes.

**Place** . . . . . . . 4 cheese triangles and 3 tomato slices alternately on each loaf; replace tops.
**Bake** . . . . . . for 5 minutes longer or until cheese is melted.
**Yields** . . . . . . 6 servings.

Photograph for this recipe on this page.

## GONDOLA SANDWICH

*1 1/2 lb. ground beef*
*1 c. chopped onion*
*1/2 green pepper, chopped*
*1  2 1/2-oz. jar sliced mushrooms, drained*
*1  8-oz. can tomato sauce*
*1  6-oz. can tomato paste*
*1/4 c. grated Parmesan cheese*
*1/4 tsp. each oregano, garlic salt, rosemary*
*1 loaf French bread, split*
*1  6-oz. package mozzarella cheese slices*

**Brown** . . . . . . ground beef in skillet, stirring until crumbly; drain.
**Add** . . . . . . . onion, green pepper and mushrooms.
**Cook** . . . . . . . for 5 minutes, stirring occasionally.
**Mix** . . . . . . . . in next 6 ingredients and 1/4 cup water.
**Simmer** . . . . . for 10 minutes, stirring occasionally.
**Scoop** . . . . . . bread from bottom half of loaf, forming a shell.
**Spoon** . . . . . . in ground beef mixture.
**Top** . . . . . . . . with cheese.
**Replace** . . . . . top of loaf.
**Bake** . . . . . . . wrapped in foil at 400 degrees for 6 to 8 minutes or until heated through.
**Cut** . . . . . . . . into sandwiches.
**Yields** . . . . . . 8 servings.

Cynthia P. Dinsdale
Ben Lomond H. S., Ogden, Utah

## KROMESKIES

*2 lb. ground beef*
*1/2 c. instant mashed potato granules*
*1/4 c. catsup*
*1 tbsp. angostura aromatic bitters*
*2 tsp. salt*

1/4 tsp. pepper
4 eggs
1 lb. sliced bacon
1/3 c. flour
1/4 tsp. marjoram
2/3 c. milk
Oil

**Combine** . . . . first 6 ingredients with 2 eggs in bowl, mixing well.
**Divide** . . . . . . into 12 equal portions.
**Shape** . . . . . . each into log and wrap with bacon to enclose completely.
**Combine** . . . . flour, marjoram, milk and remaining 2 eggs in bowl, beating until smooth.
**Dip** . . . . . . . . each log in batter.
**Fry** . . . . . . . . in 1/2-inch deep hot oil until bacon is brown and crisp.
**Serve** . . . . . . . on toasted frankfurter buns with catsup and onion, tomato and pickle slices.
**Yields** . . . . . . 6 servings.

Photograph for this recipe on page 35.

## MEXICAN BEEF HEROES

1/2 lb. ground beef
1 onion, chopped
1  4-oz. can green chilies, chopped
1/4 c. sliced ripe olives
1/4 c. catsup
1/2 tsp. each salt, chili powder
6 slices Colby cheese
6 slices crisp-cooked bacon
6 slices Muenster cheese
6 sm. French bread loaves, split

**Brown** . . . . . . ground beef with onion in skillet, stirring until crumbly.
**Add** . . . . . . . next 5 ingredients, mixing well.
**Cook** . . . . . . . for 5 minutes longer, stirring occasionally.
**Layer** . . . . . . Colby cheese, ground beef mixture, bacon and Muenster cheese on bottom halves of loaves.
**Top** . . . . . . . . with remaining loaf halves.
**Bake** . . . . . . . wrapped in foil, at 375 degrees for 10 minutes.
**Yields** . . . . . . 6 servings.

Judith A. Herman
Dublin H. S., Dublin, California

## SPOON BURGERS

2 lb. ground beef
1 med. onion, chopped
2 tsp. salt
1/2 tsp. pepper
1/4 c. flour
1 tsp. Worcestershire sauce
1 1/2 c. catsup
16 hamburger buns

**Brown** . . . . . . ground beef in skillet, stirring until crumbly.
**Mix** . . . . . . . . in onion, salt and pepper.
**Cook** . . . . . . until onion is tender.
**Add** . . . . . . . flour, mixing well.
**Mix** . . . . . . . . in 2 1/2 cups water, Worcestershire sauce and catsup.
**Simmer** . . . . . for 15 minutes, stirring frequently.
**Serve** . . . . . . . on buns.
**Yields** . . . . . . 16 servings.

Betty L. Blackburn
Intermediate H. S., Broken Arrow, Oklahoma

## TACO LOAF SANDWICHES

1 lb. ground beef
1 pkg. taco seasoning mix
2 loaves French bread
1 can refried beans
12 oz. jalapeno pepper cheese, sliced

**Prepare** . . . . . ground beef with seasoning mix, using package directions.
**Slice** . . . . . . . top fourth from each loaf.
**Hollow** . . . . . out bottom, leaving shell.
**Spread** . . . . . beans over bottoms of shells.
**Spoon** . . . . . . ground beef mixture over beans.
**Top** . . . . . . . . with cheese.
**Replace** . . . . . loaf tops.
**Bake** . . . . . . . wrapped in foil at 350 degrees for 20 to 30 minutes or until heated through.
**Yields** . . . . . . 12 servings.

Doris W. Larke
Woodruff H. S., Peoria, Illinois

## STUFFED FRENCH BREAD

*1 to 2 lb. hamburger*
*1 or 2 onions, chopped*
*Salt, pepper and garlic salt to taste*
*1  10-oz. can each tomatoes, green chilies*
*6 to 12 mushrooms, sliced*
*1 to 2 green peppers, chopped*
*1 loaf French bread*

**Brown** . . . . . . hamburger in skillet, stirring un-
til crumbly; drain.
**Add** . . . . . . . remaining ingredients, except
bread, mixing well.
**Simmer** . . . . . for 10 minutes.
**Slice** . . . . . . . bread in half.
**Remove** . . . . soft bread from inside loaf.
**Spoon** . . . . . . meat mixture into hollow crust.
**Replace** . . . . . top.
**Bake** . . . . . . . wrapped in foil at 400 degrees
for 15 to 20 minutes or until
heated through.
**Yields** . . . . . . 4 servings.

Mil Sanderson
Clayton Int. Sch., Salt Lake City, Utah

## EASY SLOPPY JOES

*1 1/2 lb. ground chuck*
*1/4 c. each mustard, barbecue sauce*
*1/2 c. catsup*
*1 can chicken gumbo soup*
*1 med. onion, chopped*
*Salt and pepper to taste*
*1 pkg. hamburger buns*

**Brown** . . . . . . ground chuck in skillet, stirring
until crumbly; drain well.
**Add** . . . . . . . next 7 ingredients, mixing well.
**Simmer** . . . . . for 20 minutes, stirring
occasionally.
**Serve** . . . . . . . on hamburger buns.
**Yields** . . . . . . 6-8 servings.

Donna Fulton
Maxwell Jr. H. S., Tucson, Arizona

## SLOPPY JOES FOR-A-CROWD

*6 lb. ground beef*
*1  32-oz. bottle of catsup*
*2 cans tomatoes*
*4 tbsp. each liquid smoke,*
*Worcestershire sauce*

*1 env. dry onion soup mix*
*2 c. chopped onion*
*1/4 tsp. garlic salt*
*2 tbsp. brown sugar*

**Brown** . . . . . . ground beef in large skillet, stir-
ring until crumbly; drain.
**Add** . . . . . . . remaining ingredients, mixing
well.
**Bake** . . . . . . . at 350 degrees for 1 hour.
**Yields** . . . . . . 25 servings.

Ella Jo Adams
Allen H. S., Allen, Texas

## FAVORITE SLOPPY JOES

*1 lb. ground chuck*
*3/4 tsp. salt*
*2 tbsp. each molasses, mustard*
*1 tbsp. Worcestershire sauce*
*1/8 tsp. hot pepper sauce*
*1/2 c. catsup*
*6 hamburger buns, toasted*

**Brown** . . . . . . ground chuck in skillet, stirring
until crumbly; drain.
**Sprinkle** . . . . salt over ground chuck.
**Blend** . . . . . . next 2 ingredients in bowl.
**Stir** . . . . . . . . into ground chuck with Worces-
tershire sauce, pepper sauce and
catsup, mixing well.
**Simmer** . . . . . covered, for 20 minutes.
**Serve** . . . . . . . on toasted hamburger buns.
**Yields** . . . . . . 6 servings.

Linda Sue James
Diamond R-4 Sch., Diamond, Missouri

## LORENE'S TAVERNS

*1 lb. hamburger*
*1 lg. onion, chopped*
*1 c. catsup*
*1 tbsp. each vinegar, mustard*
*1 tsp. sugar*

**Brown** . . . . . . hamburger in skillet, stirring un-
til crumbly; drain.
**Mix** . . . . . . . . in remaining ingredients.
**Simmer** . . . . . for 30 minutes.
**Serve** . . . . . . . on buns.
**Yields** . . . . . . 6-8 servings.

Lorene L. Arent
Wausa Public Sch., Wausa, Nebraska

# Stove Top Dishes

## DIFFERENT CHILI

2 lb. ground beef
1 c. each chopped onion, green pepper
1 c. sliced celery
3 15-oz. cans kidney beans
2 16-oz. cans tomatoes, mashed
1 6-oz. can tomato paste
2 cloves of garlic, minced
1 1/2 tbsp. chili powder
2 tsp. salt

**Saute** . . . . . . ground beef with onion, green pepper and celery in skillet until vegetables are tender, stirring frequently.
**Add** . . . . . . . remaining ingredients, mixing well.
**Simmer** . . . . . covered, for 1 1/2 hours.
**Yields** . . . . . . 8 servings.

Mary C. Martinez
Central Lafourche H. S., Mathews, Louisiana

## CHILI CON CARNE

2 lb. ground beef
1/2 c. minced onion
2 tbsp. each garlic powder,
    ground cuminseed
4 tbsp. chili powder
1 tbsp. each salt, oregano
3 tbsp. flour
1 c. finely chopped tomatoes

**Brown** . . . . . . ground beef in saucepan, stirring until crumbly.
**Add** . . . . . . . onion and spices, mixing well.
**Stir** . . . . . . . . in flour and tomatoes with 5 cups water.
**Simmer** . . . . . for 45 minutes, stirring occasionally.
**Yields** . . . . . . 4-6 servings.

Louise Norvill
Lindsay Jr.-Sr. H. S., Lindsay, Oklahoma

## CHILI CON CARNE WITH TOMATOES

1 lb. ground beef
2 med. onions, chopped
3/4 c. chopped green pepper
1 28-oz. can tomatoes
1 8-oz. can tomato sauce
2 tsp. chili powder

1 tsp. salt
1/8 tsp. each red pepper, paprika
1 15 1/2-oz. can kidney beans, drained

**Brown** . . . . . . ground beef with onions and green pepper in skillet, stirring until crumbly; drain.
**Stir** . . . . . . . . in remaining ingredients except beans, mixing well.
**Simmer** . . . . . covered, for 2 hours, stirring occasionally.
**Stir** . . . . . . . . in beans.
**Cook** . . . . . . . until heated through.

Pat Foley
Tempe H. S., Tempe, Arizona

## HOMEMADE CHILI WITH CORN

1 lb. coarsely ground beef
1 med. onion, chopped
1 1/2 tsp. salt
2 tbsp. shortening
3 1/2 tbsp. chili powder
2 tbsp. flour
1 16-oz. can tomatoes
1 can whole kernel corn
1 can ranch-style beans

**Brown** . . . . . . ground beef with onion and salt in shortening in skillet, stirring until ground beef is crumbly.
**Stir** . . . . . . . . in remaining ingredients and 1 cup water, mixing well.
**Cook** . . . . . . . covered, for 2 hours, stirring occasionally and adding water if necessary.

Ann Edwards
Duncanville H. S., Duncanville, Texas

## COMMUNITY CHILI

6 lb. ground beef, crumbled
3 12-oz. cans tomato paste
3 sm. cans chili powder
1 tsp. garlic powder
3 tbsp. ground cuminseed
1 1/2 c. flour
Salt and pepper to taste
Chopped onions (opt.)

**Place** . . . . . . . ground beef in 6 quarts water in large saucepan.
**Simmer** . . . . . for 30 minutes, stirring frequently.

**Mix** . . . . . . . . remaining ingredients in bowl.
**Add** . . . . . . . to ground beef mixture, mixing well.
**Simmer** . . . . . for 1 1/2 to 2 hours or until thickened, stirring occasionally.
**Yields** . . . . . . 25-30 servings.

Janice Dennard
Beckville H. S., Beckville, Texas

## RED BEAN CHILI CON CARNE

  *1 lb. ground beef*
  *1/2 c. chopped onion*
  *2 tbsp. shortening*
  *1 tbsp. chopped garlic*
  *1 1/2 tbsp. chili powder*
  *1 tbsp. paprika*
  *1 tsp. salt*
  *1 20-oz. can tomatoes*
  *1 8-oz. can tomato sauce*
  *3 c. cooked red beans*

**Brown** . . . . . . ground beef with onion in shortening in skillet, stirring until crumbly.
**Add** . . . . . . . remaining ingredients except beans, mixing well.
**Cook** . . . . . . . covered, over high heat until steaming.
**Simmer** . . . . . for 1 hour.
**Add** . . . . . . . beans, mixing well.
**Cook** . . . . . . . until heated through.

Ruth E. Hood
A. W. Coolidge Jr. H. S., Reading, Massachusetts

## CHILI-STYLE GREEK SAUCE

  *2 lb. ground beef*
  *1 green pepper, chopped*
  *2 onions, chopped*
  *1 tbsp. each salt, paprika*
  *1 to 2 tsp. pepper*
  *1 tsp. each garlic salt, oregano*
  *2 tsp. celery salt*
  *1/2 to 1 tsp. red pepper*
  *1/2 stalk celery, chopped*
  *Chili powder to taste*
  *1/2 to 1 tsp. cuminseed (opt.)*
  *1 12-oz. can tomato paste (opt.)*

**Brown** . . . . . . ground beef in skillet, stirring until crumbly.

**Combine** . . . . with 2 quarts water and remaining ingredients in stock pot.
**Simmer** . . . . . until reduced to desired consistency.
**Serve** . . . . . . . with hot dogs or hamburgers.

Janet Miller
Strong Vincent H. S., Erie, Pennsylvania

## ONE-POT MACARONI AND BEEF

  *1 1/2 lb. ground beef*
  *1 med. onion, chopped*
  *1 green pepper, chopped*
  *2 c. elbow macaroni*
  *2 8-oz. cans tomato sauce*
  *1 tsp. salt*
  *1/4 tsp. pepper*
  *1 tbsp. Worcestershire sauce*

**Brown** . . . . . . ground beef with onion and green pepper in large skillet, stirring until crumbly; drain.
**Add** . . . . . . . remaining ingredients and 1 1/2 cups water, mixing well.
**Simmer** . . . . . covered, for 25 minutes or until macaroni is tender, stirring occasionally, adding more water if necessary.
**Serve** . . . . . . . immediately.

Photograph for this recipe below.

## BEEF DELIGHT

1/2 lb. ground beef
1 med. onion, chopped
1/4 c. chopped green pepper
1 tbsp. oil
1 c. macaroni
1 can tomato soup

Brown ...... ground beef with onion and green pepper in oil in skillet, stirring until crumbly; remove with slotted spoon.
Add ....... macaroni.
Saute ...... until browned.
Add ....... ground beef mixture, soup and 1 soup can water, mixing well.
Simmer ..... covered, for 10 minutes or until macaroni is tender, adding additional water if necessary.
Garnish ..... with parsley flakes.
Yields ...... 4-6 servings.

Helen C. Borders
Burns Sr. H. S., Lawndale, North Carolina

## MACARONI CHILI

2 lb. ground round
3 tbsp. olive oil
1  28-oz. can tomatoes
4 c. tomato juice
2 c. chopped onion
3 cloves of garlic, minced
4 tsp. salt
2 tbsp. chili powder
1 bay leaf
1/2 tsp. each ground cuminseed, oregano, pepper
1  15-oz. can kidney beans, drained
1 c. mixed sweet pickles
2 c. elbow macaroni, cooked, drained

Brown ...... ground round in oil in soup pot, stirring until crumbly.
Add ....... next 7 ingredients with cuminseed, oregano and pepper, mixing well.
Simmer ..... covered, for 1 hour.
Stir ........ in beans and pickles.
Cook ....... for 30 minutes longer; remove bay leaf.
Add ....... macaroni, mixing well.
Yields ...... 10 servings.

Photograph for this recipe on page 2.

## ITALIAN HAMBURGER CASSEROLE

1 lb. hamburger
1 lg. onion, chopped
4 c. tomatoes
1 can cream of mushroom soup
1 tsp. chili powder
1/2 tsp. each garlic, onion salt
8 oz. macaroni, cooked

Brown ...... hamburger with onion in large skillet, stirring until crumbly.
Add ....... next 5 ingredients, stirring well.
Simmer ..... for 20 minutes.
Add ....... macaroni, mixing well.
Yields ...... 6-8 servings.

Bonnie B. Edgell
West Noble H. S., Ligonier, Indiana

## HAMBURGER HELPER MACARONI CASSEROLE

1 1/4 tsp. pepper
3 tbsp. onion powder
1 tbsp. garlic powder
5 tsp. salt
2 tbsp. dried parsley flakes
1 2/3 c. nonfat dry milk
1/3 c. onion flakes
3 1/2 tbsp. granulated beef bouillon
1 lb. hamburger
1 c. cooked macaroni

Combine .... first 8 ingredients in bowl, mixing well; set aside.
Brown ...... hamburger in skillet, stirring until crumbly; drain.
Add ....... 9 tablespoons prepared seasoning mixture, macaroni and 1 1/2 to 2 cups water, mixing well.
Bring ....... to a boil.
Simmer ..... covered, for 15 to 20 minutes, or until macaroni is tender, stirring occasionally and adding water as necessary.
Simmer ..... uncovered, until excess water has evaporated, stirring frequently.
Yields ...... 6 servings.

Sandy Swart
Marysville H. S., Marysville, Kansas

Recipe on page 28.

## BEEF SKILLET SUPPER

1 lb. ground beef
1 each med. onion, green pepper, chopped
1 c. catsup
1 can kidney beans
1  2 to 3-oz. can mushrooms
1 c. small macaroni, cooked

**Brown** . . . . . . ground beef with onion and green pepper in skillet, stirring until crumbly; drain.
**Add** . . . . . . . next 3 ingredients, mixing well.
**Cook** . . . . . . . for 10 minutes.
**Stir** . . . . . . . . in macaroni.
**Simmer** . . . . . for 30 minutes.
**Yields** . . . . . . 6-8 servings.

Ann Moore
Jackson County H. S., Gainesboro, Tennessee

## BUSY DAY BEEF AND MACARONI

1/2 lb. lean ground beef
1/4 c. each chopped onion, green pepper
2 c. tomato juice
1/8 tsp. pepper
2 tsp. sugar
1/2 tsp. salt
1/4 tsp. thyme
1 tsp. cider vinegar
1 c. macaroni

**Brown** . . . . . . ground beef with onion and green pepper in skillet, stirring until crumbly.
**Add** . . . . . . . remaining 7 ingredients, mixing well.
**Bring** . . . . . . . to a boil, stirring occasionally.
**Simmer** . . . . . covered, for 25 to 30 minutes or until macaroni is tender, stirring occasionally.
**Yields** . . . . . . 2-3 servings.

Frances V. Hamlet
Alton Park Jr. H. S., Chattanooga, Tennessee

## TURTLE SHELLS

1/2 to 3/4 lb. ground beef
Salt and pepper to taste

Recipe on page 20.

6 to 8 oz. small shell macaroni
1  8-oz. can tomato sauce
1/4 c. chopped green pepper
3 chicken bouillon cubes
1/2 tsp. cumin
1/4 tsp. each garlic salt, pepper
1 can green beans (opt.)

**Brown** . . . . . . ground beef with salt and pepper in skillet, stirring until crumbly; drain all but 2 tablespoons pan drippings.
**Add** . . . . . . . macaroni; saute until lightly browned.
**Add** . . . . . . . remaining ingredients, mixing well.
**Simmer** . . . . . for 15 minutes or until macaroni is tender.
**Yields** . . . . . . 4 servings.

Sandra Salas DeBord
Spring Oaks Jr. H. S., Houston, Texas

## HAMBURGER MASTER MIX

1 lb. ground beef
1 tsp. margarine
1/2 c. chopped onion
1 c. chopped celery
3 tbsp. chopped green pepper
1 can tomato soup
1  15-oz. can tomato sauce
1 tsp. each salt, basil
1/2 tsp. thyme
Dash of pepper

**Cook** . . . . . . . ground beef lightly in margarine in skillet, stirring until crumbly.
**Add** . . . . . . . onion, celery and green pepper.
**Saute** . . . . . . until vegetables are tender and ground beef is brown.
**Add** . . . . . . . remaining 6 ingredients, mixing well.
**Simmer** . . . . . covered, for 30 to 45 minutes.
**Yields** . . . . . . 4 servings.

May be prepared in quantity to freeze. Use for chili, sloppy Joes, spaghetti or other main dishes.

Lorna Hinson
Floyd Johnson Voc. Center, York, South Carolina

## KETTLE LASAGNA

*1 lb. ground beef*
*1 pkg. spaghetti sauce mix*
*1 pt. cottage cheese (opt.)*
*1  8-oz. package narrow egg noodles*
*4 c. tomatoes*
*8 oz. mozzarella cheese, grated*

**Brown** . . . . . . ground beef in kettle, stirring until crumbly; drain.
**Spread** . . . . . evenly over bottom.
**Sprinkle** . . . . 1/2 of the spaghetti sauce mix over beef.
**Layer** . . . . . . cottage cheese, noodles, remaining spaghetti sauce mix, tomatoes and 1 1/2 cups cold water over ground beef.
**Simmer** . . . . . covered, for 27 minutes without stirring.
**Sprinkle** . . . . mozzarella cheese over top.
**Cook** . . . . . . . for 3 minutes longer.
**Serves** . . . . . . 4-6 servings.

Katy Jo Powers
Haysi H. S., Haysi, Virginia

## MEAL-IN-ONE

*1 lb. ground beef*
*1 med. onion, chopped*
*1  8-oz. package medium noodles, cooked, drained*
*1  16-oz. can herbed tomato sauce*
*1  16-oz. can whole kernel corn, drained*
*4 slices American cheese*

**Brown** . . . . . . ground beef in skillet, stirring until crumbly; drain.
**Add** . . . . . . . onion.
**Cook** . . . . . . . until tender, stirring frequently.
**Layer** . . . . . . noodles, tomato sauce, corn and cheese slices over ground beef mixture.
**Simmer** . . . . . covered, until cheese is slightly melted.
**Cut** . . . . . . . . into squares.
**Yields** . . . . . . 6 servings.

Alma Lee Hicks
Murphysboro H. S., Murphysboro, Illinois

## CREAMY NOODLE CASSEROLE

*1/2 c. chopped onion*
*1/4 c. chopped green pepper*

*Oil*
*1 lb. hamburger*
*4 oz. noodles, cooked*
*1 can each cream of mushroom, tomato soup*
*3 or 4 slices cheese, cut into pieces*
*Garlic salt and pepper to taste*

**Saute** . . . . . . onion and green pepper in a small amount of oil in skillet until golden brown.
**Add** . . . . . . . hamburger.
**Cook** . . . . . . . stirring until crumbly and brown.
**Add** . . . . . . . noodles, soups, cheese and seasonings, mixing well.
**Serve** . . . . . . with fruit salad.
**Yields** . . . . . . 4 servings.

Carolyn Grams
Hooks H. S., Hooks, Texas

## SPANISH NOODLES

*1 lb. hamburger*
*2 slices bacon, chopped*
*1 onion, chopped*
*1 green pepper, chopped*
*1/2 tsp. each salt, Accent*
*1 tbsp. parsley flakes*
*2 c. wide noodles*
*1  16-oz. can tomatoes*
*1/2 c. chili sauce*

**Brown** . . . . . . hamburger and bacon with onion in skillet, stirring until crumbly.
**Add** . . . . . . . 1/2 cup water and remaining ingredients in order given, mixing well after each addition.
**Simmer** . . . . . for 35 minutes.
**Yields** . . . . . . 4-5 servings.

Frankie Sue Clayton
Paul H. Pewitt H. S., Omaha, Texas

## BARBECUED HAMBURGER ON RICE

*1 lb. hamburger*
*1/2 c. each chopped onion, green pepper*
*2 tbsp. oil*
*1 tbsp. Worcestershire sauce*
*2 tbsp. vinegar*
*2 tbsp. brown sugar*
*1 tbsp. dry mustard*

1/4 c. each chili sauce, catsup
1/8 tsp. pepper
1/2 tsp. paprika
4 c. cooked rice
1 tbsp. chopped parsley

Brown . . . . . . hamburger with onion and green pepper in oil in skillet, stirring until crumbly; drain.
Combine . . . . remaining ingredients except rice and parsley in bowl, mixing well.
Pour . . . . . . . over hamburger mixture.
Simmer . . . . . covered, for 30 minutes.
Serve . . . . . . . over rice with sprinkle of chopped parsley.
Yields . . . . . . 6 servings.

Mary Crossley
Conroe H. S., Conroe, Texas

## BEAN-BEEF AND RICE SKILLET

1 lb. ground beef
1 lg. onion, chopped
4 tbsp. shortening
1 tbsp. chili powder
2 tsp. salt
1 tsp. pepper
1/4 tsp. garlic salt
1 c. minute rice
1 can kidney beans
1 can tomatoes

Brown . . . . . . ground beef with onion in shortening in skillet, stirring until crumbly; drain.
Add . . . . . . . remaining ingredients, mixing well.
Bring . . . . . . . to a boil.
Simmer . . . . . for 30 minutes.
Yields . . . . . . 8-10 servings.

Beverly Plyler
Glenwood H. S., Glenwood, Arizona

## SPECIAL BEEF AND RICE SKILLET DISH

1 lb. lean ground beef
3/4 c. finely chopped onion
1/8 tsp. each oregano, thyme, garlic powder
Dash of pepper
1/2 sm. bay leaf
1 can cream of mushroom soup

1 1/2 c. tomato juice
1 c. minute rice
1 sm. can mushrooms

Brown . . . . . . ground beef in skillet, stirring until crumbly.
Add . . . . . . . remaining ingredients, mixing well.
Simmer . . . . . for 10 minutes, stirring occasionally.
Yields . . . . . . 4 servings.

Della O. Lindsay
Riverside H. S., Boardman, Oregon

## FIESTA RICE

1 lb. hamburger
1/4 c. chopped celery
3/4 c. chopped green pepper
1 7-oz. box minute rice
1 16-oz. can tomato sauce
1/4 tsp. garlic powder
1 tbsp. salt
1 tsp. each sugar, chili powder
1 bay leaf

Brown . . . . . . hamburger with celery in skillet, stirring until crumbly.
Combine . . . . hamburger mixture with remaining ingredients in large saucepan, mixing well; cover.
Bring . . . . . . . to a boil.
Simmer . . . . . for 15 to 20 minutes or until rice is tender.

Brenda Simmons
Dayton H. S., Dayton, Texas

## OH MY GOSH!

1 lb. ground beef
1 can each Spanish rice, ranch-style beans
1/4 c. catsup
2 tbsp. Worcestershire sauce

Brown . . . . . . ground beef in skillet, stirring until crumbly.
Stir . . . . . . . . in remaining ingredients.
Cook . . . . . . . until heated through.
Serve . . . . . . . over toast.
Yields . . . . . . 8 servings.

Deborah Casados
Mexia H. S., Mexia, Texas

## GERMAN SKILLET DINNER

*1 tbsp. butter*
*1  16-oz. can sauerkraut*
*2/3 c. rice*
*1 med. onion, chopped*
*1 lb. ground chuck, crumbled*
*1 1/2 tsp. salt*
*1/4 tsp. pepper*
*1  8-oz. can tomato sauce*

**Melt** . . . . . . . butter in large skillet.
**Spread** . . . . . sauerkraut over bottom.
**Layer** . . . . . . remaining ingredients in order given over sauerkraut.
**Cook** . . . . . . tightly covered, over low heat for 50 minutes.
**Yields** . . . . . . 4-5 servings.

Dorothy Winter
North Olmstead H. S., North Olmstead, Ohio

## A MALAYSIAN MEAL

*2 1/2 lb. hamburger*
*1 can evaporated milk*
*1 can mushroom soup*
*1  14-oz. can tomatoes*
*2 tsp. each curry, turmeric, salt*
*1 tsp. chili powder*
*2 1/2 c. long grain rice, cooked*
*Coconut*
*Pineapple tidbits*
*Raisins*
*Peanuts*
*Chopped cucumber*
*Sliced banana*
*Chutney*

**Brown** . . . . . . hamburger in skillet, stirring until crumbly.
**Add** . . . . . . . next 3 ingredients and seasonings, mixing well.
**Simmer** . . . . . for 15 minutes.
**Serve** . . . . . . . over rice.
**Top** . . . . . . . . each serving with remaining ingredients, as desired.

E. Klassen
Georges P. Vanier, Donnelly, Alberta, Canada

## BEVERLY'S SPAGHETTI SAUCE

*1 lb. ground beef*
*1  1 1/4-oz. box pickling spice*

*1/2 c. chopped onion*
*1  6-oz. can tomato paste*
*1  8-oz. can tomatoes*
*1/2 c. sugar*
*1 tsp. salt*
*Dash of pepper*

**Brown** . . . . . . ground beef in large skillet, stirring until crumbly.
**Tie** . . . . . . . . 1/3 of the pickling spice in cheesecloth, reserving remaining spice for later use.
**Add** . . . . . . . pickling spice and remaining ingredients to ground beef, mixing well.
**Simmer** . . . . . for 2 to 3 hours; remove spice bag.
**Yields** . . . . . . 6-8 servings.

Beverly C. Goodman
Smyth County Vocational Sch., Marion, Virginia

## IRISH-ITALIAN SPAGHETTI

*1 onion, chopped*
*2 tbsp. oil*
*1 lb. ground beef*
*1 tsp. salt*
*1/2 tsp. chili powder*
*1/2 tsp. Tabasco sauce*
*1/4 tsp. pepper*
*Dash of red pepper*
*1 can each cream of mushroom soup,*
      *tomato soup*
*Long spaghetti, cooked*
*Parmesan cheese*

**Saute** . . . . . . onion in oil in skillet until tender.
**Add** . . . . . . . next 6 ingredients.
**Cook** . . . . . . . until lightly browned, stirring frequently.
**Simmer** . . . . . covered, for 10 minutes.
**Stir** . . . . . . . . in soups.
**Simmer** . . . . . covered, for 45 minutes longer.
**Serve** . . . . . . . with long spaghetti.
**Top** . . . . . . . . with Parmesan cheese.
**Yields** . . . . . . 4-6 servings.

Mary Jo Lyle
Gatewood Sch., Eatonton, Georgia

## MARIE'S SPAGHETTI

*1 1/2 lb. ground beef*
*Olive oil*

1/2 c. finely chopped onion
1/4 c. finely chopped green pepper
1 clove of garlic, sliced
1 lg. can each tomato sauce, tomato paste
1 tsp. oregano
1 tbsp. salt
1 tsp. pepper
1 lg. box spaghetti, cooked
Cheddar cheese, grated

**Brown** . . . . . . ground beef in oil in large sauce-pan, stirring until crumbly.
**Add** . . . . . . . onion, green pepper and garlic.
**Simmer** . . . . . until vegetables are tender.
**Add** . . . . . . . tomato sauce and tomato paste with an equal amount of water, mixing well.
**Mix** . . . . . . . . in seasonings.
**Simmer** . . . . . for 20 minutes or until flavors are blended.
**Serve** . . . . . . . sauce over spaghetti.
**Sprinkle** . . . . with cheese.
**Yields** . . . . . . 12-15 servings.

Marie R. Duggan
Johnson County H. S., Wrightsville, Georgia

## SIMPLE AND QUICK SPAGHETTI SAUCE

1 med. onion, chopped
1 tbsp. margarine
1 lb. ground beef
Salt and pepper to taste
1 can tomato soup
1 1/2 tbsp. mustard
1/3 c. catsup
1/2 tsp. garlic salt
3 dashes of hot sauce
1/4 green pepper, chopped
1/4 c. grated cheese

**Saute** . . . . . . onion in margarine in large skil-let until tender.
**Add** . . . . . . . ground beef.
**Cook** . . . . . . . until brown and crumbly, stir-ring constantly.
**Season** . . . . . with salt and pepper.
**Add** . . . . . . . remaining ingredients except cheese.
**Simmer** . . . . . for 30 to 40 minutes or until heated through, stirring occasionally.
**Top** . . . . . . . . with cheese before serving.

**Cook** . . . . . . . until cheese melts.
**Yields** . . . . . . 4-6 servings.

Mrs. Maurice Eugene Eshridge
Bessemer City Jr. H. S.
Bessemer City, North Carolina

## MARY'S SPAGHETTI SAUCE

2 lb. hamburger
1 lg. onion, chopped
1/2 c. catsup
1 6-oz. can tomato paste
1 sm. can tomato sauce
1 tsp. each thyme, cinnamon, chili powder
1 tbsp. brown sugar
1 tbsp. each mustard, garlic juice
1/2 tsp. cumin
Salt and pepper to taste

**Brown** . . . . . . hamburger with onion in large skillet, stirring until crumbly.
**Add** . . . . . . . remaining ingredients with enough water to thin to desired consistency, mixing well.
**Simmer** . . . . . for 1 hour.
**Yields** . . . . . . 8-10 servings.

Mary L. Booker
Hoffman Estates H. S., Hoffman Estates, Illinois

## QUICK MEAT SAUCE AND SPAGHETTI

1 lb. ground beef
1 tsp. onion salt
1/4 tsp. seasoned salt
1/8 tsp. seasoned pepper
1 tbsp. oil
1 pkg. spaghetti sauce mix
1 8-oz. can tomato sauce
1 8-oz. package spaghetti, cooked

**Brown** . . . . . . ground beef with seasonings in oil in skillet, stirring until crum-bly; drain.
**Add** . . . . . . . next 2 ingredients and 1 1/2 cups water, mixing well.
**Simmer** . . . . . covered, for 20 minutes or longer.
**Serve** . . . . . . . with spaghetti.
**Yields** . . . . . . 4-6 servings.

Shirley Grube
Huron Jr. H. S., Huron, South Dakota

## CHEESY MEAT AND SPAGHETTI CASSEROLE

1 lb. ground beef
2 tbsp. oil
1 c. each chopped green pepper, onion,
    celery
1 clove of garlic
1 c. catsup
2 cans tomato juice
1 pkg. long spaghetti
1 tsp. each allspice, parsley
1/2 tsp. thyme
1 bay leaf
2 tbsp. each Worcestershire sauce,
    steak sauce
1/2 lb. Cheddar cheese, grated

**Brown** . . . . . . ground beef in oil in skillet, stirring until crumbly.
**Cook** . . . . . . . green pepper, onion, celery and garlic in a small amount of water in saucepan until tender.
**Add** . . . . . . . ground beef and remaining ingredients except cheese, stirring gently.
**Simmer** . . . . . until spaghetti is tender.
**Add** . . . . . . . cheese 15 minutes before serving.
**Yields** . . . . . . 10-12 servings.

Mary Anne Power
Sidney H. S., Sidney, Texas

## SPAGHETTINI WITH HOT SAUSAGE SAUCE

1 lb. Italian hot sausage, cut up
1/2 lb. mushrooms, sliced
3/4 c. shredded carrot
1 med. onion, sliced
1/2 c. chopped celery
1/4 c. chopped parsley
2 lb. ground chuck
1    28-oz. can plum tomatoes
2    6-oz. cans tomato paste
1 c. dry red wine
1 bay leaf
2 tsp. salt
1 tsp. basil
1/4 tsp. pepper (opt.)
1 1/2 lb. spaghettini, cooked

**Cook** . . . . . . . sausage in 1/4 cup water in covered saucepan for 10 minutes; remove with slotted spoon.
**Saute** . . . . . . next 5 ingredients in pan drippings until tender-crisp; remove with slotted spoon.
**Add** . . . . . . . ground chuck.
**Brown** . . . . . . in pan drippings, stirring until crumbly.
**Cook** . . . . . . . until liquid is reduced, skimming if necessary.
**Add** . . . . . . . sausage, sauteed vegetables and remaining ingredients except spaghettini.
**Simmer** . . . . . covered, for 1/2 hour.
**Simmer** . . . . . uncovered, for 1 1/2 hours longer, stirring occasionally.
**Serve** . . . . . . . over spaghettini with Parmesan cheese if desired.
**Yields** . . . . . . 12 servings.

Photograph for this recipe on page 31.

## ONE-PAN SPAGHETTI

1 lb. ground beef
1 c. each chopped celery, onion
3 cloves of garlic, finely chopped
2 tsp. each oregano, salt
1/4 to 1/2 tsp. pepper
1    46-oz. can tomato juice
6 oz. thin spaghetti, broken
Parmesan cheese

**Brown** . . . . . . ground beef with celery, onion and garlic in 4-quart saucepan, stirring until crumbly; drain.
**Add** . . . . . . . remaining ingredients except Parmesan cheese, mixing well.
**Simmer** . . . . . covered, for 30 to 35 minutes or until spaghetti is tender, stirring occasionally.
**Top** . . . . . . . . with Parmesan cheese.
**Yields** . . . . . . 6 servings.

Jeri O'Quinn
Jones County H. S., Gray, Georgia

## WAREHOUSE SPAGHETTI AND MEAT SAUCE

*1 1/2 lb. ground beef*
*1 med. onion, chopped*
*1 can each tomato, mushroom soup*
*1 sm. can tomato paste*
*1 sm. can mushroom pieces, drained*
*1 to 2 tsp. salt*
*1/4 tsp. pepper*
*1/2 tsp. garlic powder*
*1 tbsp. each oregano, Italian seasoning*

**Brown** . . . . . . ground beef with onion in large skillet, stirring until crumbly.
**Add** . . . . . . . remaining ingredients.
**Simmer** . . . . . for 45 minutes, stirring occasionally.
**Serve** . . . . . . . over spaghetti.
**Garnish** . . . . . with grated Parmesan cheese.
**Yields** . . . . . . 5-6 servings.

Charlene Green
Hawkins H. S., Hawkins, Texas

## EASY HAMBURGER STROGANOFF

*1 1/2 lb. hamburger*
*1 1/2 c. chopped onion*
*2 cans cream of mushroom soup*
*1 soup can milk*
*Salt and pepper to taste*
*1 carton sour cream*

**Brown** . . . . . . hamburger in skillet, stirring until crumbly; drain.
**Add** . . . . . . . onion.
**Cook** . . . . . . . until tender.
**Add** . . . . . . . soup, milk and seasonings, mixing well.
**Cook** . . . . . . . until heated through.
**Mix** . . . . . . . . in sour cream.
**Serve** . . . . . . . with noodles.
**Yields** . . . . . . 8 servings.

Mrs. Richard Vaughan
Fairfield H. S., Fairfield, Illinois

## EDITH'S STROGANOFF

*1 clove of garlic, minced*
*1/2 c. minced onion*
*1/4 c. butter*

*1 lb. ground beef*
*2 tbsp. flour*
*Salt and pepper to taste*
*1   8-oz. can mushrooms*
*1 can cream soup*
*1/2 c. each mayonnaise, yogurt*

**Saute** . . . . . . garlic and onion in butter in skillet until tender.
**Add** . . . . . . . ground beef.
**Cook** . . . . . . . until brown and crumbly, stirring constantly.
**Stir** . . . . . . . . in flour, seasonings and mushrooms, mixing well.
**Cook** . . . . . . . for 5 minutes.
**Add** . . . . . . . soup, mixing well.
**Simmer** . . . . . for 10 minutes, stirring occasionally.
**Stir** . . . . . . . . in mayonnaise and yogurt.
**Cook** . . . . . . . until heated through.
**Serve** . . . . . . . with rice.
**Yields** . . . . . . 6 servings.

Edith M. Kilgren
Bothell H. S., Bothell, Washington

## JIFFY BEEF STROGANOFF

*1 lb. ground beef*
*2 tbsp. shortening*
*1 env. dry onion soup mix*
*1/2 tsp. ginger*
*3 c. medium noodles*
*1   3-oz. can sliced mushrooms*
*2 tbsp. flour*
*1 c. sour cream*

**Brown** . . . . . . ground beef in shortening in skillet, stirring until crumbly.
**Sprinkle** . . . . with soup mix and ginger.
**Layer** . . . . . . noodles and mushrooms with liquid over ground beef.
**Pour** . . . . . . . 3 to 3 1/2 cups hot water over noodles until all are moistened.
**Cook** . . . . . . . covered, over low heat for 20 to 25 minutes or until noodles are tender.
**Blend** . . . . . . flour into sour cream in bowl.
**Stir** . . . . . . . . into ground beef mixture.
**Cook** . . . . . . . for 3 minutes longer.
**Yields** . . . . . . 6 servings.

Faye Lynch
Hickman County H. S., Centerville, Tennessee

## ONE-POT NOODLE STROGANOFF

1 lb. ground chuck
1 c. chopped onions
4 c. tomato juice
2 1/2 tsp. salt
1/4 tsp. pepper
2 tsp. Worcestershire sauce
1 6-oz. package medium egg noodles
1 c. sour cream

**Brown** . . . . . . ground chuck with onions in large skillet, stirring until crumbly; drain.
**Stir** . . . . . . . . in next 4 ingredients.
**Bring** . . . . . . . to a boil.
**Stir** . . . . . . . . in noodles gradually.
**Simmer** . . . . . covered, for 10 minutes or until noodles are tender, stirring occasionally.
**Stir** . . . . . . . . in sour cream. Do not boil.
**Spoon** . . . . . . into serving dish.
**Garnish** . . . . . with parsley.

Photograph for this recipe above.

## SKILLET ENCHILADAS

1 lb. ground beef
1/2 c. chopped onion
2 tbsp. minced green chilies
1 can cream of mushroom soup
1 10-oz. can enchilada sauce
1/3 c. milk
8 corn tortillas
1/4 c. oil
2 1/2 c. shredded American cheese
1/2 c. ripe olives, chopped

**Brown** . . . . . . ground beef with onion in large skillet, stirring until crumbly; drain.
**Stir** . . . . . . . . in next 4 ingredients.
**Simmer** . . . . . covered, for 20 minutes, stirring occasionally.
**Soften** . . . . . . tortillas in oil in small skillet over medium heat; drain on paper towels.
**Place** . . . . . . . 1/4 cup cheese and 1 tablespoon olives on each tortilla, rolling to enclose filling.
**Place** . . . . . . . seam side down in ground beef mixture.
**Cook** . . . . . . . covered, for 5 minutes.
**Sprinkle** . . . . remaining 1/2 cup cheese over tortillas.
**Cook** . . . . . . . covered, for 1 minute longer or until cheese is melted.
**Yields** . . . . . . 4 servings.

Betty Porter
West Jr. H. S., Liberal, Kansas

## SKILLET PIZZA

1 lb. lean ground beef
1/2 c. bread crumbs
1 sm. onion, chopped
1/2 tsp. oregano
Salt and pepper to taste
1 can tomatoes, drained, mashed
1 to 2 c. shredded cheese

**Combine** . . . . first 6 ingredients in bowl, mixing well.
**Press** . . . . . . . into skillet.
**Layer** . . . . . . with tomatoes and cheese.
**Cook** . . . . . . . over medium heat for 25 to 30 minutes or until cooked through.

Pam Eastup
Northwest H. S., Justin, Texas

## SKILLET MEAT LOAF

1 egg, beaten
1 lb. ground chuck
3/4 tsp. salt
1/4 c. minced onion
3 slices American cheese
1/4 tsp. pepper

**Combine** .... egg, ground chuck, salt and onion in bowl, mixing well.
**Pat** ........ half the ground chuck mixture into greased 8-inch skillet.
**Top** ........ with cheese slices.
**Press** ....... remaining ground chuck mixture over cheese.
**Sprinkle** .... pepper over top.
**Cut** ........ into 4 wedges.
**Cook** ....... over medium heat for about 15 minutes or until browned on bottom.
**Broil** ....... until browned on top.
**Yields** ...... 4 servings.

Myrtle Chapman
El Reno H. S., El Reno, Oklahoma

## TEXAS SOMBREROS

1 tsp. each Accent, salt
1/8 tsp. pepper
1 tsp. steak sauce
1 to 2 tsp. chili powder
1 lb. ground chuck
1/2 to 1 c. chopped onion
1 tbsp. margarine
1   16-oz. can tomatoes
1   8-oz. can tomato sauce
Corn chips
Hot sauce
Shredded lettuce
Grated cheese
Chopped onion
Chopped tomatoes
Sliced avocados
Warm refried beans

**Sprinkle** .... seasonings over ground chuck in bowl.
**Saute** ...... onion in margarine in skillet until tender.
**Add** ....... ground chuck mixture.
**Cook** ....... until brown, stirring until crumbly.

**Add** ....... tomatoes and tomato sauce, mixing well.
**Simmer** ..... for 30 minutes.
**Serve** ....... over corn chips.
**Top** ........ each serving with remaining ingredients as desired.
**Yields** ...... 4-6 servings.

Katie Johnston
Mohave Middle Sch., Scottsdale, Arizona

## KOREAN BUFFET

1 1/2 lb. ground beef
2 tbsp. oil
1/2 med. cabbage, chopped
1 sm. bunch celery, chopped
1 med. onion, chopped
1 green pepper, chopped
4 carrots, sliced
Salt and pepper to taste

**Brown** ...... ground beef in oil in skillet, stirring until crumbly.
**Add** ....... remaining ingredients.
**Cook** ....... until vegetables are tender-crisp, stirring constantly.
**Serve** ....... over egg noodles with soy sauce.
**Yields** ...... 6 servings.

Jane Woods
Wood Memorial H. S., Oakland City, Indiana

## TEENAGE SCRAMBLE

1 lb. ground beef
1 sm. onion, chopped
3 tbsp. olive oil
1 sm. can sliced mushrooms
1 pkg. frozen spinach, cooked
6 eggs, well beaten
Salt and pepper to taste

**Saute** ...... ground beef with onion in oil in skillet until ground beef is browned, stirring frequently.
**Add** ....... mushrooms and spinach, mixing well.
**Stir** ........ in eggs gradually.
**Cook** ....... until eggs are set, stirring constantly.
**Season** ..... with salt and pepper.
**Yields** ...... 6 servings.

Gail Chaid
Independence H. S., San Jose, California

## STUFFED CABBAGE ROLLS

*8 lg. cabbage leaves*
*1 lb. ground beef*
*1 1/2 c. soft bread crumbs*
*1/2 c. finely chopped onion*
*2 eggs, well beaten*
*1 1/2 tsp. salt*
*1/4 tsp. pepper*
*1/8 tsp. garlic powder*
*2 1/2 c. tomatoes*

**Cook** . . . . . . . cabbage leaves in boiling water in saucepan for 5 minutes; drain.
**Combine** . . . . next 7 ingredients in bowl, mixing well.
**Shape** . . . . . . into 8 rolls.
**Place** . . . . . . . on cabbage leaves, rolling to enclose filling.
**Place** . . . . . . . rolls on tomatoes in skillet.
**Simmer** . . . . . covered, for 35 minutes.
**Yields** . . . . . . 4 servings.

Jewell Blevins
Carl Junction H. S., Carl Junction, Missouri

## ORIENTAL HASH

*1 lb. lean ground beef*
*2 c. diagonally sliced celery*
*1 c. diagonally sliced carrots*
*1/2 c. chopped scallions*
*1 lg. clove of garlic, minced*
*1 tbsp. Worcestershire sauce*
*3/4 tsp. salt*
*1/2 lb. spinach, torn*

**Brown** . . . . . . ground beef in large skillet, stirring until crumbly.
**Stir** . . . . . . . . in next 4 ingredients.
**Sprinkle** . . . . with Worcestershire sauce and salt.
**Simmer** . . . . . covered, for 3 minutes.
**Add** . . . . . . . spinach.
**Simmer** . . . . . covered, for 3 minutes longer.
**Serve** . . . . . . . with rice.
**Yields** . . . . . . 4 servings.

Carla J. Sutton
Center Grove H. S., Greenwood, Indiana

## BEEF-BEAN CASSEROLE

*1 1/2 lb. ground beef*
*1 sm. onion, minced*
*1/2 c. catsup*
*1/2 tsp. dry mustard*
*2 tbsp. vinegar*
*3 tbsp. dark brown sugar*
*1  15-oz. can kidney beans*
*1  21-oz. can pork and beans*
*1 tsp. salt*

**Brown** . . . . . . ground beef in skillet, stirring until crumbly.
**Add** . . . . . . . onion.
**Cook** . . . . . . . until tender, stirring frequently.
**Stir** . . . . . . . . in remaining ingredients.
**Cook** . . . . . . . for 15 to 20 minutes, or until heated through.
**Yields** . . . . . . 4 servings.

Vanessa M. Napier
I. C. Norcom H. S., Portsmouth, Virginia

## T. J.'S BEEF AND BISCUITS

*1 lb. ground beef*
*1/4 c. chopped onion*
*1 tbsp. soy sauce*
*1 can cream of mushroom soup*
*Milk*
*1 1/2 c. flour*
*2 tsp. baking powder*
*1/4 tsp. salt*
*3 tbsp. shortening*

**Brown** . . . . . . ground beef with onion in large skillet, stirring until crumbly; drain.
**Add** . . . . . . . soy sauce, soup and 1 soup can milk, mixing well.
**Simmer** . . . . . for several minutes.
**Combine** . . . . remaining dry ingredients in bowl.
**Cut** . . . . . . . . in shortening until crumbly.
**Stir** . . . . . . . . in 3/4 cup milk.
**Drop** . . . . . . . by spoonfuls into ground beef mixture.
**Simmer** . . . . . for 10 minutes.
**Simmer** . . . . . covered, for 10 minutes longer, or until dough is fluffy.
**Yields** . . . . . . 4 servings.

Judith Varney
Corry Area H. S., Corry, Pennsylvania

# Meatballs

## BARBECUED MEATBALLS

1 lb. ground beef
1 tsp. salt
Dash of pepper
1/3 c. quick-cooking oatmeal
2/3 c. milk
2 tbsp. brown sugar
2 tsp. dry mustard
2 tbsp. vinegar
1 tbsp. Worcestershire sauce
3/4 c. catsup

**Mix** . . . . . . . . first 5 ingredients in bowl.
**Shape** . . . . . . into balls.
**Brown** . . . . . . in skillet.
**Place** . . . . . . . in baking dish.
**Blend** . . . . . . brown sugar and dry mustard in bowl.
**Stir** . . . . . . . . in remaining 3 ingredients, mixing well.
**Pour** . . . . . . . sauce over meatballs.
**Bake** . . . . . . . at 350 degrees for 40 minutes.
**Yields** . . . . . . 4 servings.

Debra A. Patterson
Commodore Perry H. S., Hadley, Pennsylvania

## BUTTERMILK MEATBALLS

1 lb. ground beef
3/4 c. milk
1/2 c. fine dry bread crumbs
1/4 c. finely chopped onion
1/8 tsp. pepper
1 1/2 tsp. salt
1/4 c. butter
2 tbsp. flour
2 tsp. sugar
2 c. buttermilk
2 tbsp. prepared mustard

**Combine** . . . . first 5 ingredients and 1 teaspoon salt in bowl, mixing well.
**Shape** . . . . . . into 16 balls.
**Brown** . . . . . . meatballs in 2 tablespoons butter in skillet, stirring frequently; remove meatballs with slotted spoon.
**Add** . . . . . . . remaining 2 tablespoons butter and 1/2 teaspoon salt, flour and sugar to pan drippings, stirring until blended.
**Stir** . . . . . . . . in buttermilk and mustard, mixing well.

**Cook** . . . . . . until thick, stirring constantly.
**Return** . . . . . meatballs to sauce.
**Simmer** . . . . . covered, for 20 minutes.
**Yields** . . . . . . 4-6 servings.

Photograph for this recipe above.

## BEST-EVER MEATBALLS

1 pkg. dry onion soup mix
2 eggs
1 sm. can evaporated milk
2 c. bread crumbs
2 lb. ground beef
1 can mushroom soup

**Mix** . . . . . . . . first 4 ingredients in bowl.
**Let** . . . . . . . . stand for 10 minutes.
**Add** . . . . . . . ground beef, mixing well.
**Shape** . . . . . . into 1 1/2-inch balls.
**Place** . . . . . . . on rack in broiler pan.
**Broil** . . . . . . . until brown.
**Place** . . . . . . . meatballs in casserole.
**Mix** . . . . . . . . soup with 1/2 soup can water in bowl.
**Pour** . . . . . . . over meatballs.
**Bake** . . . . . . . at 350 degrees for 45 minutes.
**Yields** . . . . . . 6-8 servings.

Mary Alsteens
Tomahawk H. S., Tomahawk, Wisconsin

## CLARETTA'S MEATBALLS

1 lb. ground beef
1/2 c. finely chopped onion
1/4 c. cream
1 egg, beaten

1 c. cracker crumbs
1/4 tsp. nutmeg
Salt to taste
1 can consomme

**Mix** . . . . . . . first 7 ingredients in bowl.
**Shape** . . . . . . into balls.
**Place** . . . . . . . in baking dish.
**Pour** . . . . . . . consomme over meatballs.
**Bake** . . . . . . . at 350 degrees for 1 hour.

Claretta Joy Beckmeyer
Snohomish H. S., Snohomish, Washington

## EASIEST-EVER MEATBALLS

5 slices bread, crumbled
1 lg. can evaporated milk
2 1/2 lb. hamburger
1 tsp. salt
1/2 tsp. pepper
3/4 tsp. sage
1 can each onion soup, chicken gumbo soup

**Soak** . . . . . . . bread in evaporated milk in large
bowl until soft.
**Add** . . . . . . . next 4 ingredients, mixing well.
**Shape** . . . . . . into balls with ice cream scoop.
**Place** . . . . . . . in large baking pan.
**Mix** . . . . . . . . soups together in bowl.
**Pour** . . . . . . . over meatballs.
**Bake** . . . . . . . at 350 degrees for 1 hour.
**Yields** . . . . . . 3 dozen.

Katherine McIlquham
Chippawa Falls Sr. H. S.,
Chippewa Falls, Wisconsin

## GOLDEN MUSHROOM MEATBALLS

1 lb. ground beef
2/3 c. fine bread crumbs
2 tbsp. each chopped onion, parsley
1 egg, slightly beaten
1 tsp. salt
1 can cream of mushroom soup
1/2 lb. cheese, cubed

**Mix** . . . . . . . . first 6 ingredients in bowl.
**Blend** . . . . . . soup and 1/4 cup water in small
bowl.
**Add** . . . . . . . 1/4 cup soup mixture to ground
beef mixture, mixing well.
**Shape** . . . . . . into balls around cheese cubes.
**Brown** . . . . . . in Dutch oven; drain.

**Pour** . . . . . . . remaining soup mixture over
meatballs.
**Bake** . . . . . . . covered, at 350 degrees for 30
minutes.
**Yields** . . . . . . 4-5 servings.

Diane Gibbs
New Bloomfield R-III H. S.
New Bloomfield, Missouri

## EASY MEATBALLS FOR SPAGHETTI SAUCE

1 slice bread
1 lb. ground beef
1 1/2 tsp. salt
1/4 tsp. basil
1 tbsp. chopped parsley
2 cloves of garlic, crushed

**Soak** . . . . . . . bread in enough water to
moisten in bowl.
**Combine** . . . . with remaining ingredients in
bowl, mixing well.
**Shape** . . . . . . into balls.
**Saute** . . . . . . in a small amount of oil in skillet
until browned and cooked
through; drain.
**Serve** . . . . . . with spaghetti sauce over
spaghetti.
**Yields** . . . . . . 4 servings.

J. Yvonne Chrane
Granbury H. S., Granbury, Texas

## LASAGNA-STYLE MEATBALLS

1 lb. ground beef
1 egg
1/4 c. each chopped onion, green pepper
1 c. cream-style cottage cheese
1 c. spaghetti sauce
1/2 c. shredded mozzarella cheese

**Mix** . . . . . . . . first 4 ingredients in bowl.
**Shape** . . . . . . into 1-inch balls.
**Place** . . . . . . . in greased 8-inch baking dish.
**Spoon** . . . . . . cottage cheese around meatballs.
**Cover** . . . . . . with spaghetti sauce.
**Sprinkle** . . . . cheese over top.
**Bake** . . . . . . . at 350 degrees for 45 minutes.
**Yields** . . . . . . 4 servings.

Marilyn Meade
LeMars Community Sch., LeMars, Iowa

## CHEESY MEATBALL PIE

1 lb. ground beef
1/2 c. quick-cooking oats
3 tbsp. chopped onion
1 tsp. salt
1/4 tsp. pepper
1/4 c. tomato sauce
1 egg, beaten
1 tbsp. Worcestershire sauce
1 tbsp. oil
1 tbsp. flour
Dash each of cayenne pepper, garlic powder
1 tbsp. butter, melted
1 c. milk
1/2 c. Parmesan cheese
1 baked 9-in. pie shell
1/2 c. grated American cheese
6 strips crisp-cooked bacon, crumbled

Combine .... first 8 ingredients in bowl, mix-
ing well.
Shape ...... into 48 balls.
Brown ...... in oil in skillet; drain.
Stir ........ flour, cayenne pepper and garlic
powder into butter in saucepan,
blending well.
Stir ........ in milk.
Bring ....... to a boil over medium heat, stir-
ring occasionally.
Simmer ..... for 1 minute.

Stir ........ in Parmesan cheese.
Cook ....... over low heat until cheese is
melted, stirring constantly.
Place ....... meatballs in pie shell.
Pour ....... sauce over meatballs, distribut-
ing evenly.
Bake ....... at 375 degrees for 25 minutes.
Top ........ with American cheese and
bacon.
Yields ...... 6 servings.

Photograph for this recipe on this page.

## MARY'S DELICIOUS GROUND BEEF ROLLS

1 20-oz. can tomatoes, mashed
1 tbsp. tomato paste
1/4 tsp. garlic salt
1 tsp. Parmesan cheese
Salt and pepper to taste
3 slices bread
Red wine
1 lb. lean ground beef
Butter

Combine .... first 4 ingredients with salt and
pepper in large saucepan, mixing
well.
Simmer ..... for 30 minutes.
Soak ....... bread in a small amount of red
wine in bowl; drain.
Add ....... ground beef, salt and pepper,
mixing well.
Shape ...... into small rolls.
Brown ...... in butter in skillet.
Add ....... to sauce.
Simmer ..... for 15 minutes longer.
Serve ....... with rice.
Yields ...... 6 servings.

Mary Kampros Graham
East H. S., Salt Lake City, Utah

## JOANNE'S MEATBALLS

1 lb. ground beef
2 tbsp. minced onion
Salt and pepper to taste
1/4 tsp. chili powder
1 egg
1/3 c. bread crumbs
Oil

1 can cream of mushroom soup
Milk

**Combine** .... first 7 ingredients in bowl, mixing well.
**Shape** ...... into small balls.
**Brown** ...... in a small amount of oil in skillet; drain.
**Blend** ...... soup with 1 soup can milk in bowl.
**Pour** ....... over meatballs.
**Simmer** ..... covered, for 15 to 20 minutes.
**Serve** ....... over rice.
**Yields** ...... 4-5 servings.

Joanne Parry Dankey
Washington Sr. H. S., Sioux Falls, South Dakota

## DIFFERENT MEATBALLS

1 1/2 lb. hamburger
1 lb. ground pork
3/4 c. cooked rice
1 sm. onion, chopped
1 1/2 c. crushed corn flakes
1 egg
Salt and pepper to taste
Flour
1 can tomato soup

**Combine** .... first 8 ingredients in bowl, mixing well.
**Form** ...... into balls using ice cream scoop.
**Coat** ....... with flour.
**Place** ....... in large baking dish.
**Pour** ....... soup over meatballs.
**Bake** ....... at 350 degrees for 1 hour.
**Yields** ...... 9 servings.

Linda Cherry
Griggsville H. S., Griggsville, Illinois

## MEATBALLS CON QUESO

1 1/2 lb. ground beef
1 1/2 c. bread crumbs
1/3 c. chopped onion
1/3 c. milk
3 tbsp. chopped parsley
1/4 tsp. pepper
1 egg
3 tbsp. oil
1 4-oz. can green chilies, chopped
16 oz. Velveeta cheese, cut into chunks
1 pkg. taco seasoning mix

**Mix** ........ first 7 ingredients in bowl.
**Shape** ...... into 1-inch balls.
**Brown** ...... meatballs in oil in skillet; remove with slotted spoon.
**Stir** ........ chilies, cheese, taco seasoning and 3/4 cup water into pan drippings, mixing well.
**Simmer** ..... until cheese is melted, stirring constantly.
**Place** ....... meatballs in cheese sauce.
**Simmer** ..... until heated through.
**Serve** ....... with corn bread and red beans.

Ann Schroeder
Texas City H. S., Texas City, Texas

## MEATBALLS IN SOUR CREAM-DILL SAUCE

2 lb. ground beef
1/2 tsp. pepper
2 eggs
1 lg. onion, chopped
1 c. soft bread crumbs
1/2 c. tomato juice
Salt
1/4 c. shortening
1/4 c. flour
1 tsp. dillseed
2 c. sour cream
Paprika to taste

**Mix** ........ first 6 ingredients and 1 1/2 teaspoons salt in bowl.
**Shape** ...... into 1 1/2-inch balls.
**Brown** ...... in shortening in skillet, stirring frequently.
**Remove** .... meatballs with slotted spoon, reserving 1/4 cup pan drippings.
**Stir** ........ in flour, 1/2 cup water, dillseed and sour cream, mixing well.
**Cook** ....... until thick and bubbly, stirring constantly.
**Add** ....... meatballs and salt and paprika to taste, mixing well.
**Cook** ....... until heated through.
**Serve** ....... with parsley noodles.
**Yields** ...... 6-8 servings.

Sharyn J. LaHaise
Medford H. S., Medford, Massachusetts

## MEATBALLS IN TOMATO SAUCE

2 lb. hamburger
2 eggs, beaten
Celery leaves, chopped
1/2 tsp. each salt, monosodium glutamate
1/4 tsp. pepper
1 c. milk
1 onion, chopped
1 sm. green pepper, chopped
4 slices bread, cubed
20 saltines, crushed
1/2 c. flour
Oil
1 sm. can tomato sauce
1 can tomato soup

Combine .... first 11 ingredients in bowl, mixing well.
Shape ...... into balls.
Coat ....... with flour.
Brown ...... in a small amount of oil in Dutch oven; drain.
Stir ........ in tomato sauce, soup and 1 soup can water.
Simmer ..... covered, for 30 minutes.
Yields ...... 8 servings.

Karen R. Collins
Greensville County H. S., Emporia, Virginia

## MEATBALLS ORIENTAL

1 lb. ground beef
1/4 c. fine dry bread crumbs
1/2 c. finely chopped onion
1 tsp. salt
Dash of pepper
2/3 c. evaporated milk
2 tbsp. butter, melted
1 c. diagonally sliced celery
1 green pepper, cut into strips
1   19-oz. can bean sprouts
1   4-oz. can sliced mushrooms
1/4 c. cornstarch
3 to 4 tbsp. soy sauce
2 med. onions, thinly sliced

Combine .... first 6 ingredients in bowl, mixing well.
Shape ...... into 12 balls.
Brown ...... in butter in skillet; push meatballs to one side.
Add ....... celery and green pepper; remove from heat.
Drain ...... bean sprouts and mushrooms, reserving liquids.
Add ....... enough water to reserved liquids to measure 1 1/2 cups.
Combine .... cornstarch with a small amount of reserved liquid in bowl, blending well.
Add ....... remaining liquid, blending well.
Stir ........ in soy sauce.
Pour ....... over meatballs and vegetables in skillet.
Bring ....... to a boil over medium heat.
Simmer ..... covered, for 20 minutes or until sauce is thickened and clear.
Add ....... drained vegetables and onions, mixing well.
Simmer ..... covered, for 5 minutes longer.
Serve ....... over rice.
Yields ...... 6 servings.

Photograph for this recipe on page 47.

## MEATBALLS PAPRIKA

1 1/2 lb. ground meat mixture
1 c. bread crumbs
1/2 c. milk
1/4 c. minced onion
1/4 tsp. Tabasco sauce
1/4 tsp. tarragon
Salt
1 pt. sour cream
2 tbsp. flour
1/2 c. milk
1 tbsp. paprika

Combine .... first 6 ingredients and 1/2 teaspoon salt in bowl, mixing well.
Shape ...... into 1-inch balls.
Boil ........ in salted water in saucepan for 12 minutes; drain.
Combine .... 1/2 teaspoon salt, sour cream and flour in saucepan, mixing well.
Mix ........ in milk and paprika.
Cook ....... over low heat until thick, stirring constantly; do not boil.
Add ....... meatballs.
Cook ....... until heated through.
Serve ....... over noodles.
Yields ...... 4 servings.

Margaret Polkabla
Memorial H. S., Campbell Ohio

## NANCY'S MEATBALLS

1 1/2 c. ground beef
1/2 c. cracker crumbs
1/4 c. milk
1 egg
1 med. onion, chopped
Salt and pepper to taste
Flour
Oil
1 can cream of mushroom soup

**Combine** .... first 7 ingredients in bowl, mixing well.
**Shape** ...... into balls.
**Coat** ....... with flour.
**Brown** ...... in a small amount of oil in skillet; drain.
**Add** ....... soup diluted with 1 soup can water.
**Simmer** .... until heated through.
**Serve** ....... over mashed potatoes.
**Yields** ...... 4 servings.

Nancy Ann Forbear
Oakridge Sr. H. S., Muskegon, Michigan

## JIFFY MEATBALL CASSEROLE

1 lb. ground beef
1/4 c. minced onion
1 1/2 tsp. salt
1/2 tsp. Tabasco sauce
1 c. rice
1  1-lb. can stewed tomatoes
1 bouillon cube

**Combine** .... ground beef, onion, 1 teaspoon salt and 1/4 teaspoon Tabasco sauce in bowl, mixing well.
**Shape** ...... into 8 balls.
**Roll** ....... in rice.
**Place** ....... in greased 2-quart casserole.
**Mix** ....... remaining 1/2 teaspoon salt and 1/4 teaspoon Tabasco sauce with tomatoes in bowl.
**Pour** ....... over meatballs.
**Dissolve** .... bouillon cube in 1 cup hot water.
**Pour** ....... over casserole.
**Sprinkle** .... remaining rice over top.
**Bake** ....... covered, at 350 degrees for 1 hour and 10 minutes or until rice is tender.
**Yields** ...... 4 servings.

Photograph for this recipe above.

## JANET'S PORCUPINE MEATBALLS

1 1/2 lb. ground beef
1 egg
Dash of salt
1 env. dry onion soup mix
3/4 c. rice
2 c. tomato juice
1 1/2 tbsp. sugar

**Mix** ........ first 3 ingredients, 1/4 envelope soup mix and 1/4 cup rice in bowl.
**Shape** ...... into 1 1/2-inch meatballs.
**Roll** ....... in remaining rice.
**Place** ....... in 9 x 13-inch casserole.
**Cook** ....... tomato juice, sugar and remaining onion soup mix in saucepan, stirring until sugar is dissolved.
**Pour** ....... over meatballs.
**Bake** ....... at 350 degrees for 50 minutes.
**Yields** ...... 8 servings.

Janet B. Miller
Roseville H. S., Roseville, Illinois

## CAROLE'S PORCUPINE MEATBALLS

*1 can tomato sauce*
*1 lb. ground beef*
*1/4 c. rice*
*1 egg, slightly beaten*
*1/4 c. minced onion*
*1 tsp. salt*

**Mix** . . . . . . . . 1/4 cup tomato sauce and remaining ingredients in bowl.
**Shape** . . . . . . into 2-inch balls.
**Place** . . . . . . . in baking dish.
**Add** . . . . . . . 1 cup water to remaining tomato sauce.
**Pour** . . . . . . . over meatballs.
**Bake** . . . . . . . covered, at 350 degrees for 1 hour.
**Yields** . . . . . . 5-6 servings.

Carole S. Curts
South Whitley Middle Sch., South Whitley, Indiana


## PRESSURE COOKER MEATBALL DINNER

*1 lb. ground beef*
*1 1/2 tsp. salt*
*Dash of pepper*
*1 egg, slightly beaten*
*2 slices bread, cubed*
*1/4 c. each finely chopped onion, celery*
*2 tbsp. shortening*
*5 med. potatoes*
*4 med. carrots, cut into pieces*

**Mix** . . . . . . . . first 7 ingredients in bowl.
**Shape** . . . . . . into 1 1/2-inch balls.
**Brown** . . . . . . in shortening in pressure cooker, stirring frequently.
**Add** . . . . . . . remaining vegetables and 1 cup water.
**Cook** . . . . . . . for 15 minutes at 10 pounds pressure, using pressure cooker directions.
**Yields** . . . . . . 5 servings.

Bonita Wiersig
Anson Jones Sch., Bryan, Texas


## SAUCY MEATBALLS

*1 egg, beaten*
*1/4 c. milk*

*1/4 c. fine dry bread crumbs*
*1 tbsp. minced parsley*
*1/4 tsp. each marjoram, thyme, pepper*
*1/2 tsp. salt*
*1 1/2 lb. ground beef*
*1 c. beef bouillon*
*1/2 c. chopped onion*
*1 c. sour cream*
*1 tbsp. flour*

**Mix** . . . . . . . . first 8 ingredients in large bowl.
**Add** . . . . . . . ground beef, mixing well.
**Shape** . . . . . . into twenty-four 1 1/2-inch balls.
**Brown** . . . . . . in skillet; drain.
**Add** . . . . . . . bouillon and onion, mixing well.
**Simmer** . . . . . covered, for 30 minutes.
**Blend** . . . . . . sour cream and flour in bowl.
**Pour** . . . . . . . over meatballs.
**Cook** . . . . . . . until sauce thickens, stirring constantly.
**Serve** . . . . . . . with noodles.
**Garnish** . . . . . with additional parsley.
**Yields** . . . . . . 4-6 servings.

Linda K. Sloan
Pryor Senior H. S., Pryor, Oklahoma


## EMILY'S SKILLET BURGER BALLS

*1 1/2 lb. ground beef*
*2 1/2 tsp. salt*
*1 egg, slightly beaten*
*1/2 c. bread crumbs*
*1/4 c. oil*
*1 c. chopped onion*
*1/2 c. chopped green pepper*
*1 clove of garlic, minced*
*2 8-oz. cans tomato sauce*
*1 tbsp. Worcestershire sauce*
*1 tsp. celery seed*
*Dash of pepper*

**Mix** . . . . . . . . ground beef, 1 1/2 teaspoons salt, egg and bread crumbs in bowl.
**Shape** . . . . . . into 1 1/2-inch balls.
**Brown** . . . . . . in oil in skillet; remove with slotted spoon.
**Saute** . . . . . . onion and green pepper in pan drippings for several minutes.
**Add** . . . . . . . 1 teaspoon salt and remaining ingredients.

**Bring** . . . . . . . to a boil, stirring frequently.
**Add** . . . . . . . meatballs.
**Simmer** . . . . . covered, for 30 minutes.
**Yields** . . . . . . 6 servings.

Emily Lewis
Capitol Hill H. S., Oklahoma City, Oklahoma

## MEATBALLS WITH SAUERKRAUT

*2 lb. hamburger*
*2 c. bread crumbs*
*3 eggs*
*1/2 c. milk*
*1 pkg. dry onion soup mix*
*1 sm. bottle of chili sauce*
*1 c. sauerkraut*
*1 can cranberries*

**Mix** . . . . . . . . first 5 ingredients in bowl.
**Shape** . . . . . . into 1-inch balls.
**Place** . . . . . . . in large baking dish.
**Mix** . . . . . . . . chili sauce with an equal amount of water in bowl.
**Layer** . . . . . . sauerkraut, cranberries and sauce over meatballs.
**Bake** . . . . . . . at 300 degrees for 2 hours.
**Serve** . . . . . . . with rice.
**Yields** . . . . . . 8-10 servings.

Marian B. Dobbins
Catalina H. S., Tucson, Arizona

## MEATBALL MEDLEY

*1 egg*
*1/4 c. milk*
*3 c. soft bread crumbs*
*1 lb. ground beef*
*1/8 tsp. pepper*
*1 tsp. salt*
*2 tbsp. oil*
*1  27-oz. can sauerkraut, drained*
*1/2 c. chopped onion*
*3/4 c. rice*
*2 c. chopped tomatoes*

**Combine** . . . . first 5 ingredients and 1/2 teaspoon salt in bowl, mixing well.
**Shape** . . . . . . into 12 meatballs.
**Brown** . . . . . . in heated oil in skillet, stirring frequently; remove with slotted spoon.

**Add** . . . . . . . sauerkraut, onion and 1/2 teaspoon salt, mixing well.
**Stir** . . . . . . . . in rice, 1 1/2 cups water, tomatoes and meatballs.
**Simmer** . . . . . covered, for 30 to 35 minutes or until rice is tender.
**Yields** . . . . . . 6 servings.

JoAnne M. Stringer
Liberty H. S., Youngstown, Ohio

## ANGELINE'S SPAGHETTI AND MEATBALLS

*4 slices bread*
*2 eggs*
*1 lb. ground beef*
*1/4 c. grated cheese*
*2 tbsp. parsley*
*2 1/2 tsp. salt*
*1 3/4 tsp. oregano*
*Pepper*
*5 tbsp. oil*
*3/4 c. chopped onions*
*1 clove of garlic, chopped*
*4 c. canned tomatoes*
*2 c. tomato sauce*
*1 tsp. sugar*
*1 bay leaf*

**Soak** . . . . . . . bread in 1/2 cup water in large bowl for 3 minutes.
**Mix** . . . . . . . . in eggs.
**Add** . . . . . . . next 3 ingredients, 1 teaspoon salt, 1/4 teaspoon oregano and pepper to taste, mixing well.
**Shape** . . . . . . into balls.
**Brown** . . . . . . in 2 tablespoons oil in skillet; remove meatballs.
**Saute** . . . . . . onions and garlic in 3 tablespoons oil in skillet until tender.
**Stir** . . . . . . . . in 1 1/2 teaspoons salt, 1/2 teaspoon pepper and 1 1/2 teaspoons oregano with remaining 4 ingredients and 2 cups water.
**Simmer** . . . . . for 30 minutes; remove bay leaf.
**Add** . . . . . . . meatballs.
**Simmer** . . . . . for 30 minutes longer.
**Serve** . . . . . . . over spaghetti.
**Yields** . . . . . . 8 servings.

Angeline Boehnke
Flatonia H. S., Flatonia, Texas

## DIANE'S SPAGHETTI SAUCE

*1 lb. ground beef*
*1 tsp. salt*
*1/4 tsp. pepper*
*1 egg*
*1/2 c. oats*
*1 onion, chopped*
*1/4 c. milk*
*Flour*
*Oil*
*2 lg. cans tomato sauce*
*2 tsp. Worcestershire sauce*
*Garlic powder to taste*
*1   12-oz. can tomato paste*

**Combine** .... first 7 ingredients in bowl, mixing well.
**Shape** ...... into balls.
**Roll** ....... in flour.
**Brown** ...... in a small amount of oil in skillet; remove meatballs.
**Stir** ........ remaining 4 ingredients and a small amount of water into pan drippings.
**Add** ....... meatballs.
**Simmer** ..... for 2 hours.
**Yields** ...... 4-6 servings.

Diane Norbury
Holton Public Sch., Holton, Michigan

## SPANISH-STYLE MEATBALLS

*1 1/2 lb. ground chuck*
*1/2 c. Italian-seasoned bread crumbs*
*1 tsp. seasoned salt*
*1/2 c. evaporated milk*
*1 tbsp. minced onion*
*Pepper*
*2 tbsp. butter, melted*
*1/4 c. each chopped green pepper,*
*    minced onion*
*1   6-oz. can tomato paste*
*1 can stewed tomatoes*
*1/2 c. sliced stuffed green olives*
*1/2 tsp. garlic salt*
*1/4 tsp. crushed red pepper*

**Combine** .... first 5 ingredients and 1/8 teaspoon pepper in bowl, mixing well.
**Shape** ...... into 12 balls.
**Brown** ...... in butter in skillet, stirring frequently.

**Add** ....... green pepper and onion.
**Saute** ...... until tender.
**Mix** ........ tomato paste with 1/2 paste can water in small bowl.
**Add** ....... to skillet with remaining ingredients, mixing well.
**Simmer** ..... tightly covered, for 30 minutes.
**Serve** ....... over noodles.
**Yields** ...... 6 servings.

Patricia M. Fritz
Bayshore H. S., Bradenton, Florida

## SPICED MEATBALLS

*3/4 c. evaporated milk*
*5 tsp. Worcestershire sauce*
*1 env. dry onion soup mix*
*1 lb. hamburger*
*2 c. catsup*
*3/4 c. packed brown sugar*

**Combine** .... evaporated milk, 2 teaspoons Worcestershire sauce and soup mix in bowl, mixing well.
**Let** ........ stand for 5 minutes.
**Mix** ........ in hamburger.
**Shape** ...... into balls.
**Brown** ...... in skillet; drain.
**Cook** ....... remaining 3 teaspoons Worcestershire sauce and remaining ingredients in saucepan until heated through, stirring constantly.
**Add** ....... meatballs, mixing gently.
**Heat** ....... to serving temperature.
**Yields** ...... 4 servings.

Earleen Williams
Williston H. S., Williston, Florida

## BAKED MEATBALLS STROGANOFF

*1 lb. ground beef*
*1 egg*
*1 c. sour cream*
*2 tsp. instant minced onion*
*1/4 tsp. each salt, pepper*
*2 slices bread, torn into pieces*
*1/2 c. milk*
*Dash of garlic powder*

**Mix** ........ ground beef, egg, 2 tablespoons sour cream, 1 1/2 teaspoons onion, salt, 1/8 teaspoon pepper and bread in bowl.

**Shape** ...... into 1 1/2-inch balls.
**Place** ....... in baking dish.
**Bake** ....... at 350 degrees for 40 minutes.
**Combine** .... remaining sour cream, pepper and onion with milk and garlic powder in bowl, mixing well.
**Pour** ....... sauce over meatballs.
**Bake** ....... for 10 minutes longer.
**Yields** ...... 4 servings.

Dorothy S. Weirick
Cottonwood H. S., Salt Lake City, Utah

## JUDY'S MEATBALLS STROGANOFF

1 lb. ground beef
Flour
1 med. onion, chopped
1 tbsp. Worcestershire sauce
1/4 tsp. garlic powder
1 can cream of mushroom soup
1/2 c. sour cream

**Shape** ...... ground beef into small balls.
**Coat** ....... with flour.
**Brown** ...... meatballs in skillet.
**Add** ....... next 4 ingredients, mixing well.
**Simmer** ..... for 15 minutes.
**Stir** ........ in sour cream, mixing well.
**Serve** ....... over noodles.
**Yields** ...... 4-6 servings.

Judy McCleery
South H. S., Salt Lake City, Utah

## STUFFED MEATBALL FONDUE

1 lb. lean ground beef
1/2 c. cracker crumbs
1 egg
3 tbsp. milk
1 tsp. seasoned salt
1/2 tsp. pepper
Cheddar cheese cubes
Oil for deep frying

**Mix** ........ first 6 ingredients in bowl.
**Shape** ...... into balls around cheese cubes.
**Chill** ....... covered, for 1 hour or longer.
**Cook** ....... in heated oil in fondue pot until browned.
**Yields** ...... 4 servings.

Brenda Brandt
Logan Middle Sch., LaCrosse, Wisconsin

## SUPER MEATBALLS

1 lb. ground beef
1/2 c. bread crumbs
1/3 c. chopped onion
1/4 c. milk
1/2 tsp. Worcestershire sauce
1 egg
1 tsp. salt
1/8 tsp. pepper
1 bottle of chili sauce
1 10-oz. jar grape jelly

**Combine** .... first 8 ingredients in bowl, mixing well.
**Shape** ...... into balls.
**Brown** ...... in skillet; drain.
**Place** ....... in casserole.
**Mix** ........ chili sauce and jelly in bowl.
**Pour** ....... over meatballs.
**Bake** ....... at 350 degrees for 30 minutes.
**Yields** ...... 6 servings.

Ramona Warwick
Castlewood H. S., Castlewood, South Dakota

## BAKED SWEDISH MEATBALLS

1/2 c. bread crumbs
Milk
1 lb. ground beef
Salt and pepper to taste
1/8 c. chopped green pepper
1 egg
1/4 c. chopped onion
1 1/2 tsp. brown sugar
1/2 tsp. nutmeg
1 can cream of mushroom soup

**Soften** ...... bread crumbs in milk in bowl.
**Add** ....... next 6 ingredients, mixing well.
**Shape** ...... into balls.
**Brown** ...... in skillet; drain.
**Place** ....... in baking dish.
**Mix** ........ remaining ingredients with 1/2 cup water in bowl.
**Pour** ....... over meatballs.
**Bake** ....... at 325 degrees until heated through.
**Yields** ...... 4-6 servings.

Carolyn Hix
Community H. S., Unionville, Tennessee

## SAUCY SWEDISH MEATBALLS

1 onion, chopped
1 green pepper, chopped
Butter
1 can each chicken with rice, tomato soup
2 slices bread, torn into pieces
2 lb. ground beef
1/4 c. evaporated milk
1 egg
1 tsp. salt

**Saute** ...... onion and green pepper in butter in skillet until tender.
**Add** ....... next 2 ingredients and 1 cup water, mixing well.
**Simmer** ..... for several minutes, stirring occasionally.
**Combine** .... bread, ground beef, milk, egg and salt in bowl, mixing well.
**Shape** ...... into balls.
**Cook** ....... in sauce for 1 hour.
**Serve** ....... over rice.

Peggy White
Califf Middle Sch., Gray, Georgia

## BRENDA'S SWEDISH MEATBALLS

1 can cream of mushroom soup
1 lb. ground beef
1/2 c. chopped onion
1/4 c. bread crumbs
1 egg
Salt and pepper to taste

**Mix** ........ soup with 1/2 cup water in small bowl.
**Combine** .... 1/4 cup soup mixture with remaining ingredients in bowl, mixing well.
**Shape** ...... into balls.
**Brown** ...... in skillet; drain.
**Pour** ....... soup mixture over meatballs.
**Serve** ....... over rice.
**Simmer** ..... for 25 to 30 minutes.

Brenda Williford
Semmes Middle Sch., Mobile, Alabama

## CHARLESTON SWEET AND SOUR MEATBALLS

2 lb. ground chuck
1 lb. ground pork

Salt and pepper to taste
Seasoned flour
3 to 4 tbsp. oil
4 lg. carrots, peeled, sliced
3 med. onions, quartered
2 c. tomato juice
3 to 4 tbsp. cider vinegar
1/2 tsp. ginger
3 to 4 tbsp. sweet pickle juice
3 to 4 tbsp. sugar
4 to 5 tsp. cornstarch
1 pkg. frozen chopped collard greens, cooked, drained
2 to 3 c. cooked rice

**Combine** .... ground chuck, ground pork, salt and pepper in large bowl, mixing well.
**Shape** ...... into 18 balls.
**Coat** ....... with seasoned flour.
**Brown** ...... in oil in heavy skillet.
**Cook** ....... covered, over low heat for 25 minutes, stirring occasionally; drain.
**Combine** .... carrots with next 5 ingredients in saucepan, mixing well.
**Cook** ....... until carrots are tender-crisp.
**Add** ....... sugar to taste.
**Blend** ...... cornstarch with a small amount of water.
**Stir** ........ into carrot mixture with half the collard greens.
**Add** ....... to meatballs in skillet.
**Simmer** ..... for 25 to 30 minutes.
**Spoon** ...... rice into ring on serving plate.
**Layer** ...... remaining collard greens and meatball mixture in center.

Garnish . . . . . with sweet pickles.
Yields . . . . . . 6 servings.

Photograph for this recipe on opposite page.

## SWEET AND SOUR MEATBALLS IN TOMATO SAUCE

*1 lb. ground beef*
*1 sm. onion, grated*
*1 egg*
*1/2 c. bread crumbs*
*Salt and pepper to taste*
*1 sm. can tomato sauce*
*1/4 c. vinegar*
*1/4 c. packed brown sugar*
*1 onion, chopped*

Combine . . . . first 6 ingredients and 1/4 cup water in bowl, mixing well.
Shape . . . . . . into small balls.
Mix . . . . . . . . tomato sauce, vinegar, brown sugar and onion in saucepan.
Bring . . . . . . . to a boil.
Add . . . . . . . meatballs.
Simmer . . . . . covered, for 1 hour.
Yields . . . . . . 4 servings.

Leigh Bookbinder
New Caney H. S., Porter, Texas

## SWEET AND SOUR MEATBALLS SUPREME

*1 c. sliced carrots*
*1  8 1/4-oz. can pineapple*
*1 tbsp. cornstarch*
*1 1/2 tbsp. sugar*
*2 tbsp. white vinegar*
*4 tbsp. soy sauce*
*1 lb. ground chuck*
*3 tbsp. minced green pepper*
*1 egg*
*1/4 tsp. each salt, ginger*
*2 tbsp. oil*
*1 green pepper, cut into strips*
*1/4 c. sliced water chestnuts*

Cook . . . . . . . carrots in water in saucepan until tender; drain, reserving liquid.
Drain . . . . . . pineapple, reserving juice; cut into bite-sized pieces.

Combine . . . . reserved juice and reserved carrot liquid with enough water to measure 1 cup.
Pour . . . . . . . into saucepan.
Stir . . . . . . . . in next 3 ingredients and 2 tablespoons soy sauce, mixing well.
Boil . . . . . . . . until thick, stirring constantly.
Combine . . . . remaining soy sauce and next 5 ingredients in bowl, mixing well.
Shape . . . . . . into balls.
Brown . . . . . . in oil in skillet.
Remove . . . . meatballs to bowl; keep warm.
Saute . . . . . . green pepper in pan drippings for 2 minutes.
Add . . . . . . . carrots, chopped pineapple and water chestnuts.
Saute . . . . . . for 3 minutes longer.
Add . . . . . . . meatballs and sauce to vegetables.
Simmer . . . . . for 5 minutes.

Cheryl Yates
Dobson H. S., Mesa, Arizona

## HARRIET'S SWEET AND SOUR MEATBALLS

*1 lb. ground beef*
*1/2 c. bread crumbs*
*2 tbsp. chopped onion*
*1 egg*
*1 tsp. salt*
*1/8 tsp. garlic powder*
*1 can tomato soup*
*1/4 c. packed brown sugar*
*1/4 c. lemon juice*
*2 tsp. Worcestershire sauce*

Mix . . . . . . . . first 6 ingredients and 3 tablespoons soup in bowl.
Shape . . . . . . into 1 1/2-inch balls.
Combine . . . . remaining soup with 1/2 cup water and remaining 3 ingredients in skillet, mixing well.
Bring . . . . . . . to a boil, covered, over medium heat.
Add . . . . . . . meatballs several at a time.
Simmer . . . . . for 40 minutes, stirring occasionally.
Yields . . . . . . 4 servings.

Harriet Chapnick
Walton H. S., Bronx, New York

## POLYNESIAN MEATBALLS

1 1/2 lb. lean ground beef
1/2 c. fine dry bread crumbs
1 sm. onion, minced
1 tsp. each cornstarch, salt
Dash of allspice
1 egg, beaten
3/4 c. cream
1/2 c. grape jelly
1 bottle of chili sauce

**Mix** . . . . . . . . first 8 ingredients in bowl.
**Shape** . . . . . . into 1-inch balls.
**Place** . . . . . . . in baking dish.
**Cook** . . . . . . . jelly and chili sauce in saucepan, stirring until bubbly.
**Pour** . . . . . . . sauce over meatballs.
**Bake** . . . . . . . at 300 degrees for 1 hour.
**Serve** . . . . . . . with rice.
**Yields** . . . . . . 3 dozen meatballs.

Leslie R. Morris
Tempe H. S., Tempe, Arizona

## LUCY'S SWEET AND SOUR BEEF

1 lb. ground beef
1 sm. onion, chopped
2 stalks celery, sliced
1  8-oz. can tomato sauce
1  15-oz. can sweet and sour sauce
1 sm. can pineapple tidbits, drained (opt.)

**Shape** . . . . . . ground beef into balls.
**Brown** . . . . . . in skillet; drain.
**Add** . . . . . . . next 4 ingredients, stirring gently.
**Simmer** . . . . . covered, for 20 minutes.
**Mix** . . . . . . . . in pineapple.
**Cook** . . . . . . . until heated through.
**Serve** . . . . . . . over rice.
**Yields** . . . . . . 4-6 servings.

Lucy Calhoun
Kelso H. S., Kelso, Washington

## THRIFTY MEATBALLS

1 lb. ground beef
1/4 c. each chopped onion, rice, cracker crumbs
1/3 c. milk

1 1/4 tsp. salt
1/8 tsp. pepper
1/4 tsp. poultry seasoning
Oil
1 can cream of mushroom soup

**Mix** . . . . . . . . all ingredients except oil and soup in bowl.
**Shape** . . . . . . into balls.
**Brown** . . . . . . in a small amount of oil in skillet.
**Blend** . . . . . . soup with 3/4 cup hot water in bowl.
**Pour** . . . . . . . over meatballs.
**Simmer** . . . . . covered, for 1 1/4 hours.
**Garnish** . . . . . with chopped parsley.

Jennifer Hemstreet
Santa Maria H. S., Santa Maria, California

## YORKSHIRE MEATBALLS

1 1/2 lb. ground beef
1/4 c. catsup
1 env. dry onion soup mix
1 tbsp. parsley flakes
1/4 tsp. pepper
5 eggs
1 1/2 c. milk
3 tbsp. butter, melted
1 1/2 c. sifted flour
1 1/2 tsp. baking powder
1 tsp. salt

**Mix** . . . . . . . . first 5 ingredients in large bowl.
**Add** . . . . . . . 1 slightly beaten egg and 1 tablespoon water, mixing well.
**Shape** . . . . . . into 24 meatballs.
**Place** . . . . . . . in well-greased 9 x 13-inch baking dish.
**Beat** . . . . . . . remaining eggs in bowl until foamy.
**Stir** . . . . . . . . in milk and butter, blending well.
**Add** . . . . . . . sifted dry ingredients, beating until smooth.
**Pour** . . . . . . . over meatballs.
**Bake** . . . . . . . at 350 degrees for 45 minutes or until golden brown.
**Serve** . . . . . . . with cheese sauce.
**Yields** . . . . . . 6-8 servings.

Debra Nelson
Donnybrook H. S., Donnybrook, North Dakota

# Loaves

## CARROT MEAT LOAF

3/4 c. milk
1 1/2 c. soft bread crumbs
2 lb. ground beef
3 sm. eggs
2 carrots, finely shredded
2 tbsp. horseradish
1 pkg. dry onion soup mix
1/4 c. catsup
3 tbsp. brown sugar
2 tbsp. prepared mustard

**Pour** . . . . . . . milk over bread crumbs in large bowl.
**Let** . . . . . . . . stand until milk is absorbed.
**Mix** . . . . . . . . in next 5 ingredients.
**Place** . . . . . . . in greased 5 x 9-inch loaf pan.
**Combine** . . . . catsup, brown sugar and mustard in bowl, blending well.
**Spread** . . . . . over meat loaf.
**Bake** . . . . . . . at 350 degrees for 1 hour.
**Yields** . . . . . . 8-10 servings.

Helen Babb Boots
Lakeland Village-Medical Lake Sch. Dist.
Cheney, Washington

## SAUCY MEAT LOAF

1/2 c. chopped onion
2 tbsp. shortening
1 can tomato soup
1 tsp. Worcestershire sauce
Dash of pepper
2 lb. lean ground beef
1 tsp. salt
3 eggs, slightly beaten
3/4 c. dry bread crumbs

**Saute** . . . . . . onion in shortening in skillet until tender.
**Add** . . . . . . . soup, Worcestershire sauce and pepper, mixing well.
**Simmer** . . . . . for several minutes.
**Combine** . . . . half the sauce with remaining 4 ingredients in bowl, mixing well.
**Press** . . . . . . . into large loaf pan.
**Pour** . . . . . . . remaining sauce over meat loaf.
**Bake** . . . . . . . at 350 degrees for 1 1/2 hours.
**Let** . . . . . . . . stand for 10 minutes for easier slicing.
**Yields** . . . . . . 8-10 servings.

Denise Potter
Alta H. S., Sandy, Utah

## JOAN'S CHEESEBURGER MEAT LOAF

2 eggs, beaten
1/4 c. light cream
1  8-oz. can tomato sauce
4 slices stale bread, crumbled
1 med. onion, finely chopped
1/4 c. celery, finely chopped
1/4 c. green pepper, chopped
1 tsp. salt
1/4 tsp. pepper
Dash of garlic salt
2 lb. lean ground beef
4 slices cheese

**Combine** . . . . first 4 ingredients in bowl.
**Let** . . . . . . . . stand until bread softens.
**Add** . . . . . . . vegetables, seasonings and ground beef, mixing well.
**Press** . . . . . . . half the mixture into well-greased loaf pan.
**Arrange** . . . . . cheese in center of ground beef layer.
**Press** . . . . . . . remaining ground beef mixture over cheese, sealing edges.
**Bake** . . . . . . . at 350 degrees for 1 hour.
**Yields** . . . . . . 6 servings.

Tomato sauce may be spread over top of loaf 5 minutes before removing from oven.

Joan W. Harmon
Bleckley County H. S., Cochran, Georgia

## TWO-MEAT LOAF

1 1/2 lb. ground chuck
1/2 lb. ground pork
2 c. bread crumbs
1 c. chopped onion
2 eggs
2 c. milk
Salt and pepper to taste
Tomato juice

**Mix** . . . . . . . . first 7 ingredients in bowl.
**Shape** . . . . . . into loaf.
**Place** . . . . . . . in baking pan.
**Pour** . . . . . . . tomato juice over top.
**Bake** . . . . . . . at 350 degrees for 45 minutes to 1 hour or until cooked through.
**Yields** . . . . . . 6-8 servings.

Frances W. Smith
Johnson County H. S., Mountain City, Tennessee

## DELICIOUS CHILI SAUCE MEAT LOAF

2 lb. ground beef
1 c. dry bread crumbs
1/2 c. sour cream
2 eggs
1 tbsp. minced onion
2 tsp. salt
1  4-oz. can mushroom pieces, drained
Chili sauce

**Combine** .... first 7 ingredients with 1/2 cup chili sauce in bowl, mixing well.
**Pat** ........ into 9 x 5-inch loaf pan.
**Bake** ....... at 350 degrees for 50 minutes.
**Pour** ....... off excess drippings.
**Invert** ...... onto warm platter.
**Spoon** ...... 2 tablespoons chili sauce over meat loaf and garnish with parsley.
**Yields** ...... 8 servings.

Alma L. Payne
Bell H. S., Hurst, Texas

## DELICIOUS MEAT LOAF

1 1/4 lb. ground beef with vegetable protein mixture
3 c. bread crumbs
1/2 c. each chopped green pepper, onion
2 eggs
1/2 c. each tomato sauce, catsup
Salt and pepper to taste

**Combine** .... all ingredients in bowl, mixing well.
**Press** ....... into well-greased loaf pan.
**Bake** ....... at 350 degrees for 1 hour.

Helen R. Kelley
Lockhart Jr. H. S., Orlando, Florida

## QUICK ITALIAN MEAT LOAF

1 1/2 lb. ground beef
1 c. dry bread crumbs
1 c. tomato sauce
1 egg, beaten
1/4 c. minced onion
1 tsp. salt
1/2 tsp. oregano

**Combine** .... all ingredients in bowl, mixing well.

**Press** ....... into loaf pan.
**Bake** ....... at 350 degrees for 1 1/4 hours.
**Yields** ...... 6-8 servings.

Marie T. Butler
Palmyra-Macedon H. S., Palmyra, New York

## OH BOY MEAT LOAF

2 lb. ground beef
2 eggs
1 1/2 c. bread crumbs
3/4 c. catsup
1 pkg. dry onion soup mix
1  8-oz. can tomato sauce
1 tsp. Accent (opt.)

**Combine** .... all ingredients together in bowl, mixing well.
**Shape** ...... into loaf.
**Place** ....... in baking dish.
**Bake** ....... at 350 degrees for 1 hour.
**Yields** ...... 6-8 servings.

Kay S. Caskey
Manogue H. S., Reno, Nevada

## SURPRISE MEAT LOAF

2 lb. lean ground beef
2 eggs, slightly beaten
1/2 c. powdered coffee creamer
1 tbsp. minced onion
3 tbsp. catsup
2 tsp. salt
1/4 tsp. pepper
1 c. dry bread crumbs
2 slices bacon
5 slices each American, Swiss cheese, cut into triangles

**Combine** .... first 8 ingredients in bowl, mixing well.
**Press** ....... into loaf pan.
**Top** ........ with bacon.
**Bake** ....... at 350 degrees for 1 hour.
**Pour** ....... off excess drippings.
**Arrange** ..... cheese triangles alternately over top.
**Garnish** ..... with paprika.
**Bake** ....... for 10 minutes longer or until cheese is melted.
**Yields** ...... 6-8 servings.

Brenda Jackson
Thackerville H. S., Thackerville, Oklahoma

## GLAZED MEAT LOAF

2 eggs
3/4 c. milk
2/3 c. fine dry bread crumbs
2 tbsp. chopped onion
3/4 tsp. salt
1/2 tsp. sage
Dash of pepper
1 1/2 lb. ground beef
1/4 c. catsup
2 tbsp. brown sugar
1 tsp. dry mustard
1 tsp. lemon juice

**Mix** . . . . . . . . first 7 ingredients in large bowl.
**Add** . . . . . . . ground beef, mixing well.
**Shape** . . . . . . into loaf in shallow baking dish.
**Bake** . . . . . . . at 350 degrees for 1 hour.
**Combine** . . . . remaining 4 ingredients, mixing well.
**Spoon** . . . . . . over meat loaf.
**Bake** . . . . . . . for 15 minutes longer.
**Yields** . . . . . . 6 servings.

Bernice Duncan
Gould H. S., Gould, Oklahoma

## QUICK SWEET AND SOUR MEAT LOAF

1 lb. ground beef
1/4 to 1/2 c. chopped onion
1/2 to 3/4 c. bread crumbs
1 egg
Salt and pepper to taste
1 can tomato sauce
3 tbsp. each mustard, vinegar
3 tbsp. brown sugar

**Combine** . . . . first 6 ingredients and half the tomato sauce in bowl, mixing well.
**Shape** . . . . . . into loaf.
**Place** . . . . . . . in baking pan.
**Combine** . . . . remaining tomato sauce, mustard, vinegar and brown sugar with 3/4 cup water in saucepan.
**Bring** . . . . . . . to a boil, stirring occasionally.
**Pour** . . . . . . . over meat loaf.
**Bake** . . . . . . . at 350 degrees for 1 hour.
**Yields** . . . . . . 4-6 servings.

Linda Richardson
R. L. Turner H. S., Carrollton, Texas

## MUSHROOM MEAT LOAF

1  4-oz. can mushrooms, drained
1 lg. carrot, chopped
1 med. onion, chopped
2 eggs
1/4 c. catsup
1 1/2 lb. ground beef
1/2 c. dry bread crumbs
1 1/2 tsp. salt
1/8 tsp. pepper
5 whole med. mushroom caps

**Place** . . . . . . . first 3 ingredients in blender container.
**Process** . . . . . for several seconds until finely chopped.
**Transfer** . . . . to bowl.
**Add** . . . . . . . eggs, catsup, ground beef, bread crumbs, salt and pepper, mixing well.
**Place** . . . . . . . half the ground beef mixture into greased 5 x 9-inch baking pan.
**Arrange** . . . . . mushroom caps in indentation in center.
**Cover** . . . . . . with remaining ground beef mixture, shaping into loaf.
**Bake** . . . . . . . at 350 degrees for 1 hour.
**Yields** . . . . . . 6 servings.

Photograph for this recipe above.

## SICILIAN MEAT ROLL

2 eggs, beaten
3/4 c. soft bread crumbs
1/2 c. tomato juice
2 tbsp. chopped parsley

1/2 tsp. oregano
1/4 tsp. each salt, pepper
1 clove of garlic, minced
2 lb. ground beef
8 thin slices ham
1 1/2 c. shredded mozzarella cheese
3 slices mozzarella cheese, cut into
    wedges

**Combine** .... first 9 ingredients in bowl, mixing well.
**Pat** ........ into rectangle on waxed paper.
**Layer** ...... ham and shredded cheese on ground beef.
**Roll** ....... as for jelly roll, sealing edge and ends.
**Place** ....... seam side down in baking pan.
**Bake** ....... at 350 degrees for 1 1/4 hours.
**Top** ........ with cheese wedges.
**Bake** ....... until cheese is melted.
**Yields** ...... 8 servings.

Cynthia Berend
Mt. Vernon H. S., Mt. Vernon, Texas

## VERY BEST MEAT LOAF

2/3 c. dry bread crumbs
1 c. milk
1 1/2 lb. ground beef
2 eggs, well beaten
1/4 c. grated onion
1 tsp. salt
1/2 tsp. sage
Dash of pepper
6 tbsp. brown sugar
1 c. catsup
1/2 tsp. nutmeg
1 tsp. mustard

**Soak** ....... bread crumbs in milk in large bowl.
**Add** ....... next 6 ingredients, mixing well.
**Press** ....... into loaf pan.
**Bake** ....... at 350 degrees for 30 minutes.
**Pour** ....... off excess drippings.
**Combine** .... brown sugar, catsup, nutmeg and mustard in small bowl, blending well.
**Spread** ..... over top of meat loaf.
**Bake** ....... for 30 minutes longer.

Debby H. Ellis
Robertson County Vocational Center
Springfield, Tennessee

## FROSTED SWEET AND SOUR MEAT LOAF

3 slices dark bread
1 lb. lean hamburger
1/3 c. chopped onion
1/3 c. chopped mushrooms
1/4 c. chopped green pepper (opt.)
2 eggs
1/2 can mushroom soup
Dash of pepper
Catsup
1/4 c. packed brown sugar
1/4 tsp. dry mustard

**Soak** ....... bread in water in bowl; squeeze to remove excess water and break into pieces.
**Combine** .... with next 7 ingredients and 1/3 cup catsup in bowl, mixing well.
**Shape** ...... into loaf in shallow baking dish.
**Mix** ........ brown sugar and dry mustard with 1/2 cup catsup in bowl.
**Spread** ..... over top of meat loaf.
**Bake** ....... at 400 degrees for 30 to 40 minutes or until cooked through.
**Yields** ...... 8 servings.

Irma M. Barbour
Exeter Area H. S., Exeter, New Hampshire

## MEAT LOAF IN A JIFFY

1 lb. ground beef
1/2 c. chopped onion
1/2 c. corn flakes
1/2 c. grated cheese
2 tsp. Worcestershire sauce
1/2 tsp. garlic salt
1 egg
2 tbsp. milk
5 tbsp. catsup
Salt and pepper to taste

**Combine** .... all ingredients in bowl, mixing well.
**Shape** ...... into loaf in baking pan.
**Bake** ....... at 350 degrees for 1 1/4 hours.
**Top** ........ with additional catsup.
**Yields** ...... 4-5 servings.

May arrange canned tomatoes and sliced potatoes around meat loaf before baking.

Audrey S. Williams
Walhalla Sr. H. S., Walhalla, South Carolina

## FAVORITE MEAT LOAF

3 c. Rice Krispies
1/2 c. milk
1/2 c. cooked tomatoes
1 egg, slightly beaten
1 1/2 tsp. salt
1/8 tsp. pepper
1/2 c. finely chopped onion
1/2 c. chopped celery
1 1/2 lb. ground beef

**Place** ....... Rice Krispies in 5 x 9-inch loaf pan.
**Add** ....... next 7 ingredients, mixing well.
**Mix** ........ in ground beef.
**Press** ....... evenly.
**Bake** ....... at 375 degrees for 1 hour.
**Let** ........ stand for 5 minutes before serving.
**Garnish** ..... with fresh parsley.
**Yields** ...... 8 servings.

Deborah Walsh
Oakdale Jr. H. S., Rogers, Arkansas

## GRAPE NUTS MEAT LOAF

1/2 c. Grape Nuts
1 c. milk
1 1/4 c. tomato sauce
2 lb. ground beef
1/2 c. grated onion
2 eggs
1 1/2 tsp. salt

**Combine** .... cereal, milk and 1 cup tomato sauce in bowl.
**Add** ....... ground beef, onion, eggs and salt, mixing well.
**Shape** ...... into 9 x 5-inch loaf in lightly greased shallow baking dish.
**Pour** ....... remaining 1/4 cup tomato sauce over loaf.
**Bake** ....... at 350 degrees for 1 hour.
**Yields** ...... 6-8 servings.

Jan Angel
J. L. Williams Jr. H. S., Copperas Cove, Texas

## CHEESE MEAT LOAF

1 lb. ground beef
1 egg
1 c. coarsely crushed crackers
1/4 c. chopped green pepper
1/4 c. finely chopped onion
1 1/4 tsp. salt
1/2 c. grated Cheddar cheese
1 1/2 tsp. Worcestershire sauce
1 tsp. sugar
1 c. tomato juice
1/8 tsp. pepper

**Combine** .... all ingredients in bowl, mixing well.
**Shape** ...... into 4 x 9-inch loaf in greased baking pan.
**Bake** ....... at 350 degrees for 50 to 55 minutes or to a rich brown.
**Cool** ....... for 10 minutes before removing to hot platter.
**Garnish** ..... with parsley.
**Yields** ...... 4-5 servings.

Elizabeth Sharp
Bismarck H. S., Bismarck, Arizona

## DIFFERENT SWEET AND SOUR MEAT LOAF

1 sm. can tomato paste
1/4 c. packed brown sugar
1/4 c. vinegar
1 tsp. dry mustard
1 lb. ground beef
1 egg
1 med. onion, chopped
1 tsp. salt
20 crackers, crushed

**Mix** ........ first 4 ingredients with 1 tomato paste can water in small bowl.
**Combine** .... ground beef, egg, onion, salt and crackers in large bowl, mixing well.
**Add** ....... half the tomato paste mixture, mixing well.
**Press** ....... into shallow baking pan.
**Spread** ..... remaining tomato paste mixture over top.
**Bake** ....... at 400 degrees for 30 minutes.
**Yields** ...... 8 servings.

Carol Harding
Florence H. S., Florence, Texas

## MEAT LOAF SUPREME

1 c. crushed crackers
1 c. sour cream

1 c. shredded carrot
1/4 c. chopped onion
1 tsp. salt
Dash of pepper
1 lb. each ground beef, ground pork

**Mix** . . . . . . . . first 6 ingredients in large bowl.
**Add** . . . . . . . ground beef and ground pork, mixing well.
**Press** . . . . . . . into loaf pan.
**Bake** . . . . . . . at 350 degrees for 1 1/4 hours.
**Let** . . . . . . . stand for 10 minutes before slicing.
**Yields** . . . . . . 8 servings.

Madge D. Tapp
Webster County H. S., Dixon, Kentucky

## SALISBURY STEAK LOAF

2 lb. ground beef
2 c. cracker crumbs
2 eggs
2 tbsp. each chopped onion, parsley
2 tsp. salt
1 tsp. Worcestershire sauce
1/2 tsp. each pepper, nutmeg, sage
1/2 c. catsup
1 can mushroom soup
2 tbsp. butter, melted
1 c. milk
1/2 tsp. garlic salt

**Combine** . . . . first 11 ingredients in bowl, mixing well.
**Shape** . . . . . . into loaf in shallow baking pan.
**Bake** . . . . . . . at 350 degrees for 45 minutes.
**Combine** . . . . soup, butter, milk and garlic salt in bowl; mixing well.
**Pour** . . . . . . . over loaf.
**Bake** . . . . . . . for 20 minutes longer.
**Yields** . . . . . . 4-6 servings.

Terri DeWerff
Plainville H. S., Plainville, Kansas

## CHEESE-FILLED MEAT LOAF

1 1/4 lb. ground beef
1 egg, slightly beaten
1/2 c. oats
1/4 c. chopped onion
1 tsp. each salt, garlic salt
1/2 tsp. thyme

2 c. tomato sauce
4 slices American cheese

**Combine** . . . . first 7 ingredients and 1 cup tomato sauce in bowl, mixing well.
**Press** . . . . . . . half the mixture in loaf pan.
**Top** . . . . . . . . with cheese slices.
**Press** . . . . . . . remaining ground beef mixture over cheese.
**Invert** . . . . . . into baking pan.
**Bake** . . . . . . . at 350 degrees for 40 minutes; drain.
**Pour** . . . . . . . remaining tomato sauce over loaf.
**Bake** . . . . . . . for 30 minutes longer.

Sandra Baron
Rye Neck H. S., Mamaroneck, New York

## FROSTED WALNUT MEAT LOAF

2 lb. ground beef
1 c. finely chopped toasted Diamond walnuts
1/2 c. oats
1 egg, beaten
1/2 c. beef bouillon
1/4 c. finely chopped onion
1 tsp. Worcestershire sauce
Salt
Pepper
2 1/2 to 3 c. mashed potatoes
1/4 c. warm milk
1/4 c. butter

**Combine** . . . . first 7 ingredients with 1 1/2 teaspoons salt and 1/8 teaspoon pepper in bowl, mixing well.
**Spoon** . . . . . . into 9 x 5-inch loaf pan.
**Bake** . . . . . . . at 350 degrees for 1 hour and 20 minutes.
**Let** . . . . . . . . stand for 5 minutes; drain.
**Turn** . . . . . . . onto baking dish.
**Combine** . . . . potatoes, milk and butter with salt and pepper to taste in bowl, mixing well.
**Cover** . . . . . . top and sides of meat loaf with potato mixture.
**Bake** . . . . . . . at 350 degrees for 10 minutes or until potatoes are lightly browned.
**Yields** . . . . . . 6 servings.

Photograph for this recipe on page 61.

## HUNGRY MAN'S MEAT LOAF

*1 1/2 lb. lean ground beef*
*2 eggs*
*1/2 onion, chopped*
*3/4 c. oats*
*1/4 c. chopped green pepper*
*1/2 c. barbecue sauce*
*1 c. chopped mushrooms*
*1/2 tsp. garlic powder*
*1 tsp. salt*
*1/4 tsp. pepper*
*2 tbsp. Worcestershire sauce*
*1 tsp. soy sauce*
*2 lg. cans tomato sauce*
*1 c. grated Cheddar cheese (opt.)*

**Combine** .... all ingredients except tomato sauce and cheese in bowl.
**Shape** ...... into loaf in greased casserole.
**Pour** ....... tomato sauce over meat loaf.
**Sprinkle** .... grated cheese on top.
**Bake** ....... covered, at 325 degrees for 1 1/2 hours.
**Yields** ...... 6-10 servings.

Dianah Sue Slusser
Carney H. S., Carney, Oklahoma

## HICKORY SMOKE MEAT LOAF

*1 1/2 lb. ground beef*
*1/4 c. chopped onion*
*1 egg*
*3/4 c. oats*
*1 c. tomato juice*
*2 tbsp. hickory smoke barbecue sauce*
*1 1/2 tsp. salt*
*1/4 tsp. pepper*
*1 slice bacon*

**Combine** .... first 8 ingredients in bowl, mixing well.
**Press** ....... into 4 x 8-inch loaf pan.
**Spread** ..... additional barbecue sauce over top of loaf.
**Top** ........ with bacon.
**Bake** ....... at 350 degrees for 1 hour.
**Let** ........ stand for 5 minutes before slicing.
**Yields** ...... 6-8 servings.

Maria Bishop
Lynn H. S., Lynn, Alabama

## SAVORY MEAT LOAF

*2 1/2 lb. hamburger*
*3/4 c. chopped onion*
*1 c. milk*
*1/2 tsp. savory*
*Salt and pepper to taste*
*2 eggs*
*3/4 c. quick-cooking oats*
*1/2 c. chili sauce*
*2 tbsp. brown sugar*

**Combine** .... first 8 ingredients in bowl, mixing well.
**Press** ....... into loaf pan lined with waxed paper.
**Chill** ....... in refrigerator.
**Turn** ....... into baking pan.
**Bake** ....... at 350 degrees for 30 minutes.
**Combine** .... chili sauce and brown sugar in bowl, blending well.
**Brush** ...... over meat loaf.
**Bake** ....... for 45 minutes longer.
**Yields** ...... 10 servings.

Jeanne Hertig
New Haven H. S., New Haven, Indiana

## MEXICAN-STYLE MEAT LOAF

*2 eggs*
*1/2 c. nonfat dry milk*
*2 tbsp. chili powder*
*1/4 c. minced onion*
*1 tbsp. mustard*
*1/4 c. catsup*
*1/2 c. whole wheat flour*
*1/2 c. oats*
*1 brick firm tofu, rinsed, crumbled*
*1 lb. ground beef*

**Mix** ........ first 6 ingredients in bowl.
**Add** ....... flour, oats and tofu, mixing well.
**Add** ....... ground beef, mixing gently.
**Press** ....... into loaf pan.
**Bake** ....... at 350 degrees for 45 minutes to 1 hour or until cooked through.
**Yields** ...... 6-8 servings.

Barsha Elzey
Terra Linda H. S., San Rafael, California

**Recipes on pages 72, 85 and 86.**

## SOY SAUCE MEAT LOAF

1 lb. ground beef
5 tbsp. each soy sauce, Worcestershire
  sauce
1 pkg. dry onion soup mix
1 tbsp. dehydrated onion
1 1/2 c. grated sharp cheese
1/2 c. oats
1/2 c. nonfat dry milk
1 egg, beaten

**Combine** . . . . all ingredients in bowl, mixing
  well.
**Shape** . . . . . . into loaf in baking pan.
**Bake** . . . . . . . at 350 degrees for 45 minutes.
**Yields** . . . . . . 6 servings.

Martha Twaddell
Cedar Hill H. S., Cedar Hill, Texas

## MEAT LOAF WITH OATS

8 oz. tomato sauce
2 tbsp. brown sugar
1 tbsp. vinegar
1 tsp. Worcestershire sauce
3/4 tsp. mustard
1/2 tsp. chili powder
1 1/2 tsp. salt
1 lb. ground beef
1/2 c. evaporated milk
1/3 c. oats
1/4 c. chopped onion
1/8 tsp. pepper

**Combine** . . . . first 6 ingredients with 1/2 teaspoon salt in saucepan, mixing
  well.
**Cook** . . . . . . . for 5 minutes, stirring
  occasionally.
**Combine** . . . . ground beef with 1 teaspoon
  salt, half the tomato sauce mix-
  ture and remaining ingredients,
  mixing well.
**Shape** . . . . . . into loaf in shallow baking pan.
**Pour** . . . . . . . remaining tomato sauce mixture
  over meat loaf.
**Bake** . . . . . . . at 350 degrees for 50 minutes.

Marilyn Davis
Van Alstyne ISD, Van Alstyne, Texas

**Recipe on page 134.**

## CHEDDAR CHEESEBURGER LOAF

2 lb. lean ground beef
1 egg, slightly beaten
1 tbsp. each Worcestershire sauce, mustard
5 oz. Cheddar cheese, grated
1 tsp. salt
1/4 tsp. pepper

**Combine** . . . . all ingredients in bowl, mixing
  well.
**Shape** . . . . . . into loaf in shallow baking pan.
**Bake** . . . . . . . at 350 degrees for 50 minutes.
**Yields** . . . . . . 6 servings.

Thelma Lee
Seneca Sr. H. S., Seneca, South Carolina

## EASY TAMALE LOAF

1 lb. ground beef
1 onion, chopped
1 can olives, sliced
1 can tomato sauce
1 can cream-style corn
1/2 c. cornmeal
3/4 tsp. each salt, pepper
1/2 tsp. chili powder

**Brown** . . . . . . ground beef with onion in skil-
  let, stirring until crumbly; drain.
**Mix** . . . . . . . . in 1/2 cup water and remaining
  ingredients.
**Pour** . . . . . . . into casserole.
**Bake** . . . . . . . at 350 degrees for 1 hour.

Judith Ann Shahenian
Mission San Jose H. S., Fremont, California

## TACO MEAT LOAF

1 lb. hamburger
1  1 1/4-oz. package taco seasoning mix
1  4-oz. can taco sauce
1 egg
8 to 10 taco shells, crushed
1 c. grated Cheddar cheese

**Combine** . . . . first 4 ingredients in bowl, mix-
  ing well.
**Mix** . . . . . . . . in taco shells and cheese.
**Shape** . . . . . . into loaf in shallow baking pan.
**Bake** . . . . . . . at 350 degrees for 45 to 50 min-
  utes or until cooked through.

Rosemary E. Cool
Western H. S., Latham, Ohio

## DEVILED BARTLETTS FOR MEAT LOAF

*1/2 c. chopped onion*
*2 tbsp. butter*
*1/2 tsp. dry mustard*
*1/8 tsp. pepper*
*1/2 c. catsup*
*1 tsp. Worcestershire sauce*
*1/4 tsp. each salt, basil*
*2 fresh Bartlett pears, peeled, sliced*
*1 recipe beef meat loaf*

**Saute** ...... onion in butter in saucepan until golden.
**Stir** ........ in next 4 ingredients with salt and basil.
**Add** ....... sliced pears.
**Simmer** ..... until tender, stirring constantly.
**Spoon** ...... sauce over cooked meat loaf.

Photograph for this recipe above.

## MOZZARELLA MEAT LOAF

*1 1/2 lb. ground beef*
*1/2 c. dry bread crumbs*
*1 egg, slightly beaten*
*1 tsp. instant minced onion*
*3/4 tsp. salt*
*1/2 tsp. oregano*
*1 15-oz. can tomato sauce*
*1 1/2 c. shredded mozzarella cheese*
*1 4-oz. can mushrooms, drained (opt.)*

**Combine** .... first 6 ingredients with 3/4 cup tomato sauce in bowl, mixing well.
**Shape** ...... into 9 x 13-inch rectangle on waxed paper.

**Top** ........ with cheese and mushrooms.
**Roll** ....... as for jelly roll.
**Place** ....... seam side down in greased baking pan.
**Bake** ....... at 375 degrees for 30 minutes.
**Pour** ....... off excess drippings.
**Pour** ....... remaining tomato sauce over meat loaf.
**Bake** ....... for 30 minutes longer.
**Yields** ...... 8 servings.

JoAnne M. Stringer
Liberty H. S., Youngstown, Ohio

## MEAT ROLL WITH TOMATO SAUCE

*1/2 c. chopped onion*
*1/3 c. chopped green pepper*
*Mazola corn oil*
*1/2 lb. ground beef*
*Parsley*
*1 tsp. Worcestershire sauce*
*2 c. sifted flour*
*1 tbsp. baking powder*
*Salt*
*2/3 c. milk*
*1 tbsp. Argo cornstarch*
*1 16-oz. can stewed tomatoes*
*2 tbsp. Mazola margarine*
*Dash of pepper*

**Saute** ...... onion and green pepper in 2 tablespoons oil in skillet.
**Add** ....... ground beef.
**Cook** ....... over high heat for 2 minutes, stirring constantly; drain.
**Stir** ........ in 1 tablespoon parsley and Worcestershire sauce; cool.
**Sift** ........ flour, baking powder and 1 1/2 teaspoons salt into bowl.
**Add** ....... 1/3 cup oil to milk.
**Stir** ........ into flour mixture until soft dough forms.
**Knead** ...... lightly on floured surface.
**Roll** ....... into 12 x 10-inch rectangle.
**Spread** ..... ground beef mixture over dough, leaving 1/2-inch margin on all sides.
**Roll** ....... as for jelly roll from short side.
**Place** ....... on baking sheet.
**Bake** ....... at 425 degrees for 30 minutes or until golden brown.

**Mix** . . . . . . . . cornstarch with 1/4 cup water in saucepan.

**Add** . . . . . . . tomatoes.

**Simmer** . . . . . until thickened, stirring frequently.

**Stir** . . . . . . . . in margarine, pepper, additional parsley to taste and 1/4 teaspoon salt.

**Serve** . . . . . . . with meat roll.

**Yields** . . . . . . 6-8 servings.

Photograph for this recipe on page 69.

## ROMA BEEF PINWHEEL

*1 1/2 lb. ground beef*
*3/4 c. soft bread crumbs*
*1 egg*
*1/8 tsp. pepper*
*1 1/4 tsp. salt*
*1   10-oz. package frozen chopped spinach, thawed, drained*
*3/4 c. shredded mozzarella cheese*
*3 tbsp. Parmesan cheese*
*1 tsp. Italian seasoning*
*1/8 tsp. garlic powder*
*3 tbsp. catsup*

**Combine** . . . . first 4 ingredients and 1 teaspoon salt in bowl, mixing well.

**Pat** . . . . . . . . ground beef mixture into 10 x 14-inch rectangle on waxed paper.

**Combine** . . . . spinach, 1/2 cup mozzarella cheese, Parmesan cheese, Italian seasoning, garlic powder and remaining salt in bowl, mixing well.

**Spread** . . . . . over ground beef, leaving 3/4-inch margin.

**Roll** . . . . . . . as for jelly roll, pressing ends to seal.

**Place** . . . . . . . seam side down on rack in broiler pan.

**Bake** . . . . . . . at 350 degrees for 1 hour.

**Spread** . . . . . catsup over loaf.

**Bake** . . . . . . . for 15 minutes longer.

**Sprinkle** . . . . remaining mozzarella cheese over loaf.

**Garnish** . . . . . with Italian seasoning.

**Yields** . . . . . . 6 servings.

Photograph for this recipe on cover.

## MEXICALI MINI MEAT LOAVES

*1 egg*
*2 lb. ground beef*
*1 c. dry bread crumbs*
*1 med. onion, chopped*
*1/4 c. catsup*
*3/4 c. milk*
*1/2 c. finely chopped dill pickles*
*1 tbsp. Worcestershire sauce*
*1/4 tsp. pepper*
*Salt*
*1 clove of garlic*
*3 tbsp. dill pickle juice*
*2 tbsp. olive oil*
*2 or 3 dashes of Tabasco sauce*
*1 ripe avocado, chopped*

**Beat** . . . . . . . egg in large bowl until fluffy.

**Add** . . . . . . . next 8 ingredients and 2 teaspoons salt, mixing lightly.

**Shape** . . . . . . into 8 loaves.

**Place** . . . . . . . in shallow baking pan.

**Bake** . . . . . . . at 350 degrees for 30 minutes.

**Place** . . . . . . . remaining 5 ingredients and salt to taste into blender container.

**Process** . . . . . until smooth.

**Chill** . . . . . . . covered, until serving time.

**Place** . . . . . . . loaves in shredded lettuce, if desired; serve with guacamole sauce.

Photograph for this recipe above.

## ROLL-IN-ONE MEAT LOAF

1 can tomato soup
1 1/2 lb. ground beef
1/2 c. fine dry bread crumbs
1/4 c. minced onion
2 tbsp. chopped parsley
1 egg, slightly beaten
1 tsp. salt
Dash of pepper
1 can green beans, drained

Combine .... 1/2 cup soup and next 7 ingredients in bowl, mixing well.
Shape ...... into 9 x 12-inch rectangle on waxed paper.
Press ....... beans over surface.
Roll ....... as for jelly roll.
Place ...... in baking pan.
Bake ....... at 350 degrees for 40 minutes; drain.
Pour ....... remaining soup over meat loaf.
Bake ....... for 10 minutes longer.

Kristine Bown
American Fork H. S., American Fork, Utah


## ITALIAN MEAT LOAF WITH MOZZARELLA CHEESE

1 1/2 lb. ground beef
1/2 c. bread crumbs
1/4 tsp. pepper
1 egg
1 tsp. salt
1 8-oz. can tomato sauce
1 tsp. oregano
1 1/2 c. grated mozzarella cheese
1/4 c. Parmesan cheese

Combine .... first 5 ingredients, 1/2 cup tomato sauce and 1/2 teaspoon oregano in bowl, mixing well.
Pat ........ into rectangle on waxed paper.
Sprinkle .... with mozzarella cheese.
Roll ....... as for jelly roll, sealing edge and ends.
Place ....... in loaf pan.
Mix ........ remaining tomato sauce with 1/2 teaspoon oregano.
Pour ....... over loaf.
Sprinkle .... with Parmesan cheese.
Bake ....... at 350 degrees for 1 hour.

Nancy A. Marrow
Salisburg H. S., Salisburg, North Carolina


## SPICY ITALIAN MEAT LOAVES

1 lb. ground beef
6 tbsp. oats
1 egg
2 1/2 tbsp. finely chopped onion
2 1/2 tbsp. catsup
1 tsp. each salt, basil
1/2 tsp. oregano
1/4 to 1/2 c. pizza sauce
1/2 c. shredded mozzarella cheese
4 tsp. grated Parmesan cheese

Combine .... first 5 ingredients with seasonings in bowl, mixing well.
Shape ...... into four 4 x 2-inch loaves.
Place ....... in baking dish.
Bake ....... at 375 degrees for 20 minutes.
Top ........ each loaf with 1 to 2 tablespoons pizza sauce, 1 to 2 tablespoons mozzarella cheese and 1 teaspoon Parmesan cheese.
Bake ....... for 5 minutes longer.
Serve ....... with remaining pizza sauce.

Sally A. Goode
Norwayne H. S., Creston, Ohio


## STUFFED GROUND BEEF LOGS

1 1/2 lb. lean ground beef
3/4 c. fine dry bread crumbs
1/2 c. chopped onion
1 egg, slightly beaten
1 tsp. salt
Worcestershire sauce
6 3 x 1 x 1/8-in. strips Cheddar cheese
6 strips bacon

Combine .... first 5 ingredients with 2 tablespoons Worcestershire sauce in bowl, mixing well.
Divide ...... into 6 portions.
Shape ...... each portion around cheese strip and wrap with bacon strip.
Place ....... in shallow baking pan.
Brush ...... with additional Worcestershire sauce.
Bake ....... at 400 degrees for 30 minutes, basting every 5 minutes with Worcestershire sauce.

Marilyn Kay Clark
Fremont Jr. H. S., Fremont, Nebraska
Sandra St. Pierre
Raceland Jr. H. S., Raceland, Louisiana

# Patties

## BEEF CORDON BLEU

3 lb. ground beef
1 tsp. each salt, dried vegetable flakes
4 slices Swiss cheese, cut in half
8 slices Canadian bacon
2 eggs
1 c. bread crumbs
1/3 c. butter
1 can each golden mushroom, cream of
 mushroom soup
1 c. milk

Combine .... first 3 ingredients in bowl, mix-
 ing well.
Shape ...... into 8 patties.
Top ........ each patty with cheese and
 Canadian bacon.
Roll ....... each patty as for jelly roll, seal-
 ing edges.
Mix ........ eggs and 1/4 cup water in shal-
 low bowl.
Dip ........ each roll in egg mixture, then in
 bread crumbs.
Saute ...... in butter in skillet for 25 min-
 utes, turning frequently.
Place ....... ground beef rolls in heated serv-
 ing dish.
Add ....... soups and milk to pan drippings,
 mixing well.
Cook ....... over low heat until heated
 through, stirring to loosen
 sediment.
Pour ....... sauce over rolls.
Serve ....... with rice.

Elsa Terry
Pleasant Grove Jr. H. S., Pleasant Grove, Utah

## BEEF PATTIES IN BEER SAUCE

1 1/2 lb. ground chuck
2 tsp. salt
1/4 tsp. pepper
Beer
2 tbsp. butter, melted
1/2 c. chili sauce
1 tsp. Worcestershire sauce
1 tsp. sugar
1/8 tsp. Tabasco sauce

Combine .... ground chuck, 1 teaspoon salt,
 pepper and 2 tablespoons beer in
 bowl, mixing well.
Shape ...... into patties.
Brown ...... on both sides in butter in skillet.

Combine .... 1 teaspoon salt, 2/3 cup beer
 and remaining 4 ingredients in
 bowl, mixing well.
Pour ....... over patties.
Simmer ..... for 15 minutes.
Yields ...... 6-8 servings.

Patricia Ann Zuanich
Mariner H. S., Everett, Washington

## BURGERS AND VEGETABLES

1 lb. ground beef
1/4 to 1/2 c. finely chopped onion
1/2 tsp. salt
1/8 tsp. pepper
1 can golden mushroom soup
1 tsp. Worcestershire sauce
1 c. thinly sliced carrots
1 pkg. frozen green beans

Combine .... ground beef, onion, salt and pep-
 per in bowl, mixing well.
Shape ...... into 4 oval patties.
Brown ...... on both sides in skillet; drain.
Stir ........ in remaining ingredients with
 1/4 cup water.
Cook ....... covered, over low heat for 20
 minutes or until vegetables are
 tender, stirring occasionally.
Yields ...... 4 servings.

Barbara K. Hillman
Twin Springs H. S., Nickelsville, Virginia

## GROUND BEEF SWISS STEAKS

4 1/4-lb. frozen ground chuck patties
Salt and pepper to taste
Worcestershire sauce to taste
4 tbsp. flour
1/4 c. shortening, melted
2 tomatoes, chopped
1 green pepper, chopped
1 tsp. minced onion

Sprinkle .... both sides of each patty with
 salt, pepper, Worcestershire
 sauce and flour.
Place ....... in hot shortening in skillet with
 remaining ingredients.
Cook ....... slowly for 45 minutes, turning
 once.
Yields ...... 4 servings.

Patricia Donahoo
Webster County H. S., Dixon, Kentucky

## BAKED HAMBURGER SURPRISES

*1 lb. hamburger*
*1/4 c. butter*
*6 med. potatoes, thinly sliced*
*4 med. carrots, sliced*
*2 med. onions, thinly sliced*
*1 green pepper, sliced into rings*
*Salt and pepper to taste*

**Shape** ...... hamburger into 4 patties.
**Layer** ...... butter, hamburger patties, vegetables, salt and pepper on 4 squares foil.
**Fold** ....... foil and seal edges.
**Place** ....... in baking pan.
**Bake** ....... at 350 degrees for 45 minutes or until vegetables are tender.
**Yields** ...... 4 servings.

Donna N. Chappell
Eastern Guilford H. S., Gibsonville, North Carolina

## HOT DAGOS

*2  12-oz. cans tomato puree*
*2  6-oz. cans tomato paste*
*4 tsp. basil*
*3 tsp. garlic salt*
*2 tsp. salt*
*1/2 tsp. each oregano, red pepper*
*4 lb. hamburger*
*2 lb. lean sausage*

**Combine** .... first 7 ingredients and 3 cups water in bowl, mixing well.
**Pour** ....... into 9 x 13-inch baking dish.
**Mix** ........ hamburger and sausage in bowl.
**Shape** ...... into 16 patties.
**Place** ....... in sauce.
**Bake** ....... at 275 degrees for 3 hours.
**Serve** ....... on French bread.
**Yields** ...... 16 servings.

Kathleen Hammer
Cradock H. S., Portsmouth, Virginia

## MOCK PEPPER STEAK

*1 lb. hamburger*
*1 1/2 tsp. oil*
*2 beef bouillon cubes*
*2 tbsp. cornstarch*
*1 tbsp. soy sauce*
*1 green pepper, cut into strips*

**Shape** ...... hamburger into 4 patties.
**Brown** ...... in oil in large skillet.
**Dissolve** .... bouillon cubes in 1 1/2 cups hot water.
**Add** ....... to patties in skillet.
**Simmer** ..... covered, for 1 hour.
**Blend** ...... cornstarch into 1 cup cold water and soy sauce in bowl.
**Add** ....... to patties in skillet.
**Cook** ....... until thick, stirring constantly.
**Add** ....... green pepper.
**Cook** ....... covered, for 8 to 10 minutes longer.
**Serve** ....... with rice.
**Yields** ...... 3-4 servings.

Beulah Faulstick
New Haven H. S., New Haven, Indiana

## OPEL'S HOT BEEF SAUSAGE

*1 1/2 lb. ground beef*
*2 slices wheat bread, crumbled*
*1 1/2 tsp. salt*
*1 tbsp. sage*
*1 tsp. red pepper*

**Combine** .... all ingredients in bowl with 2/3 cup water, mixing well.
**Shape** ...... by 1/4 cupfuls into 1/4-inch thick patties.
**Brown** ...... on both sides in skillet.
**Yields** ...... 10-12 patties.

Opel Askew
Frederick Douglass H. S., Atlanta, Georgia

## EASY SALISBURY STEAK

*1 lb. ground beef*
*1 tsp. chili powder*
*1 egg*
*1/2 c. crumbs*
*1 sm. onion, chopped*
*Salt and pepper to taste*
*1 can cream of mushroom soup*

**Combine** .... first 7 ingredients, mixing well.
**Shape** ...... into oval patties.
**Brown** ...... on both sides in a small amount of oil in skillet; drain.
**Stir** ........ in soup and 1 soup can water.
**Simmer** ..... covered, for several minutes.

Norma Dabney
Liberty Jr. H. S., Orlando, Florida

## SALISBURY SAUERBRATEN

1 can Franco-American beef gravy
1 lb. ground beef
1/3 c. fine dry bread crumbs
2 tbsp. chopped onion
1/2 tsp. each grated lemon rind, ground
    ginger
1  1-lb. can small whole potatoes
4 gingersnaps, finely crushed
1 tbsp. brown sugar
1 tbsp. wine vinegar

**Combine** .... 1/3 cup gravy with next 5 ingre-
                dients in bowl, mixing well.
**Shape** ...... into 4 patties.
**Place** ....... in shallow baking dish.
**Bake** ....... at 350 degrees for 20 minutes;
                drain.
**Arrange** ..... potatoes around patties.
**Combine** .... remaining gravy with remaining
                ingredients in bowl, mixing well.
**Pour** ....... over patties and potatoes.
**Bake** ....... covered, for 20 minutes longer.
**Yields** ...... 4 servings.

Photograph for this recipe on page 75.

Photograph for this recipe above.

## SAUERBRATEN BURGERS WITH NOODLES

1 1/2 lb. ground chuck
1/4 tsp. salt
1/8 tsp. pepper
1/4 c. dry bread crumbs
1/4 c. dill pickle liquid
1 c. finely chopped onion
2 tbsp. butter
2 tbsp. oil
1/3 c. white vinegar
1/2 tsp. caraway seed
Dash of ground cloves
2 beef bouillon cubes
1/2 c. gingersnap crumbs
1 tbsp. brown sugar
1/2 c. sliced dill pickles
1  8-oz. package noodles, cooked

**Combine** .... first 5 ingredients with 1/3 cup
                onion in bowl, mixing well.
**Shape** ...... into 6 patties.
**Brown** ...... over high heat on both sides in
                butter and oil in skillet; drain
                patties and set aside.
**Saute** ...... remaining 2/3 cup onion in skil-
                let for 2 minutes.
**Add** ....... remaining ingredients except
                pickles and noodles with 1 3/4
                cups water, mixing well.
**Simmer** ..... covered, for 10 minutes, stirring
                frequently and adding water if
                necessary.
**Add** ....... patties, basting with sauce.
**Simmer** ..... covered, until patties are of de-
                sired doneness.
**Add** ....... pickles.
**Serve** ....... with noodles.
**Yields** ...... 6 servings.

## SALISBURY STEAK DELUXE

1 can golden mushroom soup
1 tbsp. mustard
1 tsp. horseradish
2 tsp. Worcestershire sauce
1 1/2 lb. ground beef
1 egg, slightly beaten
1/4 c. fine dry bread crumbs
1/4 c. finely chopped onion
1/2 tsp. salt
Dash of pepper
2 tsp. chopped parsley

**Mix** ........ first 4 ingredients in bowl.
**Combine** .... 1/4 cup soup mixture, ground
                beef, egg, bread crumbs, onion,
                salt and pepper in bowl, mixing
                well.
**Shape** ...... into 6 patties.
**Brown** ...... in skillet; drain.

Add ....... remaining soup mixture, 1/2 cup water and parsley, stirring well.
Cook ....... covered, over low heat for 20 minutes, stirring occasionally.
Serve ....... with mashed potatoes.
Yields ...... 6 servings.

Cora Ann Ferrara
Smithsburg H. S., Smithsburg, Maryland

## SAUCY HAMBURGER STEAK

2 lb. hamburger
2 c. tomato sauce
1/4 c. chopped green onion
1/4 c. packed brown sugar
2 tsp. each Worcestershire sauce, mustard

Shape ...... hamburger into patties.
Brown ...... on both sides in skillet; drain.
Combine .... remaining ingredients in bowl, mixing well.
Pour ....... over patties.
Simmer ..... for 10 minutes.
Yields ...... 6-8 servings.

Julia A. Arnett
Madison County Technical Center, Huntsville, Alabama

## SUPREME BURGER CASSEROLE

1 lb. ground beef
1/2 tsp. pepper
1 tsp. salt
1 egg
2 tbsp. chopped onion
12 saltines, crumbled
1 c. milk
Flour
Oil
1 can cream of mushroom soup

Combine .... first 5 ingredients in bowl, mixing well.
Mix ........ saltines and milk in small bowl until crumbs are soft.
Add ....... to ground beef mixture, mixing well.
Shape ...... into 3-inch patties.
Coat ....... with flour.
Brown ...... in oil in skillet.
Place ....... in 2-quart casserole.
Mix ........ soup with 1 soup can water in bowl.

Pour ....... over patties.
Bake ....... at 350 degrees for 45 to 55 minutes to desired degree of doneness.
Yields ...... 6-8 servings.

Nell Vaden
Lufkin-West, Lufkin, Texas

## BEEF PATTIES WITH MUSHROOM SAUCE

1 lb. ground beef
1 tsp. salt
1/3 c. bread crumbs
1 tbsp. minced onion
1 tsp. Worcestershire sauce
1/3 c. cream
1 can mushroom soup

Combine .... all ingredients except soup in bowl, mixing well.
Shape ...... into 4 patties.
Place ....... on rack in broiler pan.
Broil ....... to desired degree of doneness, turning once or twice; drain.
Cover ...... with soup.
Broil ....... until soup is bubbly.
Yields ...... 4 servings.

Elanor P. Hamme
Lake Gibson Jr. H. S., Lakeland, Florida

## BRAN BURGERS

1 lb. each ground beef, ground veal
2 eggs, slightly beaten
1/4 c. milk
1 c. bran cereal
1/2 c. finely chopped onion
1/4 c. chopped parsley
1 tsp. each salt, caraway seed
1/4 tsp. pepper

Mix ........ first 4 ingredients and 1/4 cup water in large bowl.
Add ....... remaining ingredients, mixing well.
Shape ...... into 6 patties.
Place ....... on rack in broiler pan.
Broil ....... 3 inches from heat source to desired degree of doneness, turning once.
Yields ...... 6 servings.

Marjory M. Peters
Talawanda H. S., Oxford, Ohio

## SURPRISE BEEF PATTIES IN SAUCE

2 slices bacon
1 lb. ground beef
1 c. cooked chopped spinach, well drained
1/2 c. fine dry bread crumbs
1/4 tsp. garlic salt
Dash of pepper
1/4 c. chopped onion
1 can Campbell's tomato soup

Saute ...... bacon in skillet until crisp; drain and crumble.
Combine .... next 5 ingredients in bowl, mixing well.
Shape ...... into 4 oval patties.
Brown ...... patties and onion in pan drippings in skillet; drain.
Add ....... soup, 1/2 cup water and bacon.
Simmer ..... covered, for 20 minutes, stirring occasionally.
Yields ...... 4 servings.

Photograph for this recipe above.

## TRISCUIT BURGERS

1 1/2 c. crushed Triscuits
3/4 c. milk
1 tsp. salt
1/4 tsp. pepper
1/4 c. chopped onion
1 lb. ground beef

Soak ....... Triscuits in milk in large bowl until soft.
Add ....... remaining ingredients, mixing well.
Shape ...... into patties.
Saute ...... in skillet to desired degree of doneness.
Yields ...... 6 servings.

Nancy A. Pearson
Sacred Heart H. S., Hallettsville, Texas

## CHA-CHA HAMBURGERS

1 lb. ground beef
1 egg
1/4 c. bread crumbs
1 1/2 tbsp. minced onion
3/4 tsp. salt
1 tsp. Tabasco sauce
1/4 c. chopped sweet pickle
2 tbsp. chili sauce

Combine .... all ingredients in bowl in order listed, mixing well after each addition.
Shape ...... into 4 patties.
Place ....... on rack in broiler pan.
Broil ....... to desired degree of doneness, basting with additional chili sauce.
Yields ...... 4 servings.

Dorothy G. Rothermel
Pasadena H. S., Pasadena, Texas

## BROILED HAMBURGER-ON-A-BUN

1 lb. ground beef
1/2 c. milk
1/4 c. catsup
1 tbsp. each mustard, Worcestershire sauce
1 tsp. vinegar
1 tsp. sugar
10 hamburger buns, split

Mix ........ first 7 ingredients in bowl.
Spread ..... thin layer of ground beef mixture on each bun half.
Place ....... on broiler rack.

Broil ....... for 5 minutes.
Yields ...... 10 servings.

Stella Heath
John Marshall H. S., Oklahoma City, Oklahoma

## THE GIANT OF HAMBURGERS

2/3 c. each catsup, mustard
2/3 c. dry red wine
1/4 c. packed brown sugar
3/4 tsp. Tabasco sauce
2 lb. ground beef
1 tsp. salt
1 tbsp. grated onion
1 tomato, chopped
2/3 c. each chopped cucumber, green pepper

Combine .... catsup, mustard, wine, brown sugar and 1/2 teaspoon Tabasco sauce in small saucepan, mixing well.
Simmer ..... for 20 minutes.
Combine .... ground beef, salt, onion and remaining 1/4 teaspoon Tabasco sauce in bowl, mixing well.
Shape ...... into patty.
Place ....... on rack in broiler pan.
Baste ....... with wine sauce.
Broil ....... 6 inches from heat source for 12 to 15 minutes on each side or to desired degree of doneness, basting occasionally with wine sauce.
Mix ........ tomato, cucumber and green pepper in bowl.
Top ........ patty with tomato mixture and remaining wine sauce.
Yields ...... 8 servings.

Photograph for this recipe on page 104.

## GRANNY'S BROILER BURGERS

1 lb. ground beef
1 egg
1 tbsp. Worcestershire sauce
1/2 c. catsup
1/4 c. pepper relish
1 tsp. salt
1/4 tsp. each pepper, garlic powder
1 c. bread crumbs
1 sm. onion, minced
8 hamburger buns

Mix ........ first 10 ingredients in bowl.
Shape ...... into 8 patties.
Brown ..... patties on each side in skillet.
Place ....... on bottom halves of buns on baking sheet.
Broil ....... 4 to 5 inches from heat source for 15 minutes or to desired degree of doneness.
Yields ...... 8 servings.

Nancy Buffington
Marshall County H. S., Benton, Kentucky

## EASY GROUND BEEF FILLETS

2 lb. ground beef
1 tbsp. Worcestershire sauce
1/4 tsp. liquid smoke
Dash of garlic powder
1/2 tsp. salt
1/4 tsp. pepper
8 to 10 slices bacon

Combine .... all ingredients except bacon in bowl, mixing well.
Shape ...... into 1/2-inch thick patties.
Wrap ....... each with 1 slice bacon, securing with toothpick.
Place ....... on rack in broiler pan.
Broil ....... to desired doneness.
Yields ...... 8-10 servings.

Eveline C. Kennedy
Elmore City H. S., Elmore City, Oklahoma

## GRILLED HAMBURGER WITH PINEAPPLE

1 lb. hamburger
Salt and pepper to taste
1 sm. can sliced pineapple
Barbecue sauce (opt.)

Combine .... hamburger with salt and pepper in bowl, mixing well.
Shape ...... into patties.
Place ....... 1 slice of pineapple between 2 patties.
Grill ....... over hot coals to desired degree of doneness.
Baste ....... with barbecue sauce.
Yields ...... 4 servings.

Mary Roddam
Clio Sch, Clio, Alabama

## HAMBURGER-BACON ROLL-UPS

2 lb. ground beef
1/4 c. chopped onion
1 egg
1 c. shredded cheese
2 tbsp. Worcestershire sauce
1 tsp. salt
1/2 tsp. pepper
3 tbsp. catsup
8 to 10 slices bacon

**Combine** .... all ingredients except bacon in bowl, mixing well.
**Shape** ...... into eight to ten 1-inch thick patties.
**Wrap** ....... each patty with 1 slice bacon; secure with toothpick.
**Place** ....... on rack in broiler pan.
**Broil** ....... for 10 minutes on each side.
**Yields** ...... 8-10 servings.

Frances Tharpe
North Wilkes H. S., Hays, North Carolina

## HAMBURGERS DELUXE

1 lb. ground beef
1 tbsp. parsley flakes
1 med. onion, finely chopped
1/2 tsp. each seasoned salt, garlic salt
1 tsp. thyme
5 drops of Worcestershire sauce
3 drops of Tabasco sauce

**Combine** .... all ingredients in bowl, mixing well.
**Shape** ...... into 4 patties.
**Place** ....... on broiler rack.
**Broil** ....... to desired degree of doneness, turning once.
**Serve** ....... on buns, if desired.
**Yields** ...... 4 servings.

Helen L. Rattray
Adena H. S., Frankfort, Ohio

## PIZZA BURGERS

1 8-oz. can tomato sauce
1 clove of garlic, minced

1/4 tsp. oregano
1/2 tsp. pepper
1 tsp. salt
1 lb. ground beef
3 hamburger buns, split
6 slices mozzarella cheese

**Combine** .... first 3 ingredients and half the pepper in saucepan, mixing well.
**Cook** ....... for 5 minutes.
**Mix** ........ remaining pepper, salt and ground beef in bowl.
**Shape** ...... into 6 patties.
**Place** ....... on rack in broiler pan.
**Broil** ....... 3 inches from heat source for 5 minutes; turn.
**Place** ....... 1 tablespoon sauce on each patty.
**Broil** ....... for 3 minutes longer.
**Place** ...... patties on bun halves.
**Top** ........ with cheese.
**Broil** ....... for 2 minutes longer or until cheese is melted.
**Yields** ...... 6 servings.

Bernita Wessel
Trimble Middle Sch., Glouster, Ohio

## PIZZA-IN-A-BURGER

1 1/2 lb. ground beef
1/3 c. grated Parmesan cheese
1/4 c. each finely chopped onion, chopped ripe olives
1 tsp. each salt, oregano
1/4 tsp. pepper
1 6-oz. can tomato paste
8 slices mozzarella cheese
8 slices tomato
8 slices French bread

**Mix** ........ first 8 ingredients in bowl.
**Shape** ...... into 8 oval patties.
**Place** ....... on rack in broiler pan.
**Broil** ....... for 3 to 6 minutes on each side or to desired degree of doneness.
**Top** ........ each patty with cheese and tomato.
**Broil** ....... for 3 to 6 minutes longer or until cheese melts.
**Serve** ....... on bread slices.
**Yields** ...... 8 servings.

Naomi Mayes
Warren East H. S., Bowling Green, Kentucky

# Pies

# BEEF AND VEGETABLE PIE WITH CHERRY PEPPERS

1 1/2 lb. lean ground beef
2 c. chopped onions
1 lg. clove of garlic, crushed
1 c. chopped pickled mild cherry peppers
3/4 c. Italian-flavored bread crumbs
2 tsp. salt
1  16-oz. can whole tomatoes, mashed
1  10-oz. package frozen peas and
  carrots, thawed
2 eggs
6 tbsp. milk
2 tbsp. butter, melted
2 c. buttermilk baking mix

Brown . . . . . . ground beef with onions and garlic in skillet, stirring until crumbly; drain.
Stir . . . . . . . . in next 5 ingredients with 1 beaten egg and 1 beaten egg white.
Cook . . . . . . . until heated through, stirring constantly.
Add . . . . . . . milk, butter and beaten egg yolk to baking mix in bowl, stirring to make soft dough.
Knead . . . . . . 5 times on floured surface.
Divide . . . . . . dough in half and roll into 2 circles.
Fit . . . . . . . . 1 circle into pie plate.
Spoon . . . . . . half the ground beef mixture into pie shell.
Cut . . . . . . . . 5-inch circle from center of remaining circle.
Place . . . . . . . over ground beef mixture, sealing and fluting edge.

Spoon . . . . . . remaining ground beef mixture into center.
Bake . . . . . . . at 375 degrees until lightly browned.
Garnish . . . . . with cherry peppers.

Photograph for this recipe on this page.

# CORNISH PASTIES WITH MUSHROOM SAUCE

Flour
1/4 tsp. salt
1/3 c. shortening
1/4 to 1/2 lb. lean ground beef
2 tbsp. chopped onion
1 chopped cooked potato
1 tbsp. each tomato paste, chili sauce
1  3-oz. can sliced mushrooms
2 tbsp. margarine, melted
1 beef bouillon cube, crushed

Combine . . . . 1 cup flour and salt in bowl.
Cut . . . . . . . . in shortening until crumbly.
Mix . . . . . . . . in 2 tablespoons cold water.
Chill . . . . . . . in refrigerator.
Brown . . . . . . ground beef with onion in skillet, stirring until crumbly; drain.
Add . . . . . . . next 3 ingredients, mixing well; set aside.
Roll . . . . . . . dough on floured surface.
Cut . . . . . . . . into 4 squares.
Spoon . . . . . . filling onto half of each square.
Fold . . . . . . . into triangles to enclose filling; seal edges.
Place . . . . . . . on baking sheet.
Bake . . . . . . . at 400 degrees for 10 to 12 minutes or until golden brown.
Drain . . . . . . mushrooms, reserving liquid.
Add . . . . . . . enough water to reserved liquid to measure 1 cup.
Mix . . . . . . . . 2 tablespoons flour with margarine in saucepan.
Add . . . . . . . liquid gradually, stirring constantly.
Stir . . . . . . . . in mushrooms and bouillon cube.
Cook . . . . . . . over medium heat until thick, stirring constantly.
Pour . . . . . . . over pasties.
Yields . . . . . . 4 servings.

Eliza Olson
Lord Tweedsmuir Sch., Scurrey, British Columbia

# HEARTY GROUND BEEF PIE

*1 med. onion, chopped*
*1 lb. ground beef*
*Salt and pepper to taste*
*2 1/2 c. cooked green beans, drained*
*1 can tomato soup*
*1/2 c. warm milk*
*1 egg, beaten*
*5 med. potatoes, peeled, cooked, mashed*

**Saute** ...... onion in skillet.
**Add** ....... ground beef and seasonings.
**Cook** ....... until ground beef is brown and crumbly, stirring constantly; drain.
**Add** ....... beans and soup, stirring gently.
**Add** ....... milk and egg to potatoes gradually, mixing well after each addition.
**Place** ....... ground beef mixture in casserole.
**Drop** ....... potatoes by spoonfuls onto meat mixture.
**Bake** ....... at 350 degrees for 30 minutes.
**Yields** ...... 6 servings.

Connie M. Amendola
Johnsonburg Area Jr.-Sr. H. S.
Johnsonburg, Pennsylvania

# HAMBURGER SHORTCAKE

*1 lb. ground beef*
*1/4 c. minced onion*
*Mazola corn oil*
*1/4 tsp. pepper*
*Salt*
*1 tbsp. pickle relish*
*1/4 c. catsup*
*2 c. sifted flour*
*3 tsp. baking powder*
*2/3 c. milk*

**Brown** ...... ground beef and onion in 1 tablespoon oil, stirring until crumbly.
**Add** ....... pepper, 1 teaspoon salt, pickle relish and catsup, mixing well.
**Sift** ........ flour, baking powder and 1 teaspoon salt together into bowl.
**Cut** ........ in 1/3 cup oil with pastry blender.
**Add** ....... milk, mixing until dough forms.

**Knead** ...... 15 to 20 times on floured surface.
**Divide** ..... into halves, rolling each into 8-inch square.
**Place** ....... 1 square in 8-inch square baking dish.
**Spoon** ...... in meat mixture.
**Top** ........ with remaining dough.
**Cut** ........ slits for steam; seal edges.
**Bake** ....... at 425 degrees for 25 minutes or until top is brown.
**Yields** ...... 6 servings.

Photograph for this recipe on page 69.

# CRAZY CRUST TACO

*1 lb. hamburger*
*1/2 c. chopped onion*
*1   16-oz. can kidney beans*
*2 tsp. chili powder*
*1/4 to 1/2 tsp. Tabasco sauce*
*1   6-oz. can tomato sauce*
*1 1/2 tsp. salt*
*1/2 c. flour*
*1/2 tsp. baking powder*
*1/4 c. shortening*
*1/2 c. sour cream*
*1 egg*

**Brown** ...... hamburger in skillet, stirring until crumbly.
**Add** ....... onion.
**Saute** ...... until brown.
**Stir** ........ in next 4 ingredients and 1 teaspoon salt.
**Simmer** ..... for 10 minutes.
**Combine** .... remaining ingredients and 1/2 teaspoon salt in bowl, stirring 60 to 70 strokes.
**Spread** ..... dough in thin layer over bottom, and thicker layer over side of greased 9-inch pie plate.
**Fill** ........ with hamburger mixture.
**Bake** ....... at 425 degrees for 20 to 30 minutes or until crust is golden brown.
**Garnish** ..... with grated cheese, shredded lettuce, chopped tomatoes and taco sauce.
**Cut** ........ into thin slices.

Karen Ferre
American Fork Jr. H. S., American Fork, Utah

## BEEF PANCAKE

*1 lb. ground beef*
*2 c. milk*
*3 eggs*
*2 c. frozen diced potatoes with onion*
*    and pepper, thawed*
*1/2 c. flour*
*1/4 c. minced parsley*
*1 tsp. each salt, oregano*
*1 c. spaghetti sauce (opt.)*

**Brown** . . . . . . ground beef in skillet, stirring until crumbly; drain, reserving 3 tablespoons pan drippings.
**Combine** . . . . ground beef, reserved pan drippings and next 7 ingredients, mixing well.
**Pack** . . . . . . . into greased 8 x 12-inch baking dish.
**Bake** . . . . . . . at 375 degrees for 25 minutes.
**Garnish** . . . . . with parsley and serve with spaghetti sauce.
**Yields** . . . . . . 4-6 servings.

Pamela Tutt
Van-Cove H. S., Cove, Arkansas

## HAMBURGER UPSIDE-DOWN PIE

*1 lb. ground beef*
*1/2 c. chopped green pepper*
*1/4 c. finely chopped onion*
*Mazola salad oil*
*1  8-oz. can tomato sauce*
*1/4 tsp. pepper*
*Salt*
*2 c. flour*
*1 tbsp. baking powder*
*2/3 c. milk*

**Brown** . . . . . . ground beef with next 2 ingredients in 1/4 cup oil in Dutch oven, stirring until crumbly.
**Add** . . . . . . . tomato sauce, pepper and 1 teaspoon salt, mixing well.
**Combine** . . . . flour, baking powder and 1 teaspoon salt in bowl.
**Cut** . . . . . . . . in 1/3 cup oil with pastry blender.
**Add** . . . . . . . milk, mixing until dough forms.
**Knead** . . . . . . 15 to 20 times on floured surface.
**Roll** . . . . . . . to fit Dutch oven.
**Place** . . . . . . . over ground beef mixture.

**Cut** . . . . . . . . slits for steam.
**Seal** . . . . . . . . and flute edge.
**Bake** . . . . . . . at 400 degrees for 25 minutes or until topping is lightly browned.
**Invert** . . . . . . onto serving plate.
**Yields** . . . . . . 6 servings.

Photograph for this recipe on page 69.

## PASTRIES FOR PARTIES

*1 lb. ground beef, crumbled*
*1/4 lb. ground pork, crumbled*
*1/2 onion, minced*
*2 or 3 potatoes, chopped*
*3 or 4 carrots, chopped*
*Salt and pepper to taste*
*1 recipe 2-crust pie pastry*

**Combine** . . . . all ingredients except pastry in large bowl, mixing well.
**Roll** . . . . . . . and cut pastry into 3 1/2-inch circles on floured surface.
**Spoon** . . . . . . ground beef mixture onto half of each circle.
**Fold** . . . . . . . to enclose filling, sealing edges and cutting slits.
**Place** . . . . . . . on baking sheet.
**Bake** . . . . . . . at 350 degrees for 15 to 20 minutes or until golden brown.
**Yields** . . . . . . 4-6 servings.

Karen Rackow
Algoma H. S., Algoma, Wisconsin

## QUICK SHEPHERD'S PIE

*1/3 c. chopped onion*
*1 clove of garlic, crushed*
*1 to 2 tbsp. oil*
*1 1/2 lb. ground beef*
*1 can cream of mushroom soup*
*1  8-oz. can sliced carrots, drained*
*1/2 c. chopped dill pickles*
*1/4 tsp. salt*
*1/8 tsp. pepper*
*1  6-serving env. mashed potatoes*
*2 tbsp. Parmesan cheese*
*2 tbsp. heavy cream*
*1 tbsp. chopped parsley*

**Saute** . . . . . . onion and garlic in oil in skillet.
**Brown** . . . . . . ground beef with sauteed vegetables, stirring until crumbly.
**Stir** . . . . . . . . in next 5 ingredients.

**Simmer** . . . . . for 15 to 20 minutes, stirring occasionally.
**Spoon** . . . . . . into casserole.
**Prepare** . . . . . mashed potatoes according to package directions adding cheese, cream and parsley.
**Spoon** . . . . . . over ground beef mixture.
**Brown** . . . . . . under broiler.
**Serve** . . . . . . . at once.

Photograph for this recipe above.

## CRAZY CRUST MEAT PIE

*3/4 lb. lean ground beef*
*3/4 c. chopped onion*
*2 tbsp. oil*
*3 8-oz. cans tomato sauce*
*1 env. Italian salad dressing mix*
*2 tbsp. sugar*
*3/4 c. biscuit mix*
*1/2 c. sour cream*
*1 egg*
*1/2 tsp. onion salt*
*1/2 c. grated cheese*

**Brown** . . . . . . ground beef with onion in oil in skillet, stirring until crumbly.
**Add** . . . . . . . next 3 ingredients, mixing well.
**Simmer** . . . . . covered, for 10 minutes.

**Combine** . . . . biscuit mix, sour cream, egg and onion salt in bowl, stirring just until mixed.
**Spread** . . . . . very thinly over bottom and thickly over side to within 1/4 inch of top of greased and floured pie plate.
**Place** . . . . . . . 1/2 of the ground beef mixture in prepared pie plate, reserving remainder for future use.
**Bake** . . . . . . . at 400 degrees for 20 to 25 minutes or until brown.
**Sprinkle** . . . . with cheese.

Minta Palmer
Crockett H. S., Austin, Texas

## IMPOSSIBLE LASAGNA PIE

*1 lb. ground beef*
*1 tsp. oregano*
*1/2 tsp. basil*
*1 6-oz. can tomato paste*
*1 c. shredded mozzarella cheese*
*1 c. cottage cheese*
*1/4 c. grated Parmesan cheese*
*1 c. milk*
*2/3 c. biscuit mix*
*2 eggs*
*1 tsp. salt*
*1/4 tsp. pepper*

**Brown** . . . . . . ground beef in skillet, stirring until crumbly; drain.
**Add** . . . . . . . oregano, basil, tomato paste and 1/2 cup mozzarella cheese, mixing well.
**Layer** . . . . . . cottage cheese and Parmesan cheese in greased 10-inch pie plate.
**Spoon** . . . . . . ground beef mixture over cheese.
**Combine** . . . . milk, biscuit mix, eggs, salt and pepper in blender container.
**Process** . . . . . on high for 15 seconds.
**Pour** . . . . . . . over ground beef mixture.
**Bake** . . . . . . . at 400 degrees for 30 to 35 minutes or until knife inserted near center comes out clean.
**Sprinkle** . . . . with remaining mozzarella cheese.
**Yields** . . . . . . 6 servings.

Mary C. James
Greenville H. S., Greenville, Alabama

## TEXAS BEER HAUL PIE

*Biscuit mix*
*1/3 c. milk*
*1 lb. ground beef*
*1 thinly sliced onion*
*1 tbsp. oil*
*1 tsp. salt*
*1/4 tsp. pepper*
*3 tbsp. catsup*
*2 eggs, slightly beaten*
*1 c. cottage cheese*

**Mix** . . . . . . . . 1 cup biscuit mix with milk in bowl.
**Roll** . . . . . . . on floured surface into 12-inch circle.
**Fit** . . . . . . . . into greased 9-inch pie plate.
**Brown** . . . . . . ground beef with onion in oil in skillet, stirring until crumbly.
**Add** . . . . . . . 2 tablespoons biscuit mix, salt, pepper and catsup, mixing well.
**Spoon** . . . . . . into prepared pie plate.
**Mix** . . . . . . . . eggs with cottage cheese in bowl.
**Pour** . . . . . . . over ground beef mixture.
**Bake** . . . . . . . at 350 degrees for 30 minutes.
**Garnish** . . . . . with paprika and parsley.
**Yields** . . . . . . 4-6 servings.

Cindy Schwartz
Bridgeport H. S., Bridgeport, Texas
Lynne Hatle
Vermillion Public Sch., Vermillion, South Dakota

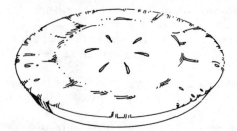

## BARBARA'S GROUND BEEF CASSEROLE

*1 1/2 lb. ground beef*
*1 onion, chopped*
*1 green pepper, chopped*
*4 oz. Cheddar cheese, grated*
*3 eggs*
*1 1/2 c. milk*
*2/3 c. biscuit mix*

**Brown** . . . . . . ground beef with onion and green pepper in skillet, stirring until crumbly; drain.

**Layer** . . . . . . ground beef mixture and cheese in casserole.
**Place** . . . . . . . remaining 3 ingredients in blender container.
**Process** . . . . . for 5 seconds.
**Pour** . . . . . . . over layers.
**Bake** . . . . . . . at 400 degrees for 30 minutes.
**Yields** . . . . . . 4-6 servings.

Barbara Gaylor
Michigan Department of Education, Lansing, Michigan

## BEEF AND BISCUIT CASSEROLE

*1 to 1 1/4 lb. ground beef*
*1/2 c. chopped onion*
*1/4 c. chopped green pepper*
*1  8-oz. can tomato sauce*
*1 tsp. chili powder*
*1/2 tsp. garlic salt*
*1 egg, slightly beaten*
*1/2 c. sour cream*
*1 1/2 c. grated Cheddar cheese*
*1 can refrigerator biscuits*

**Brown** . . . . . . ground beef with onion and green pepper in skillet, stirring until crumbly.
**Combine** . . . . tomato sauce with chili powder and garlic salt in saucepan.
**Simmer** . . . . . for several minutes; remove from heat.
**Combine** . . . . egg and sour cream with 1 cup cheese in bowl, mixing well.
**Stir** . . . . . . . . into tomato mixture.
**Line** . . . . . . . bottom of 8 x 8-inch baking pan with biscuits, sealing seams.
**Layer** . . . . . . tomato sauce and ground beef mixture over dough.
**Top** . . . . . . . . with remaining 1/2 cup cheese.
**Bake** . . . . . . . at 375 degrees for 25 to 30 minutes or until crust is brown.
**Yields** . . . . . . 6 servings.

Gloria Lloyd
Taylorsville H. S., Salt Lake City, Utah

## HAMBURGER CRESCENTS

*1 lb. ground beef*
*2 tbsp. butter*
*1  3-oz. package cream cheese, softened*

1 med. onion, chopped
1/4 c. slivered almonds
1/4 c. chopped green pepper
1 pkg. refrigerator crescent rolls
1/2 c. shredded Cheddar cheese

**Brown** . . . . . . ground beef in skillet, stirring until crumbly.
**Add** . . . . . . . 1 tablespoon butter and next 4 ingredients, mixing well.
**Place** . . . . . . . roll dough flat on baking sheet.
**Spoon** . . . . . . ground beef mixture onto center of roll.
**Fold** . . . . . . . corners to center to enclose filling; seal.
**Brush** . . . . . . with 1 tablespoon melted butter.
**Top** . . . . . . . with cheese.
**Bake** . . . . . . at 350 degrees for 30 minutes or until golden brown.
**Yields** . . . . . . 8 servings.

Kimberly Hux
Frank W. Cox H. S., Virginia Beach, Virginia

## QUICK HAMBURGER AND VEGETABLE CASSEROLE

1 1/2 lb. hamburger
1 onion, chopped
1 green pepper, chopped
1 can tomato sauce
1 can whole kernel corn, drained
1 pkg. refrigerator crescent rolls
1 egg, beaten
2 c. grated Cheddar cheese

**Brown** . . . . . . hamburger with onion and green pepper in skillet, stirring until crumbly; drain.
**Add** . . . . . . . tomato sauce and corn, mixing well.
**Line** . . . . . . . pie plate with roll dough, sealing seams.
**Combine** . . . . egg and cheese in bowl, mixing well.
**Layer** . . . . . . cheese mixture and ground beef mixture in prepared pie plate.
**Top** . . . . . . . . with additional grated cheese.
**Bake** . . . . . . . at 375 degrees for 20 minutes.
**Let** . . . . . . . stand for 10 minutes before serving.
**Yields** . . . . . . 6-8 servings.

Edith Carter
Hamlin H. S., Hamlin, Texas

## JUDY'S HAMBURGER PIE

1 1/4 lb. hamburger
1/4 to 1/2 c. each chopped onion, green pepper
1/4 to 1/2 tsp. each garlic salt, salt
1/2 tsp. ground cuminseed
1 c. each tomato sauce, green beans
1 pkg. refrigerator crescent rolls
1/2 c. shredded Cheddar cheese

**Brown** . . . . . . hamburger with onion and green pepper in skillet, stirring until crumbly.
**Add** . . . . . . . next 5 ingredients, mixing well.
**Simmer** . . . . . until seasonings are well blended.
**Line** . . . . . . . pie plate with crescent roll dough, sealing seams.
**Spoon** . . . . . . hamburger mixture into pie shell.
**Sprinkle** . . . . cheese over top.
**Bake** . . . . . . . at 350 degrees for 30 minutes.

Judy Newcomb
Lake Hamilton Jr. H. S., Pearcy, Arkansas

## QUICK CRESCENT TACO PIE

1 1/4 lb. ground beef
1 pkg. taco seasoning mix
1/3 c. sliced stuffed green olives
1 pkg. refrigerator crescent rolls
1 1/2 to 2 c. crushed corn chips
1 c. sour cream
6 slices American cheese

**Brown** . . . . . . ground beef in skillet, stirring until crumbly; drain.
**Add** . . . . . . . taco mix, olives and 1/2 cup water, mixing well.
**Simmer** . . . . . for 5 minutes.
**Separate** . . . . crescent dough into triangles.
**Press** . . . . . . . triangles over bottom and side of 9-inch pie plate, sealing seams.
**Layer** . . . . . . 1 cup corn chips, ground beef mixture, sour cream, cheese and remaining corn chips over dough.
**Bake** . . . . . . . at 375 degrees for 20 to 25 minutes or until brown.
**Yields** . . . . . . 8 servings.

Kay C. Moore
Thibodaux H. S., Thibodaux, Louisiana

## CHILI GROUND BEEF WITH CORN BREAD TOPPING

1 lb. ground beef
2 c. tomato sauce
Chili powder to taste
4 to 6 slices American cheese
1 sm. box corn muffin mix

Brown . . . . . . ground beef in skillet, stirring until crumbly; drain.
Add . . . . . . . tomato sauce and chili powder, mixing well.
Spoon . . . . . . into casserole.
Top . . . . . . . . with cheese.
Prepare . . . . . corn muffin mix, using package directions.
Pour . . . . . . . over cheese.
Bake . . . . . . . at 400 degrees until corn bread tests done.
Yields . . . . . . 6 servings.

Billie Rickard
Sharon H. S., Sharon, Kansas

## EASY ITALIAN CASSEROLE

1 lb. ground beef
2 cloves of garlic, crushed
1/2 c. chopped onion
1   16-oz. can tomato sauce
1 sm. can mushroom stems and pieces
1 tsp. sugar
1/2 tsp. each oregano, basil
1/4 tsp. each salt, pepper
1 pkg. corn muffin mix
8 slices American cheese

Brown . . . . . . ground beef with garlic and onion in skillet, stirring until crumbly; drain.
Stir . . . . . . . . in next 7 ingredients, mixing well.
Simmer . . . . . for 10 minutes.
Prepare . . . . . muffin mix using package directions.
Layer . . . . . . 1/2 of the batter, 4 slices cheese, ground beef mixture, remaining cheese slices and remaining batter in 8 x 8-inch baking dish.
Bake . . . . . . . at 400 degrees for 20 minutes.
Yields . . . . . . 4-6 servings.

Suzanne Stone Evans
Snohomish H. S., Snohomish, Washington

## CORN BREAD-TOPPED HAMBURGER PIE

1 lb. ground beef
1 med. onion, chopped
1 tsp. Worcestershire sauce
1/4 c. catsup
1 sm. can tomato sauce
1 can whole kernel corn, drained
1 tsp. chili powder
Salt and pepper
1/4 c. flour
1/2 tsp. soda
1 c. cornmeal
1 egg
1 c. buttermilk
2 tbsp. shortening, melted

Brown . . . . . . ground beef with onion in skillet, stirring until crumbly.
Add . . . . . . . next 5 ingredients and salt and pepper to taste.
Simmer . . . . . for 5 minutes.
Pour . . . . . . . into large baking dish.
Sift . . . . . . . . flour, soda and 1/2 teaspoon salt together into bowl.
Add . . . . . . . cornmeal, mixing well.
Combine . . . . remaining 3 ingredients in small bowl, mixing well.
Pour . . . . . . . into dry ingredients, stirring until just moistened.
Pour . . . . . . . over ground beef mixture.
Bake . . . . . . . at 400 degrees for 30 minutes.
Yields . . . . . . 6-8 servings.

Glenda Gray
Rosebud-Lott H. S., Rosebud, Texas

## MEXICAN CORN PONE PIE

1 lb. ground beef
1/4 c. chopped onion
2 tsp. chili powder
1 tsp. salt
1 tsp. Worcestershire sauce
1 c. tomatoes
1 c. kidney beans
1 pkg. corn bread mix

Brown . . . . . . ground beef in skillet, stirring until crumbly.
Add . . . . . . . next 6 ingredients, mixing well.
Simmer . . . . . for 15 minutes.
Pour . . . . . . . into pie plate.

**Prepare** ..... corn bread mix, using package directions.
**Spoon** ...... thin layer of corn bread batter over ground beef mixture.
**Bake** ....... at 450 degrees until golden brown.
**Yields** ...... 6 servings.

Gail M. Skelton
Biggersville H. S., Corinth, Mississippi

## HAMBURGER-CORN PIE

*1 lb. hamburger*
*1/4 lb. pork sausage*
*1 sm. onion, chopped*
*1 clove of garlic, finely chopped*
*1   16-oz. can whole tomatoes*
*1   16-oz. can whole kernel corn, drained*
*20 to 24 pitted ripe olives, sliced*
*1 1/2 to 3 tsp. chili powder*
*1 1/2 tsp. salt*
*1 c. cornmeal*
*1 c. milk*
*2 eggs, beaten*
*1 c. shredded Cheddar cheese*

**Brown** ...... hamburger and sausage with onion and garlic in skillet, stirring until crumbly; drain.
**Stir** ........ in next 5 ingredients.
**Bring** ....... to a boil.
**Pour** ....... into 2-quart baking dish.
**Combine** .... cornmeal, milk and eggs in bowl, mixing well.
**Pour** ....... over hamburger mixture.
**Sprinkle** .... cheese over top.
**Bake** ....... at 350 degrees for 40 to 50 minutes or until golden brown.
**Garnish** ..... with parsley sprigs and additional ripe olives.
**Yields** ...... 8 servings.

Shelire L. Miller
Scott H. S., Huntsville, Tennessee

## MOM'S CORN PONE PIE

*1 lb. ground beef*
*1/3 c. chopped onion*
*1 c. canned tomatoes*
*3/4 tsp. salt*
*1 tsp. Worcestershire sauce*

*1 can kidney beans, drained*
*1 c. corn bread batter*

**Brown** ...... ground beef with onion in skillet, stirring until crumbly.
**Add** ....... tomatoes with salt and Worcestershire sauce, mixing well.
**Simmer** ..... for 15 minutes.
**Stir** ........ in beans.
**Pour** ....... into greased casserole.
**Spread** ..... corn bread batter over ground beef mixture using wet knife.
**Bake** ....... at 425 degrees for 20 minutes.
**Yields** ...... 4-6 servings.

Emely Sundbeck
Manor H. S., Manor, Texas

## RAILROAD PIE

*1 lb. ground beef*
*1 onion, chopped*
*1 can tomato soup*
*1/2 c. chopped green pepper*
*1 tbsp. (or more) chili powder*
*Dash of pepper*
*1 can kidney beans, drained (opt.)*
*1 can whole kernel corn, drained (opt.)*
*2 tsp. salt*
*3/4 c. cornmeal*
*1 tbsp. flour*
*1/4 tsp. soda*
*1 egg, beaten*
*1/2 c. buttermilk*
*1 tbsp. bacon drippings*

**Brown** ...... ground beef with onion in skillet, stirring until crumbly.
**Add** ....... next 6 ingredients and 1 teaspoon salt, mixing well.
**Simmer** ..... for 15 minutes.
**Pour** ....... into 2-quart casserole.
**Combine** .... remaining 1 teaspoon salt with cornmeal and remaining 5 ingredients in bowl, mixing well.
**Spoon** ...... over ground beef mixture.
**Bake** ....... at 350 degrees for 30 to 40 minutes or until corn bread tests done.
**Yields** ...... 6 servings.

Kay Keen
Lake Wales Jr. H. S., Lake Wales, Florida

## MEATZA PIE

1 lb. ground beef
1/2 to 1 tsp. garlic salt
1/2 c. fine dry bread crumbs
2/3 c. evaporated milk
1/3 c. catsup
1  2-oz. can sliced mushrooms, drained
2 to 3 slices Cheddar cheese, cut
    into strips
1/4 tsp. oregano
2 tbsp. Parmesan cheese

Combine .... first 4 ingredients in 9-inch pie plate, mixing lightly with fork.
Spread ..... over bottom and side of pie plate, shaping rim around edge.
Layer ...... catsup and mushrooms over ground beef mixture.
Arrange ..... cheese strips in crisscross pattern over top.
Sprinkle .... with remaining ingredients.
Bake ....... at 400 degrees for 20 minutes or until cheese is lightly browned.
Cut ........ into wedges.

Photograph for this recipe on page 83.

## MEATY SPANISH RICE PIE

3/4 c. crushed corn flakes
1/2 c. milk
1/4 c. chopped onion
1 tsp. salt
1 lb. ground beef
1  15-oz. can tomato sauce
1 c. minute rice
2 tbsp. finely chopped green pepper
1/4 tsp. chili powder
1/2 c. shredded American cheese

Combine .... first 5 ingredients in large bowl, mixing well.
Press ....... over bottom and side of 9-inch pie plate.
Combine .... tomato sauce, rice, green pepper and chili powder in bowl, mixing well.
Spoon ...... over ground beef.
Bake ....... at 350 degrees for 30 minutes.
Sprinkle .... with cheese.
Bake ....... for 3 minutes longer or until cheese melts.

Cut ........ into wedges to serve.
Yields ...... 6 servings.

Janet M. Burns
Newaygo H. S., Newaygo, Michigan

## HAMBURGER-BROCCOLI PIE WITH MUSHROOMS

1 lb. ground round
1/4 c. chopped onion
2 tbsp. flour
Salt to taste
1/4 tsp. garlic salt
Milk
1  3-oz. package cream cheese, softened
1  6-oz. can mushrooms
1 egg, beaten
1  10-oz. package frozen chopped broccoli, cooked, drained
1 recipe 2-crust pie pastry
4 oz. Cheddar cheese, grated

Brown ...... ground round with onion in skillet, stirring until crumbly; drain.
Add ....... flour, salt and garlic salt, mixing well.
Stir ........ in 1 1/4 cups milk and cream cheese.
Cook ....... until bubbly, stirring constantly.
Stir ........ mushrooms and a small amount of hot mixture into egg; stir egg mixture into ground round mixture.
Cook ....... over medium heat until thick, stirring constantly.
Stir ........ in broccoli.
Line ....... 9-inch pie plate with half the pastry.
Spoon ...... ground round mixture into pie shell.
Top ........ with cheese.
Cover ...... with remaining pastry, sealing edge and cutting slits.
Brush ...... with milk.
Bake ....... at 350 degrees for 40 to 45 minutes or until crust is golden brown.
Let ........ stand for 10 minutes before serving.
Yields ...... 6 servings.

Lillian Wilhelm
Hamilton H. S., Hamilton, Texas

## CHEEZY BEEF-BROCCOLI PIE

1 lb. ground beef
1/4 c. chopped onion
2 tbsp. flour
3/4 tsp. salt
1/4 tsp. garlic salt
Milk
1   3-oz. package cream cheese, softened
1 egg, beaten
1 pkg. frozen broccoli, cooked, drained
1 recipe 2-crust pie pastry
4 oz. Monterey Jack cheese, sliced

Brown ...... ground beef with onion in skil-
            let, stirring until crumbly; drain.
Stir ........ in flour, salt and garlic salt.
Add ....... 1 1/4 cups milk and cream
            cheese.
Cook ....... until bubbly.
Stir ........ a small amount of ground beef
            mixture into beaten egg; stir egg
            mixture into ground beef
            mixture.
Cook ....... until thick, stirring constantly.
Stir ........ in broccoli.
Line ....... 9-inch pie plate with half the
            pastry.
Spoon ...... hamburger mixture into pie
            shell.
Top ....... with cheese slices and remaining
            pastry; seal and prick with fork.
Brush ...... milk over top of pastry.
Bake ....... at 350 degrees for 40 to 45 min-
            utes or until golden brown.
Let ........ stand for 10 minutes before
            cutting.
Yields ...... 6 servings.

Brandy Harris
Texas City H. S., Texas City, Texas
Barbara Ann Talbot
Natick H. S., Natick, Massachusetts

## CHEESEBURGER PIE DELUXE

1 lb. ground beef
1 tsp. oregano
1 1/2 tsp. salt
1/4 c. each chopped onion, green pepper
1  8-oz. can tomato sauce
1 egg
1/4 c. milk

1/2 tsp. dry mustard
1/2 tsp. Worcestershire sauce
8 oz. grated sharp cheese
1 unbaked 9-in. pie shell

Brown ...... ground beef in skillet, stirring
            until crumbly.
Add ....... oregano, 1 teaspoon salt and
            next 3 ingredients, mixing well.
Cook ....... for 5 minutes.
Mix ........ egg, milk, remaining 1/2 tea-
            spoon salt, mustard, Worcester-
            shire sauce and cheese in bowl.
Spoon ...... ground beef mixture into pie
            shell.
Pour ....... cheese mixture over ground
            beef.
Bake ....... at 425 degrees for 30 minutes.
Yields ...... 6 servings.

Doris Patterson
Fairview H. S., Cullman, Alabama

## FAVORITE CHEESEBURGER PIE

1 lb. ground beef
1/2 c. each evaporated milk, catsup
1/3 c. fine dry bread crumbs
1/4 c. chopped onion
1/2 tsp. oregano
3/4 tsp. salt
1/8 tsp. pepper
1 recipe pie pastry
4 oz. American cheese, grated
1 tsp. Worcestershire sauce

Combine .... first 8 ingredients in bowl, mix-
            ing well.
Line ....... pie plate with pastry.
Spoon ...... in ground beef mixture.
Bake ....... at 350 degrees for 35 to 40 min-
            utes or until pastry is lightly
            browned.
Toss ....... cheese with Worcestershire sauce
            in small bowl.
Sprinkle .... over pie.
Bake ....... for 10 minutes longer.
Let ........ stand for 10 minutes before
            cutting.
Garnish ..... with pickle slices.
Yields ...... 6 servings.

Tyran Lee Fox
Austin Jr. H. S., San Juan, Texas

## DEEP-DISH ITALIAN MEAT PIE

1 lb. ground beef
1/3 c. chopped green pepper
1 sm. onion, chopped
1   6-oz. can tomato paste
1 env. spaghetti sauce mix
1/3 c. grated Parmesan cheese
1/4 c. grated mozzarella cheese
1 deep-dish pie shell

**Brown** . . . . . . ground beef in skillet, stirring until crumbly; drain.
**Add** . . . . . . . green pepper and onion.
**Saute** . . . . . . until vegetables are tender.
**Add** . . . . . . . tomato paste and spaghetti sauce mix with water according to package directions.
**Simmer** . . . . . for 10 minutes.
**Layer** . . . . . . ground beef mixture and cheeses alternately into pie shell until all ingredients are used, ending with cheeses.
**Bake** . . . . . . . at 400 degrees for 15 to 20 minutes or until crust is golden brown.

Emily B. Fallaw
Lockhart H. S., Lockhart, South Carolina

## MEAT AND POTATO PIE

2 sticks pie crust mix
1 lb. ground beef
1/2 c. milk
1/2 env. dry onion soup mix
Dash each of pepper, allspice
1   12-oz. package frozen hashed brown potatoes, thawed

**Prepare** . . . . . pie crust, using package directions.
**Line** . . . . . . . 9-inch pie plate with half the pastry.
**Combine** . . . . ground beef with milk, soup mix and seasonings in bowl, mixing well.
**Pat** . . . . . . . . lightly into prepared pie plate.
**Top** . . . . . . . . with potatoes.
**Cover** . . . . . . with remaining pastry, sealing and fluting edge.
**Cut** . . . . . . . . slits in top crust.
**Bake** . . . . . . . at 350 degrees for 1 hour or until golden brown.

**Serve** . . . . . . . with warm catsup.
**Yields** . . . . . . 6-8 servings.

K. Alicia Hampton
Pewitt H. S., Omaha, Texas

## NACHO PIE

1 lb. ground beef
1 med. onion, chopped
1 16-oz. can refried beans
1 8-oz. jar taco sauce
1 baked 9-in. pie shell
1 c. grated Monterey Jack cheese

**Brown** . . . . . . ground beef in skillet, stirring until crumbly.
**Add** . . . . . . . onion.
**Cook** . . . . . . . u n t i l   t e n d e r ,   s t i r r i n g occasionally.
**Mix** . . . . . . . . in refried beans and taco sauce.
**Spoon** . . . . . . into pie shell.
**Top** . . . . . . . . with cheese.
**Bake** . . . . . . . at 350 degrees for 15 minutes or until cheese is melted.
**Yields** . . . . . . 12-16 servings.

Debora A. Dillon
Princess Anne Jr. H. S., Virginia Beach, Virginia

## RICE-A-BURGERS

1 lb. ground beef
2 eggs, slightly beaten
3 c. cooked rice
2 tsp. seasoned salt
3/4 c. catsup
1/2 tsp. oregano
4 slices Cheddar cheese

**Combine** . . . . ground beef, eggs, rice and salt in large mixing bowl, mixing well.
**Spread** . . . . . into 8 foil "pans" or 1 large pizza pan. Use 8-inch circles of aluminum foil, 3 layers each, crimping edges of foil.
**Spread** . . . . . with catsup and sprinkling of oregano.
**Bake** . . . . . . . at 450 degrees for 10 minutes.
**Top** . . . . . . . . with cheese triangles.
**Bake** . . . . . . . at 450 degrees for 5 minutes longer or until cheese is bubbly.
**Yields** . . . . . . 8 servings.

Photograph for this recipe on page 1.

## SPICY BEEF CUPS

*3 sticks pie crust mix*
*1 1/2 med. green peppers, chopped*
*2 tbsp. margarine*
*2 lb. ground chuck*
*1/2 lb. hot pork sausage*
*2 eggs, well beaten*
*2 tbsp. lemon-pepper marinade*
*1 tbsp. Accent*
*2 tsp. sage*
*1 tsp. garlic juice*
*1 c. sliced green onions*
*24 stuffed olives (opt.)*

**Prepare** ..... pie crust, using package directions.
**Fit** ........ into 24 muffin cups; prick with fork.
**Bake** ....... at 350 degrees until lightly brown.
**Saute** ...... green peppers in margarine in large skillet until tender.
**Add** ....... ground chuck, sausage and next 6 ingredients.
**Saute** ...... until brown and crumbly.
**Fill** ........ crusts 3/4 full with ground chuck mixture.
**Top** ........ with remaining pastry.
**Bake** ....... at 350 degrees until golden brown.
**Top** ........ with olives on toothpicks.
**Yields** ...... 24 servings.

Gertrude M. Smith
Sherwood Middle Sch., Baton Rouge, Louisiana

## DEEP-DISH BEEF-MOZZARELLA PIZZA

*1  1-lb. loaf frozen bread dough, thawed*
*1 lb. ground beef*
*1/4 c. chopped onion*
*1  16-oz. can tomatoes*
*1  6-oz. can tomato paste*
*2 tsp. oregano*
*2  6-oz. packages mozzarella cheese slices*
*Grated Parmesan cheese*

**Let** ........ dough stand at room temperature for 1 hour.
**Brown** ...... ground beef in skillet, stirring until crumbly; drain.
**Add** ....... onion.
**Cook** ....... until tender, stirring frequently.
**Stir** ........ in next 3 ingredients.
**Simmer** ..... for 15 minutes.
**Roll** ....... dough on lightly floured surface into 11 x 15-inch rectangle.
**Press** ....... into bottom and 1 inch up sides of greased 9 x 13-inch baking pan.
**Layer** ...... ground beef mixture and mozzarella cheese alternately over dough until all ingredients are used.
**Sprinkle** .... with Parmesan cheese.
**Bake** ....... at 425 degrees for 20 minutes.
**Let** ........ stand for 10 minutes before cutting.
**Yields** ...... 8 servings.

Clarazina H. Lovett
Seabreeze Jr. H. S., Daytona Beach, Florida

## EASY BURGER PIZZA

*1 1/2 lb. ground chuck*
*1 c. seasoned bread crumbs*
*2/3 c. evaporated milk*
*1 egg, slightly beaten*
*1/2 c. chopped onion*
*1 tsp. salt*
*1 c. pizza sauce*
*1/2 c. each shredded Cheddar, mozzarella cheese*
*Chopped green peppers (opt.)*
*Sliced mushrooms (opt.)*
*Sliced olives (opt.)*
*Chopped chilies (opt.)*

**Combine** .... first 6 ingredients in bowl, mixing well.
**Press** ....... over bottom and side of 12-inch pizza pan, forming 1/2-inch rim around edge.
**Spread** ..... pizza sauce over top.
**Sprinkle** .... cheeses over sauce.
**Garnish** ..... with chopped green peppers, sliced mushrooms, olives, chilies or additional chopped onion as desired.
**Bake** ....... at 350 degrees for 20 to 25 minutes or until crust is brown; drain.
**Cut** ........ into wedges.

Doris M. Swinhart
Necedah Area H. S., Necedah, Wisconsin

## QUICK MEXICAN BURGER PIZZA PIE

*1 lb. ground beef*
*1/4 c. fine dry bread crumbs*
*1 egg, slightly beaten*
*1/2 c. chopped onion*
*1/2 c. pizza sauce*
*1  4-oz. can green chilies, finely chopped*
*1/2 c. sliced ripe olives*
*1/2 to 3/4 c. grated Cheddar cheese*

**Combine** .... first 4 ingredients in bowl, mixing well.
**Press** ....... into 8-inch pie plate.
**Spread** ..... pizza sauce over ground beef mixture.
**Top** ........ with chilies, olives and cheese.
**Bake** ....... at 350 degrees for 20 to 25 minutes or until crust is brown; drain.
**Garnish** ..... with shredded lettuce, chopped tomatoes and hot sauce.
**Yields** ...... 4-6 servings.

Nancy A. Gearhart
Westwood H. S., Mesa, Arizona

## POP-UP PIZZA

*1  lb. ground chuck*
*1 onion, chopped*
*1 pkg. spaghetti sauce mix*
*1  15-oz. can tomato sauce*
*2 c. shredded mozzarella cheese*
*2 eggs*
*1 c. milk*
*1 tbsp. oil*
*1 c. flour*
*1/2 tsp. salt*
*1/2 c. grated Parmesan cheese*

**Brown** ...... ground chuck with onion in skillet, stirring until crumbly.
**Add** ....... spaghetti sauce mix, tomato sauce and 1/2 cup water, mixing well.
**Simmer** ..... for 10 minutes.
**Spoon** ...... into greased 9 x 13-inch baking dish.
**Sprinkle** .... with mozzarella cheese.
**Beat** ....... eggs, milk and oil in bowl until foamy.
**Add** ....... flour and salt, beating until smooth.

**Pour** ....... over ground chuck mixture.
**Sprinkle** .... with Parmesan cheese.
**Bake** ....... at 400 degrees for 30 minutes or until puffy.
**Yields** ...... 8 servings.

Pam Byce
Greene County H. S., Greensboro, Georgia
Marla Hartry
Central Elgin C. I., St. Thomas, Ontario

## TACO PIZZA

*3/4 c. cornmeal*
*1 tsp. each salt, baking powder*
*1 1/4 c. flour*
*2/3 c. milk*
*1/4 c. oil*
*1 lb. hamburger*
*8 oz. tomato sauce*
*1/2 to 1 pkg. taco seasoning mix*
*1 c. shredded cheese*
*2 c. chopped lettuce*
*1 c. chopped tomato*
*1 c. chopped avocado*

**Combine** .... first 6 ingredients in bowl, mixing well.
**Knead** ...... lightly on floured surface.
**Press** ....... into greased pizza pan.
**Bake** ....... at 400 degrees for 10 minutes.
**Brown** ...... hamburger in skillet, stirring until crumbly.
**Stir** ........ in tomato sauce and taco seasoning.
**Simmer** ..... for 3 minutes.
**Spoon** ...... onto crust, distributing evenly.
**Sprinkle** .... 1/2 cup cheese over top.
**Bake** ....... at 400 degrees for 10 minutes longer.
**Top** ........ with remaining 1/2 cup cheese and remaining ingredients.
**Yields** ...... 8-10 servings.

Thyra K. Davis
Auburn Middle Sch., Auburn, Kansas

## TWO PIZZAS

*1 pkg. dry yeast*
*Flour*
*1/2 tsp. salt*
*1 tsp. olive oil*
*1 lb. hamburger*

2 tbsp. each chopped onion, green pepper
1/4 tsp. seasoned salt
2 tsp. steak sauce
4 tsp. Worcestershire sauce
1 8-oz. can tomato sauce
1 tsp. garlic salt

**Dissolve** ..... yeast in 1 cup lukewarm water.
**Place** ....... 3 cups flour in bowl; make a well.
**Mix** ......... in salt and oil.
**Add** ....... yeast mixture gradually, mixing well.
**Knead** ...... on floured surface until smooth and elastic.
**Place** ....... in greased bowl.
**Let** ........ rise, covered, in warm place until doubled in bulk.
**Press** ....... into two 12-inch pizza pans.
**Let** ........ rise for 20 minutes.
**Brown** ...... hamburger in skillet, stirring until crumbly; drain.
**Add** ....... onion and green pepper.
**Cook** ....... until slightly brown, stirring frequently.
**Stir** ........ in remaining ingredients.
**Spoon** ...... over dough.
**Bake** ....... at 475 degrees for 10 minutes.
**Yields** ...... 2 pizzas.

Martha Pearce
Muskogee H. S., Muskogee, Oklahoma

## QUICK CRUST PIZZA

1 1/2 c. flour
2 pkg. dry yeast
Sugar
1 tsp. salt
2/3 c. shortening
1 8-oz. can pizza sauce
1 tsp. oregano
1/4 tsp. garlic salt
3/4 lb. ground beef
1/4 lb. pepperoni, sliced
1 can chopped mushrooms, drained
1 c. shredded mozzarella cheese

**Sift** ........ 1/2 cup flour, yeast, 1 teaspoon sugar and salt together into bowl.
**Cut** ........ in shortening until crumbly.
**Add** ....... 1/2 cup hot water.
**Beat** ....... for 1 minute or until smooth.

**Stir** ........ in enough flour to make moderately stiff dough.
**Knead** ...... on floured surface for 3 to 5 minutes or until smooth and elastic.
**Let** ........ rise, covered, for 20 minutes.
**Press** ....... into greased 12-inch pizza pan; prick with fork.
**Bake** ....... at 425 degrees for 10 minutes.
**Combine** .... pizza sauce, oregano, garlic salt and 1 teaspoon sugar, if desired, in saucepan.
**Bring** ....... to a boil.
**Spread** ..... over crust.
**Brown** ...... ground beef in skillet, stirring until crumbly; drain.
**Layer** ...... with remaining 3 ingredients over sauce.
**Bake** ....... at 425 degrees for 15 minutes.

Patricia Ann Duncan
Halton Jr. H. S., Fort Worth, Texas

## PIZZA CUPS

1 sm. onion, minced
1 tbsp. oil
1/2 lb. ground beef
1 can tomato sauce
1/2 tsp. Italian seasoning
1/4 tsp. each garlic salt, oregano
1 can refrigerator biscuits
4 oz. mozzarella cheese, shredded

**Saute** ...... onion in oil in skillet until tender.
**Add** ....... ground beef.
**Cook** ....... until brown, stirring until crumbly.
**Add** ....... tomato sauce and seasonings, mixing well.
**Simmer** ..... for 3 to 5 minutes or until heated through.
**Press** ....... biscuit dough into greased muffin cups, pulling edges up sides to make high ridge.
**Spoon** ...... ground beef mixture into biscuit-lined muffin cups.
**Bake** ....... at 400 degrees for 15 minutes.
**Sprinkle** .... with cheese.
**Bake** ....... for 5 minutes longer or until cheese is melted.

F. Tymosko
Derby H. S., Derby, Connecticut

## PRONTO PIZZA

1 pkg. refrigerator crescent rolls
1 lb. ground beef
1  8-oz. can tomato sauce
1 tbsp. sugar
1 tsp. basil
1 tsp. oregano
1 tbsp. spaghetti sauce mix
Parmesan cheese (opt.)
Sliced mushrooms (opt.)
Sliced ripe olives (opt.)
4 oz. mozzarella cheese, shredded

**Arrange** . . . . . roll dough in pizza pan, sealing seams and shaping ridge around edge.

**Brown** . . . . . . ground beef in skillet, stirring until crumbly; drain.

**Combine** . . . . next 5 ingredients in bowl, mixing well.

**Spread** . . . . . over dough.

**Layer** . . . . . . ground beef and remaining ingredients in order given over sauce.

**Bake** . . . . . . . at 450 degrees for 12 to 15 minutes or until crust is brown.

**Yields** . . . . . . 4 servings.

Carla Seippel
Fort Osage Jr. H. S., Independence, Missouri

## QUICK PIZZAS

1  8-oz. can tomato sauce
1/8 tsp. garlic powder
1/2 tsp. oregano
Dash of pepper
1/2 lb. ground beef
2 cans refrigerator biscuits
1 c. shredded Cheddar cheese
1/4 c. grated Parmesan cheese

**Mix** . . . . . . . . first 4 ingredients in bowl.

**Brown** . . . . . . g round beef in skillet, stirring until crumbly.

**Press** . . . . . . . biscuits into 2 greased 12-inch pizza pans, forming shallow rim.

**Layer** . . . . . . sauce mixture, ground beef and cheeses over dough.

**Bake** . . . . . . . in moderately hot oven for 10 to 15 minutes or until crust is golden brown.

**Yields** . . . . . . 20 servings.

Patricia A. Giles
Chidester H. S., Chidester, Arkansas

## BLENDER HAMBURGER QUICHE

1/2 lb. ground beef
1 sm. onion, chopped
1/2 c. grated Cheddar cheese
1/2 c. milk
1/2 c. mayonnaise
1 tbsp. cornstarch
3 eggs
Salt and pepper to taste
1 deep-dish pie shell

**Brown** . . . . . . ground beef with onion in skillet, stirring until crumbly.

**Place** . . . . . . . next 7 ingredients in blender container.

**Process** . . . . . until foamy.

**Spoon** . . . . . . ground beef mixture into pie shell.

**Pour** . . . . . . . egg mixture over ground beef.

**Bake** . . . . . . . at 350 degrees for 30 minutes.

**Yields** . . . . . . 6 servings.

Patsy S. Coble
Arab H. S., Arab, Alabama

## HAMBURGER-ONION QUICHE

1/2 lb. hamburger
1 c. thinly sliced onion
1 tbsp. butter
3 tbsp. flour
1 tsp. salt
1/4 tsp. pepper
2 eggs, beaten
2 c. milk
1 tsp. Worcestershire sauce
2 c. shredded cheese
1 unbaked 9-in. pie shell

**Saute** . . . . . . hamburger and onion in butter in skillet until onion is tender.

**Mix** . . . . . . . . in flour, salt and pepper.

**Combine** . . . . eggs with milk, Worcestershire sauce and 1 cup cheese in large bowl, mixing well.

**Add** . . . . . . . hamburger mixture.

**Spoon** . . . . . . into pie shell.

**Sprinkle** . . . . remaining 1 cup cheese over top.

**Bake** . . . . . . . at 425 degrees for 20 to 25 minutes or until center is set.

**Let** . . . . . . . . stand for 15 minutes before cutting.

**Yields** . . . . . . 6-8 servings.

Elizabeth Bowdin
Kinston H. S., Kinston, Alabama

# Company Fare

## BEEFBURGERS WELLINGTON

*1 1/2 lb. lean ground beef*
*1 egg*
*1/4 c. milk*
*1 tsp. Worcestershire sauce*
*Salt and pepper to taste*
*Grated cheese*
*Crisp-cooked bacon, crumbled*
*1 frozen pie shell, thawed, quartered*

**Combine** .... first 6 ingredients in bowl, mixing well.
**Shape** ...... 3/4 of the mixture into 4 loaves.
**Make** ....... oblong-shaped well in each loaf.
**Fill** ........ with cheese and bacon.
**Top** ........ with remaining ground beef mixture, pressing to seal well.
**Place** ....... pastry over each loaf, tucking edges underneath.
**Place** ....... pastry side up on rack in baking pan.
**Bake** ....... at 350 degrees for 30 minutes or to desired degree of doneness.
**Broil** ....... for 2 minutes to brown pastry.

Photograph for this recipe above.

## SISTER RENEE'S BEEF CAKE

*1 c. ground beef, crumbled*
*1 c. each sugar, raisins*

*1/2 c. shortening*
*1 tsp. each salt, cinnamon, nutmeg*
*1/4 tsp. cloves*
*1 3/4 c. flour*
*2 tsp. baking powder*
*1 tsp. soda*
*1 egg*
*Nuts (opt.)*

**Combine** .... ground beef with next 3 ingredients, seasoning and 1 1/2 cups water in saucepan, mixing well.
**Bring** ....... to a boil, stirring frequently; cool.
**Add** ....... remaining ingredients, mixing well.
**Press** ....... into greased and floured loaf pan.
**Bake** ....... at 350 degrees for 45 to 50 minutes.
**Yields** ...... 8-10 servings.

Sister Renee Washut
St. Pius X H. S., Kansas City, Missouri

## CHILI FOR ONE-HUNDRED

*30 lb. hamburger*
*12 No. 10 cans tomato juice*
*12 No. 10 cans beans*
*20 c. elbow macaroni, cooked*
*3/4 c. dried onions*
*2 1/2 c. chili powder*
*Salt and pepper to taste*

**Brown** ...... hamburger in large skillets, stirring until crumbly.
**Add** ....... remaining ingredients, mixing well.
**Simmer** ..... until flavors are blended.
**Yields** ...... 100 servings.

Mrs. Mary Jane Smith
Pleasant View Jr. H. S., Richmond, Indiana

## CALIFORNIA CASSEROLE

*1 lb. ground beef*
*1/2 c. chopped onion*
*1 clove of garlic, chopped*
*1 c. rice*
*1 c. sliced ripe olives*
*1  4-oz. can mushrooms*
*1  16-oz. can whole tomatoes*
*1/2 c. Sherry*

Salt and pepper to taste
1 c. grated Cheddar cheese
2 tbsp. chopped parsley

Brown . . . . . . ground beef with onion and garlic in skillet, stirring until crumbly.
Add . . . . . . . next 7 ingredients, mixing well.
Bring . . . . . . . to a boil.
Pour . . . . . . . into 2-quart casserole.
Bake . . . . . . . covered, at 350 degrees for 30 minutes.
Stir . . . . . . . . in cheese.
Bake . . . . . . . covered, for 15 minutes longer; stir.
Top . . . . . . . . with parsley.
Garnish . . . . . with paprika.
Yields . . . . . . 4 servings.

Karen Wagner
Branham H. S., San Jose, California

## FABULOUS BURGER CASSEROLE

1 lb. ground beef
1/2 c. chopped green pepper
4 green onions, chopped
Dash of garlic salt
1/4 c. margarine
2 1/2 tbsp. flour
1 c. milk
1 can cream of mushroom soup
3 c. grated mild Cheddar cheese
1/2 c. Parmesan cheese
1/2 c. chopped celery
1/2 c. shaved almonds
Salt and pepper to taste
3/4 lb. thin spaghetti, cooked, drained

Brown . . . . . . ground beef in skillet, stirring until crumbly; drain.
Saute . . . . . . green pepper and green onions with garlic salt in margarine in skillet until tender.
Mix . . . . . . . . in flour.
Add . . . . . . . milk gradually, stirring constantly.
Cook . . . . . . . until thick, stirring constantly.
Stir . . . . . . . . in soup.
Simmer . . . . . for several minutes.
Add . . . . . . . ground beef and cheeses, mixing well.
Cook . . . . . . . over low heat until cheeses melt, stirring frequently.

Mix . . . . . . . . in celery, almonds, salt and pepper.
Combine . . . . with spaghetti in baking dish, mixing well.
Bake . . . . . . . at 350 degrees until bubbly.

Deanna Hardesty
Tuttle Public Schools, Tuttle, Oklahoma

## GROUND BEEF COMPANY SURPRISE

1 1/2 lb. ground chuck
1 egg, slightly beaten
1/2 c. milk
1/3 c. quick oats
1/4 c. finely chopped onion
1 tbsp. chopped parsley
1 1/2 tsp. salt
1/2 tsp. monosodium glutamate
1/8 tsp. pepper
1/3 c. each chopped onion, celery
3 tbsp. margarine
1 c. herb-seasoned stuffing mix
4 carrots, cooked, cut into strips
6 slices bacon
1/4 c. chili sauce
2 tbsp. dark corn syrup

Combine . . . . first 9 ingredients in large bowl, mixing well.
Shape . . . . . . into 9 x 12-inch rectangle on waxed paper.
Saute . . . . . . chopped onion and celery in margarine in skillet until tender.
Add . . . . . . . stuffing and 1/3 cup water, mixing well.
Spread . . . . . over ground beef rectangle.
Arrange . . . . . carrots along center of stuffing mixture.
Roll . . . . . . . as for jelly roll.
Place . . . . . . . seam side down in baking dish.
Wrap . . . . . . . with bacon slices.
Bake . . . . . . . at 325 degrees for 45 minutes.
Combine . . . . chili sauce and syrup, blending well.
Brush . . . . . . onto ground beef roll.
Bake . . . . . . . for 5 minutes longer.
Let . . . . . . . . stand for 5 minutes; remove to serving dish.
Yields . . . . . . 6 servings.

Marjorie Yandell
Caldwell County H. S., Princeton, Kentucky

## PICADILLO PEPPERS

4 lg. green peppers
1 1/2 lb. ground beef
2 tbsp. olive oil
1 clove of garlic, minced
1/3 c. chopped celery
1/2 c. chopped onion
1 1/4 tsp. ground cumin or chili powder
3/4 c. sliced pimento-stuffed olives
1/3 c. raisins
2 tbsp. chopped capers
3/4 tsp. salt
1/4 tsp. pepper
1/8 tsp. ground allspice
1 1/2 c. cooked brown rice
1   8-oz. can tomato sauce

Cut . . . . . . . . peppers in half lengthwise, removing seeds.
Parboil . . . . . in boiling salted water for 5 minutes; drain.
Brown . . . . . . ground beef in olive oil in skillet, stirring until crumbly; drain, reserving pan drippings.
Saute . . . . . . garlic, celery and onion in pan drippings in skillet until tender.
Stir . . . . . . . . in ground beef, 3/4 teaspoon cumin and remaining ingredients except tomato sauce.
Spoon . . . . . . into peppers in baking dish.
Bake . . . . . . . at 350 degrees for 30 minutes.
Mix . . . . . . . . remaining 1/2 teaspoon cumin with tomato sauce in saucepan.
Cook . . . . . . . until heated through, stirring constantly.
Spoon . . . . . . over peppers.
Garnish . . . . . with parsley sprigs.
Yields . . . . . . 8 servings.

Photograph for this recipe on page 6.

## COMPANY DOWN-EAST MEATBALLS-FOR-A-CROWD

2 c. stale bread crumbs
Milk
6 lb. ground beef
4 eggs, beaten
2 tsp. each garlic salt, pepper
1/2 c. parsley, finely chopped
2 med. onions, finely chopped
4 stalks celery, finely chopped
1/2 lb. mushrooms, coarsely chopped
Oil
2 lg. cans barbecue sauce
2 cans cream of mushroom soup

Soak . . . . . . . bread crumbs in a small amount of milk in bowl.
Combine . . . . with remaining ingredients except oil, barbecue sauce and soup in large bowl; mixing well.
Shape . . . . . . into bite-sized balls.
Brown . . . . . . in a small amount of oil in skillet; drain.
Place . . . . . . . in large slow cooker.
Combine . . . . barbecue sauce and soup in bowl, mixing well.
Pour . . . . . . . over meatballs.
Cook . . . . . . . on Low for several hours.
Yields . . . . . . 400 meatballs.

Brenda L. Little
Farmville Central H. S., Farmville, North Carolina

## POOR BOY FILETS

5 slices bacon
1 lb. lean ground beef
Salt and pepper to taste
1/4 c. Parmesan cheese
1   2-oz. can mushroom pieces, drained
3 tbsp. finely chopped pimento-stuffed olives
2 tbsp. each finely chopped onion, green pepper

Saute . . . . . . bacon in skillet until partially cooked; drain on paper towels.
Press . . . . . . . ground beef into 7 x 12-inch rectangle on waxed paper.
Sprinkle . . . . lightly with salt and pepper.
Top . . . . . . . . with Parmesan cheese.
Combine . . . . remaining ingredients in bowl.
Sprinkle . . . . evenly over ground beef.
Roll . . . . . . . as for jelly roll.
Cut . . . . . . . . into 1 1/2-inch slices.
Wrap . . . . . . . edge of each slice with strip of bacon, securing with toothpick.
Place . . . . . . . on rack in broiling pan.
Broil . . . . . . . for 8 minutes on each side.
Yields . . . . . . 5 servings.

Agatha Fods
Tri-Valley H. S., Lyons, South Dakota

Recipe on page 146.

## MOCK FILET MIGNON

*1 1/2 lb. lean ground beef*
*2 c. cooked rice*
*1 c. minced onion*
*1 clove of garlic, crushed*
*2 tbsp. Worcestershire sauce*
*1 1/2 tsp. salt*
*1/4 tsp. pepper*
*8 slices bacon*

**Combine** .... first 7 ingredients in bowl, mixing well.
**Shape** ...... into 8 patties 3/4 inch thick.
**Wrap** ....... bacon slice around each patty, fastening with toothpick.
**Place** ....... in shallow baking pan.
**Bake** ....... at 450 degrees for 15 minutes.
**Serve** ...... with mushroom sauce.
**Yields** ...... 8 servings.

Photograph for this recipe on page 99.

## VANESSA'S SPAGHETTI SAUCE

*2 med. onions, chopped*
*1 stalk celery, chopped*
*3/4 stick margarine*
*2 1/2 lb. ground beef*
*1 lg. can mushrooms*
*1 6-oz. can tomato paste*
*1 15-oz. can tomato sauce*
*1 8-oz. can tomato sauce*
*1/4 tsp. garlic powder*
*5 bay leaves*
*2 tbsp. brown sugar*
*Oregano, thyme, chili powder, salt and pepper to taste*
*Worcestershire sauce to taste*

**Saute** ...... onions and celery in margarine in skillet; remove vegetables.
**Brown** ...... ground beef in skillet, stirring until crumbly; drain.
**Combine** .... with sauteed vegetables and remaining ingredients in large saucepan.
**Simmer** ..... covered, for 2 hours.
**Yields** ...... 6-8 servings.

Vanessa L. Robinson
Seabreeze Sr. H. S., Daytona Beach, Florida

Recipe on page 81.

## MEXICAN SPAGHETTI SAUCE

*2 lb. ground round*
*1 Bermuda onion, chopped*
*1 lg. jar spaghetti sauce*
*8 jalapeno peppers, chopped*
*2 lg. cans mushrooms*
*2 tbsp. butter*
*2 c. white wine*
*1 sm. can tomato paste*
*1 tbsp. pepper*
*Oregano to taste*

**Brown** ...... ground round in skillet, stirring until crumbly.
**Add** ....... remaining ingredients, mixing well.
**Simmer** ..... for 4 hours, stirring occasionally.
**Serve** ...... with spaghetti and garnish with Parmesan cheese.

JoAnn Bauer
Hurst Jr. H. S., Hurst, Texas

## WARREN POND GROUND BEEF

*2 lb. ground chuck*
*1/4 lb. Italian sausage, skinned*
*1 med. onion, chopped*
*1/4 c. chopped green pepper*
*1 32-oz. jar spaghetti sauce*
*1 4-oz. can mushroom pieces*
*2 oz. dry red wine*
*1 tsp. oregano*
*2 tbsp. Parmesan cheese*
*1/2 lb. size 22 pasta shells, cooked*
*Garlic salt to taste*
*1 tbsp. margarine*
*1/4 lb. Port du Salut cheese, thinly sliced*

**Brown** ...... ground chuck and sausage with onion and green pepper in skillet, stirring until crumbly.
**Add** ....... next 5 ingredients, mixing well.
**Simmer** ..... for 30 minutes.
**Mix** ........ pasta shells, garlic salt and margarine in shallow casserole.
**Add** ....... spaghetti sauce mixture, mixing well.
**Arrange** ..... Port du Salut cheese on top.
**Bake** ....... at 350 degrees for 30 minutes.
**Yields** ...... 8-10 servings.

Sandra S. Roman
Cheshire Vocational Center, Keene H. S.
Keene, New Hampshire

## FAVORITE BEEF LASAGNA

2 lb. ground beef
1 med. onion, chopped
1 clove of garlic, minced
1  16-oz. can tomatoes
2  8-oz. cans pizza sauce
1 tsp. each salt, oregano
1/2 tsp. basil
1  8-oz. package lasagna noodles,
    cooked, drained
1  8-oz. carton cottage cheese
2 c. grated mozzarella cheese
1/2 c. Parmesan cheese

**Brown** ...... ground beef with onion and garlic in skillet, stirring until
crumbly; drain.
**Add** ...... tomatoes, pizza sauce and seasonings, mixing well.
**Simmer** ..... covered, for 20 minutes.
**Pour** ....... 1 cup sauce over bottom of
greased 9 x 13-inch baking dish
and reserve 1 cup for topping.
**Layer** ..... half the noodles, remaining
sauce, cottage cheese and mozzarella cheese in baking dish; repeat layers.
**Top** ........ with reserved sauce.
**Sprinkle** .... with Parmesan cheese.
**Bake** ....... at 350 degrees for 30 minutes.
**Let** ........ stand for 10 minutes before
cutting.
**Yields** ...... 8 servings.

Evelyn B. Willey
Gates County H. S., Gatesville, North Carolina

## BONNIE'S COMPANY CASSEROLE

1 lb. lean ground beef
1 med. onion, finely chopped
1 clove of garlic, crushed
1  8-oz. can stewed tomatoes
1  3-oz. can sliced mushrooms, drained
7 oz. spaghetti sauce
4 oz. shell macaroni, cooked
1/2 pt. sour cream
4 oz. provolone cheese, sliced
4 oz. mozzarella cheese, sliced

**Brown** ...... ground beef in skillet, stirring
until crumbly; drain.
**Stir** ........ in next 5 ingredients.
**Simmer** ..... for 20 minutes.

**Layer** ...... macaroni, sour cream, provolone
cheese, mozzarella cheese and
ground beef mixture in greased
casserole.
**Bake** ....... at 350 degrees for 35 to 40 minutes or until bubbly.
**Yields** ...... 6 servings.

Mary M. Vorpahl
Gaston H. S., Gaston, Oregon

## MAZETTI

1 green pepper, chopped
1 lg. onion, chopped
2 stalks celery, chopped
2 lb. ground beef
1 can each tomato, cream of mushroom
    soup
2 tbsp. oil
1 tsp. each salt, pepper
1/4 tsp. chili powder
Dash of garlic salt
1 pkg. shell macaroni, cooked
1 c. grated cheese

**Saute** ...... green pepper, onion and celery
in skillet until tender.
**Add** ....... ground beef.
**Cook** ....... until brown and crumbly, stir-
ring constantly.
**Stir** ........ in next 8 ingredients with 1 soup
can water.
**Spoon** ...... into greased casserole.
**Top** ........ with cheese.
**Bake** ....... covered, at 350 degrees for 35
minutes.
**Yields** ...... 12 servings.

Barbara D. Ayers
Phil Campbell H. S., Phil Campbell, Alabama

## STUFFED JUMBO SHELLS

1 lb. ground beef
1/2 med. onion, minced
1 sm. can mushrooms
1 clove of garlic, minced
1/2 c. finely chopped celery
1 tsp. salt
1/2 tsp. pepper
1 tbsp. oil
1/2 tsp. each oregano, paprika
2 tbsp. Worcestershire sauce
1/2 c. walnuts, chopped

3 c. bottled spaghetti sauce
1/2 pkg. jumbo shell macaroni, cooked
1  8-oz. package mozzarella cheese,
    shredded

**Brown** ...... ground beef with next 6 ingredients in oil in 12-inch skillet, stirring until crumbly; remove from
heat.

**Add** ....... oregano, paprika, Worcestershire
sauce, walnuts and 1 cup sauce,
mixing well.

**Fill** ........ each shell with rounded table-
spoonful of ground beef mix-
ture, reserving remaining ground
beef mixture.

**Spoon** ...... 1 cup sauce into casserole.

**Sprinkle** .... remaining ground beef mixture
over sauce.

**Place** ....... shells in casserole.

**Pour** ....... remaining sauce over shells.

**Sprinkle** .... with cheese.

**Bake** ....... at 350 degrees for 20 minutes.

**Yields** ...... 4-5 servings.

Phyllis Dunlap
Dysart-Geneseo Community Sch., Dysart, Iowa

## BEEF-PEACH PIE

1  29-oz. can cling peach halves
1 1/2 lb. lean ground beef
1 1/2 c. soft bread crumbs
1/2 c. finely chopped onion
1 1/4 tsp. salt
2 eggs, beaten
1  8-oz. can tomato sauce with mushrooms

**Drain** ...... peaches, reserving 1/4 cup syrup.

**Combine** .... next 5 ingredients with reserved
peach syrup and 1/2 cup tomato
sauce in bowl, mixing well.

**Spoon** ...... into 9-inch pie plate. Do not
pack.

**Make** ....... depressions around edge of
ground beef mixture with back
of spoon.

**Place** ....... peach halves in depressions, cup-
sides up.

**Bake** ....... covered, at 350 degrees for 1
hour.

**Spoon** ...... remaining tomato sauce into
peach halves and over top of
ground beef mixture.

**Bake** ....... uncovered for 15 to 20 minutes
longer or to desired degree of
doneness.

**Yields** ...... 6-7 servings.

Photograph for this recipe above.

## SOUR CREAM-NOODLE BAKE

1 lb. ground beef
1 tbsp. butter
1 tsp. salt
1/2 tbsp. pepper
1/4 tsp. garlic salt
1 c. tomato sauce
1 c. cream-style cottage cheese
1 c. sour cream
1 c. chopped green pepper
1 c. grated sharp Cheddar cheese
1  8-oz. package med. noodles, cooked

**Brown** ...... ground beef in butter in skillet,
stirring until crumbly.

**Add** ....... salt, pepper, garlic salt and
tomato sauce, mixing well.

**Simmer** ..... for 5 minutes.

**Combine** .... remaining 5 ingredients in bowl,
mixing well.

**Layer** ...... noodle and ground beef mixtures alternately in 2-quart casserole until all ingredients are
used, ending with ground beef
mixture.

**Bake** ....... at 350 degrees for 20 to 25 minutes or unril bubbly.

**Yields** ...... 8 servings.

Dona M. McCloud
Kempsville Jr. H. S., Virginia Beach, Virginia

## COMPANY GROUND BEEF CASEROLE

1 lb. green peppers, chopped
1 lb. onions, chopped
1 bunch celery, chopped
1/2 lb. butter
1 lb. ground beef
1 lb. lean ground pork
1 sm. can sliced mushrooms
1  20-oz. can tomato sauce
1 sm. jar stuffed olives, chopped
1 can tomato paste
Salt to taste
2  10-oz. packages egg noodles, cooked
1 can cream of mushroom soup
1/2 lb. cheese, grated

Saute ...... green peppers, onions and celery in butter in large skillet until tender.
Brown ...... ground beef and ground pork in Dutch oven, stirring until crumbly.
Add ...... sauteed vegetables and next 7 ingredients, mixing well.
Cook ....... over low heat for 30 minutes.
Spoon ...... into casserole.
Sprinkle .... with cheese.
Bake ....... at 350 degrees for 30 minutes.
Yields ...... 12 servings.

Carolyn L. Kelly
Bainbridge H. S., Bainbridge, Georgia

## IMPERIAL HAMBURGER

1/2 c. blanched slivered almonds
1 tbsp. butter
3/4 lb. hamburger
1/4 tsp. salt
1 c. fine noodles
1 pkg. Japanese-style vegetables with seasoned sauce
1 tbsp. soy sauce

Saute ...... almonds lightly in butter in skillet; remove to small bowl.
Brown ...... hamburger in butter remaining in skillet, stirring occasionally; drain.
Stir ........ in salt and 1 cup water.
Bring ....... to a boil.
Add ...... noodles, mixing well.
Simmer ..... covered, for 2 minutes.
Add ...... vegetables.
Boil ........ until sauce cubes dissolve, stirring frequently.
Stir ........ in almonds, reserving 2 tablespoons.
Simmer ..... covered, for 3 minutes.
Add ...... soy sauce, mixing well.
Top ........ with reserved almonds.
Yields ...... 4 servings.

Beverly Perry
Putnam City Central Jr. H. S.
Oklahoma City, Oklahoma

## GROUND BEEF-CASHEW CASEROLE

2 lb. ground beef
2 onions, minced
1/2 c. mushrooms, chopped
1/2 c. ripe olives, chopped
1/2 lb. American cheese, grated
2 cans mushroom soup
1/2 c. sour cream
2 tbsp. Sherry
8 oz. noodles, cooked
1/2 c. cashews
1/2 c. chow mein noodles

Brown ...... ground beef with onions in skillet, stirring until crumbly.
Combine .... next 6 ingredients in saucepan.
Cook ....... until cheese is melted.
Layer ...... ground beef mixture, cooked noodles and cheese mixture in 9 x 13-inch casserole.
Bake ....... at 325 degrees for 35 minutes.
Top ........ with cashews and chow mein noodles.
Bake ....... for 10 minutes longer.
Yields ...... 12-15 servings.

Sandra Nelson
Cavalier H. S., Cavalier, North Dakota

## FAVORITE WILD RICE CASEROLE

1 1/2 lb. ground beef
2 tbsp. chopped onion
2 tbsp. butter
1 pkg. wild rice, cooked
1 can each cream of mushroom, cream of chicken soup

1/4 c. slivered almonds (opt.)
3/4 c. buttered croutons (opt.)

**Brown** . . . . . . ground beef with onion in butter in skillet, stirring until crumbly; drain.
**Stir** . . . . . . . . in remaining ingredients except croutons, mixing well.
**Spoon** . . . . . . into greased 1 1/2-quart casserole.
**Bake** . . . . . . . at 350 degrees for 45 minutes.
**Top** . . . . . . . . with croutons.
**Yields** . . . . . . 4 servings.

Kathleen Ann McConkie
Southwest Jr. H. S., Hot Springs, Arkansas

## FOUR-BEAN-BEEF BAKE

2 lb. lean ground beef
6 slices bacon, chopped
1 med. onion, chopped
1 can each green beans, wax beans, drained
1 can each kidney beans, garbanzo
    beans, rinsed, drained
1 lg. can baked beans
1 tbsp. vinegar
1 tsp. prepared mustard
1/2 c. catsup
1/2 c. packed brown sugar
1 tsp. salt

**Brown** . . . . . . ground beef with bacon in skillet, stirring until crumbly; drain.
**Combine** . . . . with remaining ingredients in 9 x 13-inch baking pan, mixing well.
**Bake** . . . . . . . at 325 degrees for 50 to 60 minutes or until heated through.
**Yields** . . . . . . 8-12 servings.

Sally Mace Gallagher
Capuchino H. S., San Bruno, California

## GRANDMA'S BEEF CASSEROLE

1 1/2 lb. ground round
1 med. onion, chopped
1 sm. green pepper, chopped (opt.)
Oil
1 lg. can whole kernel corn
3 cans tomato soup
1 sm. jar stuffed olives, sliced
1 tbsp. Worcestershire sauce
1/4 tsp. cayenne pepper

1 sm. can mushroom pieces
1 sm. package egg noodles, cooked
1 1/2 to 2 c. grated American cheese
1/2 c. slivered almonds (opt.)

**Brown** . . . . . . ground round with onion and green pepper in a small amount of oil in skillet, stirring until crumbly.
**Stir** . . . . . . . . in next 7 ingredients and 1 cup cheese.
**Spoon** . . . . . . into casserole.
**Sprinkle** . . . . remaining cheese over top.
**Top** . . . . . . . . with slivered almonds.
**Bake** . . . . . . . at 350 degrees for 20 minutes or until heated through.
**Yields** . . . . . . 8 servings.

Doris Bradley
Kelso H. S., Kelso, Washington

## SPINACH CASSEROLE FANTASTIQUE

1 lb. ground beef
1 med. onion, chopped
1 or 2 cloves of garlic, minced
2 dashes of hot pepper sauce
1 tsp. oregano
1  10-oz. can mushrooms, drained
Salt and pepper to taste
2  10-oz. packages frozen spinach, cooked
1 c. sour cream
1 can cream of mushroom soup
8 oz. Monterey Jack cheese, sliced

**Brown** . . . . . . ground beef with onion and garlic in skillet, stirring until crumbly.
**Stir** . . . . . . . . in next 5 ingredients.
**Simmer** . . . . . for 5 minutes.
**Squeeze** . . . . excess moisture from spinach.
**Add** . . . . . . . to ground beef mixture with sour cream and mushroom soup, mixing well.
**Cook** . . . . . . . until heated through. Do not boil.
**Spoon** . . . . . . into greased casserole.
**Top** . . . . . . . . with cheese slices.
**Bake** . . . . . . . at 350 degrees for 15 to 20 minutes or until bubbly.
**Yields** . . . . . . 6-8 servings.

Carol K. Allen
Independence Jr. H. S., Virginia Beach, Virginia

## BEEF-POTATO PINWHEEL

*1 1/2 lb. ground beef*
*1 1/2 c. soft bread crumbs*
*1 1/2 tsp. salt*
*1 egg, beaten*
*1/4 tsp. each Italian seasoning, pepper*
*3/4 c. condensed beef broth*
*Instant minced onion*
*1/2  12-oz. package frozen hashed*
*brown potatoes, thawed*
*3/4 c. grated Monterey Jack cheese*
*1 tbsp. parsley flakes*
*1 tsp. each mustard, Worcestershire sauce*
*1  8-oz. can tomato sauce*
*1 tbsp. brown sugar*

Combine .... first 6 ingredients, 1/2 cup broth and 1 tablespoon minced onion in bowl, mixing well.
Shape ...... into 10-inch square on waxed paper.
Mix ........ 1 teaspoon minced onion and next 3 ingredients in bowl.
Spoon ...... over ground beef, leaving 1 inch uncovered on opposite sides.
Roll ....... as for jelly roll from uncovered end.
Place ....... seam side down into lightly greased baking pan.
Bake ....... at 375 degrees for 35 minutes.
Mix ........ remaining 1/4 cup broth, mustard, Worcestershire sauce, tomato sauce and brown sugar in bowl.
Pour ....... over ground beef roll.
Bake ....... for 5 to 10 minutes longer or until sauce is bubbly.

Joan Jacobsen
Boyden-Hull Community Sch., Hull, Iowa

## POTATO BOATS

*4 med. potatoes, baked*
*Butter to taste*
*Salt and pepper to taste*
*Milk*
*1 lb. ground beef*
*1 onion, chopped (opt.)*
*1 green pepper, chopped (opt.)*

Slice ....... tops from potatoes.
Remove .... soft potato from skin, reserving shells.

Mash ....... soft potato and butter with salt and pepper and enough milk to whip to desired consistency.
Brown ...... ground beef with onion and green pepper in skillet, stirring until crumbly; drain.
Add ....... to potato mixture, mixing well.
Spoon ...... into potato shells.
Bake ....... at 250 degrees for 15 minutes or until brown.
Garnish ..... with cheese, pimento and sour cream.
Yields ...... 4 servings.

Dorothy Moore
Central Jr. H. S., Sand Springs, Oklahoma

## BEEF AND ZUCCHINI CASSEROLE

*3 lb. zucchini, sliced*
*1 lb. ground beef*
*1 lg. onion, chopped*
*1 c. minute rice*
*1 tsp. each seasoned salt, garlic salt, oregano*
*1 pt. ricotta cheese*
*1 can cream of mushroom soup*
*1 c. grated Cheddar cheese*

Cook ....... zucchini in salted water in saucepan until tender-crisp; drain well.
Brown ...... ground beef with onion in skillet, stirring until crumbly.
Stir ........ in rice and seasonings, mixing well.
Layer ...... half the zucchini, all the ground beef mixture and ricotta cheese in shallow casserole.
Top ........ with remaining zucchini, soup and Cheddar cheese.
Bake ....... at 350 degrees for 35 to 40 minutes or until bubbly.
Yields ...... 12 servings.

Brenda Oxspring
Butler Middle Sch., Salt Lake City, Utah

## ROMA MEAT ROLL

*2 lb. ground beef*
*1 egg, beaten*
*3/4 c. cracker crumbs*
*1/2 c. finely chopped onion*

1 tsp. salt
1/2 tsp. oregano
1/8 tsp. pepper
Pinch of sugar
2 8-oz. cans tomato sauce
2 c. shredded mozzarella cheese

**Combine** .... first 8 ingredients with 1/3 cup tomato sauce in bowl, mixing well.
**Shape** ...... into 10 x 12-inch rectangle on waxed paper.
**Sprinkle** .... cheese evenly over rectangle.
**Roll** ....... as for jelly roll, pressing ends to seal.
**Place** ....... in baking dish, seam side down.
**Bake** ....... at 350 degrees for 1 hour.
**Pour** ....... remaining tomato sauce over roll.
**Bake** ....... for 15 minutes longer.
**Yields** ...... 6-8 servings.

Barbara Fitch
West Bend H. S., West Bend, Iowa

## INDIVIDUAL BEEF WELLINGTONS

2 c. biscuit mix
Milk
1 lb. ground beef
1/2 c. sour cream
1/2 c. oats
1 tsp. Worcestershire sauce
1/4 c. chopped onion
1 egg
1 tsp. salt
Pepper to taste
1 tsp. dry mustard
1 can Cheddar cheese soup

**Combine** .... biscuit mix and 2/3 cup milk in bowl, mixing well.
**Knead** ...... lightly on floured surface.
**Roll** ....... into 8 x 12-inch rectangle.
**Cut** ........ into 8 equal rectangles.
**Combine** .... next 8 ingredients and 1/2 teaspoon dry mustard in bowl, mixing well.
**Shape** ...... into eight 4-inch long rolls.
**Place** ....... 1 roll on each dough rectangle, rolling to enclose filling.
**Seal** ........ seam leaving ends open.
**Place** ....... seam side down in shallow baking dish.

**Bake** ....... at 375 degrees for 35 minutes.
**Mix** ........ soup, 1/2 cup milk and remaining 1/2 teaspoon dry mustard in saucepan.
**Cook** ....... until heated through, stirring frequently.
**Pour** ....... over ground beef rolls.
**Yields** ...... 8 servings.

Linda M. Frank
Dublin H. S., Dublin, Texas

## COMPANY MEAT LOAF WELLINGTON

3 lb. ground beef
1/4 c. minced onion
1/2 c. dry bread crumbs
1 c. tomato juice
4 eggs
1/2 tsp. thyme
1/4 tsp. each pepper, oregano
2 tbsp. parsley flakes
4 tsp. salt
5 c. flour
5 tsp. baking powder
1/2 c. shortening
1 1/2 c. milk

**Combine** .... first 4 ingredients with 3 eggs, next 4 spices and 2 teaspoons salt in bowl, mixing well.
**Shape** ...... into loaf in baking pan.
**Bake** ....... at 350 degrees for 1 hour; cool.
**Sift** ........ flour, baking powder and remaining 2 teaspoons salt into bowl.
**Cut** ........ in shortening until crumbly.
**Add** ....... milk, mixing well.
**Knead** ...... until smooth on floured surface.
**Roll** ....... into rectangle.
**Place** ....... cooked meat loaf upside down in center of rectangle, folding dough to enclose loaf.
**Beat** ....... remaining egg with 1 teaspoon water in small bowl.
**Seal** ........ seams with egg mixture.
**Place** ....... seam side down on baking sheet; slash top.
**Brush** ...... with remaining egg mixture.
**Bake** ....... at 375 degrees for 20 minutes.
**Yields** ...... 12-14 servings.

Helen P. Hart
East Montgomery H. S., Biscoe, North Carolina

## PARTY DEEP-DISH PIZZA

*1 pkg. dry yeast*
*1/4 c. sugar*
*1 tsp. salt*
*3 1/4 to 3 1/2 c. flour*
*1 egg*
*2 tbsp. shortening*
*2 lb. ground beef*
*1/2 lb. Italian sausage*
*1  8-oz. can tomato sauce*
*1  4-oz. can mushrooms, drained*
*2 c. grated mozzarella cheese*
*1 c. grated American cheese*

**Dissolve** .... yeast in 1 cup warm water in bowl.
**Stir** ........ in sugar, salt and half the flour.
**Beat** ....... for 2 minutes.
**Add** ....... egg, shortening and remaining flour, mixing well.
**Spread** ..... on well-greased baking pan to desired thickness.
**Bake** ....... at 375 degrees for 10 minutes.
**Brown** ...... ground beef and sausage in skillet, stirring until crumbly; drain.
**Spoon** ...... tomato sauce over partially baked crust.
**Layer** ...... ground beef mixture, mushrooms, mozzarella and American cheeses over sauce.
**Bake** ....... at 375 degrees for 10 to 12 minutes or until cheese is melted.
**Yields** ...... 8-10 servings.

Linda J. Stolp
Atkinson H. S., Atkinson, Illinois

## BISCUIT-TOPPED STROGANOFF

*1 lb. ground beef*
*1/2 c. chopped onion*
*1/2 tsp. salt*
*2 cloves of garlic, crushed*
*1  4-oz. can mushrooms*
*1 can cream of chicken soup*
*2 c. sour cream*
*2 c. biscuit mix*
*1 egg*
*1 tbsp. chopped parsley*

**Brown** ...... ground beef with onion in skillet, stirring until crumbly.
**Stir** ........ in next 4 ingredients.

**Cook** ....... until bubbly.
**Mix** ........ in 1 1/2 cups sour cream.
**Pour** ....... into 2-quart baking dish.
**Mix** ........ biscuit mix with 1/2 cup water in bowl.
**Knead** ...... gently on floured surface.
**Roll** ....... 1/2 inch thick; cut with biscuit cutter.
**Arrange** ..... biscuits over ground beef mixture.
**Mix** ........ remaining 1/2 cup sour cream with egg and parsley.
**Spoon** ...... over biscuits.
**Bake** ....... at 425 degrees for 20 minutes or until golden brown.
**Yields** ...... 6 servings.

Marilyn Gornto
Perry Jr. H. S., Perry, Georgia

## STACK-A-ROLL STROGANOFF

*1 to 1 1/4 lb. ground beef*
*1  3 1/2-oz. can French-fried onions*
*1 can cream of mushroom soup*
*1 c. sour cream*
*1  10-oz. can refrigerator biscuits*
*1 egg*
*1 tsp. celery seed*
*1/2 tsp. salt*

**Brown** ...... ground beef in skillet, stirring until crumbly; drain.
**Mix** ........ ground beef and onions in 2 1/2-quart shallow casserole, reserving 1/2 cup onions.
**Combine** .... soup and 1/2 cup sour cream in saucepan, mixing well.
**Bring** ....... to a boil.
**Pour** ....... over ground beef mixture.
**Cut** ........ each biscuit in half.
**Arrange** ..... biscuits cut side down around edge of casserole.
**Sprinkle** .... reserved onions in center.
**Combine** .... remaining 1/2 cup sour cream and remaining 3 ingredients in bowl, mixing well.
**Pour** ....... over biscuits.
**Bake** ....... at 375 degrees for 25 to 30 minutes or until biscuits are golden brown.
**Yields** ...... 4-5 servings.

Laura Lewis Henderson
Versailles H. S., Versailles, Missouri

# Crock·Pot & Microwave

## BARBECUED BEANS

1 1/2 lb. ground beef
1 lb. bacon, chopped
1 c. chopped onion
2 16-oz. cans pork and beans
1 16-oz. can butter beans
1 c. catsup
1/4 c. packed brown sugar
1 tbsp. liquid smoke
3 tbsp. white vinegar
1 tsp. salt
Dash of pepper

**Brown** . . . . . . ground beef in skillet, stirring until crumbly; drain.
**Saute** . . . . . . bacon with onion in skillet until brown; drain.
**Combine** . . . . with ground beef and remaining ingredients in Crock•Pot, mixing well.
**Cook** . . . . . . . on Low for 4 to 6 hours.
**Yields** . . . . . . 8-10 servings.

Anne F. Farris
Soldan H. S., St. Louis, Missouri

## BEEFY TACO DIP

1 lb. ground beef
1 c. chopped onion
1 lb. process cheese
1/2 to 1 4-oz. can green chilies, chopped
1 tomato, chopped
1/3 c. chopped ripe olives
1/4 c. chopped green pepper

**Brown** . . . . . . ground beef with onion in skillet, stirring until crumbly; drain.
**Add** . . . . . . . cheese.
**Cook** . . . . . . . until cheese is melted, stirring occasionally.
**Stir** . . . . . . . . in remaining ingredients.
**Transfer** . . . . to Crock•Pot.
**Cook** . . . . . . . on Low until heated through.
**Serve** . . . . . . warm with corn chips.

Suzanne Tenley
Anamosa H. S., Anamosa, Iowa

## CROCK•POT SOMBRERO DIP

1 lb. ground beef
1/2 onion, chopped
16 oz. mild taco sauce
1/4 c. chopped jalapeno peppers
1/2 c. green olives, chopped
2 tsp. chili powder
2 c. shredded Cheddar cheese
1 can refried beans

**Brown** . . . . . . ground beef with onion in skillet, stirring until crumbly.
**Combine** . . . . with remaining ingredients in Crock•Pot, mixing well.
**Cook** . . . . . . . on High until bubbly.
**Serve** . . . . . . with corn chips.

Rita Poncelet
Irene H. S., Irene, South Dakota

## CROCK•POT CHOW MEIN

1 1/2 lb. ground beef
1 onion, sliced, separated into rings
1 can each cream of mushroom, chicken soup
2/3 c. rice
2 tbsp. soy sauce
1/2 c. diagonally sliced celery

**Brown** . . . . . . ground beef in skillet, stirring until crumbly; drain.
**Combine** . . . . with remaining ingredients and 1 soup can water in Crock•Pot, mixing well.
**Cook** . . . . . . . on Low for 5 to 6 hours.
**Serve** . . . . . . over chow mein noodles.
**Yields** . . . . . . 6 servings.

Nancy Roop
Caldwell H. S., Caldwell, Kansas

## GAIL'S CROCK•POT CHILI

1 to 1 1/2 lb. ground beef
1 can kidney beans
1 can tomatoes, chopped
1 env. dry onion soup mix
2 to 3 tbsp. chili powder
3 tbsp. sugar
Salt and pepper to taste
Hot sauce to taste

**Brown** . . . . . . ground beef in skillet, stirring until crumbly; drain.
**Combine** . . . . with remaining ingredients in Crock•Pot, mixing well.

**Cook** . . . . . . . on Low for 8 to 10 hours or on High for 5 to 6 hours.
**Yields** . . . . . . 6 servings.

Gail Helms
Enterprise H. S., Enterprise, Alabama

## CROCK•POT HOMEMADE CHILI

*1 1/2 lb. ground beef*
*1/2 c. chopped onion*
*1 clove of garlic, crushed*
*1   16-oz. can tomatoes*
*1   15 1/2-oz. can kidney beans, drained*
*1   6-oz. can tomato paste*
*1 tbsp. chili powder*
*2 tsp. sugar*
*1 tsp. salt*
*1/4 tsp. pepper*
*Cheddar cheese, shredded*

**Brown** . . . . . . ground beef with onion and gar-lic in skillet, stirring until crumbly; drain.
**Combine** . . . . ground beef mixture with next 7 ingredients in Crock • Pot.
**Cook** . . . . . . . on Low for 6 to 8 hours.
**Top** . . . . . . . . with cheese.
**Yields** . . . . . . 8 servings.

Photograph for this recipe above.

## CROCK•POT HAMBURGER-VEGETABLE STEW

*1 1/2 lb. hamburger*
*2 lg. potatoes, sliced*
*2 lg. carrots, sliced*
*1   16-oz. can peas, drained*
*3 med. onions, sliced*
*2 stalks celery, sliced*
*Salt and pepper to taste*
*1 can tomato soup*

**Brown** . . . . . . ground beef in skillet, stirring until crumbly.
**Layer** . . . . . . vegetables in Crock•Pot in order listed, seasoning each layer with salt and pepper.
**Spoon** . . . . . . ground beef over celery.
**Pour** . . . . . . . soup with 1 soup can water in bowl, mixing well.
**Pour** . . . . . . . over ground beef.
**Cook** . . . . . . . covered, on Low for 6 to 8 hours or on High for 2 to 4 hours, stirring occasionally.
**Yields** . . . . . . 6-8 servings.

Anne E. Shadwick
Seneca H. S., Seneca, Missouri

## STROGANOFF FOR TWO

*1 lb. ground beef*
*1 med. onion, chopped*
*1 clove of garlic, minced*
*1   4-oz. can mushrooms*
*1 1/2 tsp. salt*
*1/4 tsp. pepper*
*1 c. beef bouillon*
*3 tbsp. tomato paste*
*3/4 c. sour cream*
*2 tbsp. flour*

**Brown** . . . . . . ground beef in skillet, stirring until crumbly.
**Stir** . . . . . . . . in onion, garlic and mushrooms.
**Add** . . . . . . . next 4 ingredients, mixing well.
**Pour** . . . . . . . into Crock•Pot.
**Cook** . . . . . . . on Low for 5 to 7 hours.
**Mix** . . . . . . . . sour cream and flour in small bowl.
**Stir** . . . . . . . . into ground beef mixture.
**Cook** . . . . . . . for 1 hour longer.
**Yields** . . . . . . 2 servings.

Mary Beth Talerico
Maplewood Area JVS, Ravenna, Ohio

## CHEESEBURGER QUICHE

1/2 lb. ground beef, crumbled
1/3 c. onion, chopped
1/2 c. milk
1/2 c. mayonnaise
1/2 tsp. salt
1/8 tsp. each pepper, oregano
3 eggs, beaten
1 1/2 c. grated Cheddar cheese
1 baked 9-in. pie shell

Combine .... ground beef and onion in glass baking dish, mixing well.
Microwave .. on High for 3 minutes, stirring once; drain.
Beat ....... next 5 ingredients together in bowl.
Stir ........ in eggs.
Add ....... ground beef mixture and 1 cup cheese, mixing well.
Pour ....... into pie shell.
Microwave .. on High for 6 minutes, turning once.
Microwave .. on Medium for 7 minutes, turning twice.
Sprinkle .... remaining 1/2 cup cheese on top.
Microwave .. on High for 3 minutes.
Let ........ stand for 10 minutes.
Yields ...... 6 servings.

Mary W. Hull
Pickens Sr. H. S., Pickens, South Carolina

## GOOD MICROWAVE CHILI

1 1/2 lb. ground beef, crumbled
1 28-oz. can tomatoes
1 6-oz. can tomato paste
2 16-oz. cans kidney beans
1 med. green pepper, chopped
1 med. onion, chopped
1 to 2 tbsp. chili powder
Salt to taste

Combine .... all ingredients in 3-quart glass casserole, mixing well.
Microwave .. covered, on High to 190 degrees on temperature probe.
Let ........ stand for 10 minutes before serving.
Yields ...... 6-8 servings.

Phyllis Pope
Medford Jr. H. S., Medford, Wisconsin

## SPICY MICROWAVE BEEF CHILI

2 lb. ground beef, crumbled
1 lg. onion, chopped
1 lg. green pepper, chopped
1 29-oz. can tomatoes, chopped
2 to 3 tbsp. chili powder
1 tsp. salt
Dash each of cayenne pepper, paprika
1 15-oz. can kidney beans, drained
1 6-oz. can tomato sauce

Brown ...... ground beef in glass baking dish in microwave for 7 minutes, stirring twice; drain.
Microwave .. onion and green pepper in 2 tablespoons water in glass baking dish for 2 minutes.
Combine .... with ground beef and remaining ingredients in large ovenproof serving bowl, mixing well.
Microwave .. covered, for 12 minutes, stirring once.
Let ........ stand, covered, for 5 minutes before serving.
Yields ...... 8 servings.

Jan Tuchscherer
Durango Sr. H. S., Durango, Colorado

## NANCY'S SWEET AND SOUR MEATBALLS

1 lb. hamburger
1 sm. onion, chopped
2 slices bread, cubed
1 egg
1/4 c. milk
1 tsp. salt
1/8 tsp. pepper
1 tsp. Worcestershire sauce
2 tbsp. cornstarch
1 15 1/4-oz. can pineapple chunks
1/2 c. chopped green pepper
1/2 c. packed brown sugar
1/4 c. vinegar
1 tbsp. soy sauce

Combine .... first 8 ingredients in bowl, mixing well.
Shape ...... into 2-inch balls.
Place ....... in glass baking dish.
Microwave .. loosely covered, for 7 to 8 minutes or until cooked through, stirring once; drain.

Combine .... cornstarch and pineapple with juice in 4-cup glass measuring cup, mixing well.

Stir ........ in remaining ingredients.

Microwave .. for 1 1/2 minutes or to boiling point.

Boil ........ for 2 1/2 to 3 1/2 minutes or until thick.

Pour ....... over meatballs.

Microwave .. for 4 to 5 minutes or until meatballs are heated through.

Yields ...... 4-6 servings.

Nancy Weis
Glasgow H. S., Glasgow, Kentucky

## MICROWAVE PARTY MEATBALLS

*1 lb. ground beef*
*1 tbsp. each finely chopped onion, parsley*
*1/2 c. soft bread crumbs*
*1 egg, slightly beaten*
*2 tbsp. milk*
*1 tsp. salt*
*1/4 tsp. garlic salt*
*1/8 tsp. each allspice, cloves*

Combine .... all ingredients in bowl, mixing well.

Shape ...... into 1-inch balls.

Place ....... 8 meatballs at a time on paper plate.

Microwave .. loosely covered, on High for 2 1/2 to 3 minutes.

Yields ...... 40 meatballs.

Doris J. Schwausch
Pflugerville H. S., Pflugerville, Texas

## SPEEDY SPRINGTIME SUPPER

*1 tsp. salt*
*1/8 tsp. each nutmeg, cumin*
*Dash of pepper*
*1 lb. ground beef*
*1 sm. clove of garlic, minced (opt.)*
*1 pkg. frozen peas*
*1 med. red pepper, cut into thin strips*
*1 tbsp. flour*

Sprinkle .... first 4 seasonings over ground beef in bowl.

Mix ........ in garlic.

Shape ...... into 12 balls.

Place ....... peas, red pepper and 2 tablespoons water in baking dish.

Cover ...... dish with plastic wrap, vented at one end.

Microwave .. on High for 2 minutes; stir.

Place ....... meatballs around sides of baking dish.

Microwave .. covered, on High for 2 minutes longer.

Combine .... flour and 2 tablespoons water in bowl, mixing well.

Stir ........ into meatballs.

Microwave .. covered, on High for 4 minutes, stirring once.

Photograph for this recipe on page 113.

## EASY CHEESY MEAT LOAF

*1 1/2 lb. ground beef*
*1 egg*
*1 tbsp. Worcestershire sauce*
*2 tsp. salt*
*1/4 tsp. pepper*
*2/3 c. milk*
*1 tbsp. dry onion soup mix*
*1/3 c. dry bread crumbs*
*1 c. grated Cheddar cheese*
*1   2 1/2-oz. can mushroom pieces, drained*
*2 tsp. brown sugar*
*1/2 tsp. dry mustard*
*2 tbsp. catsup*

Combine .... first 8 ingredients in bowl, mixing well.

Shape ...... into flat rectangle on waxed paper.

Sprinkle .... with cheese and mushrooms.

Roll ....... as for jelly roll.

Place ....... in glass baking dish.

Microwave .. on Roast for 25 to 30 minutes or to 140 degrees internal temperature.

Combine .... brown sugar, mustard and catsup in bowl, blending well.

Pour ....... over meat loaf.

Yields ...... 6-8 servings.

Sauce may be poured over meat loaf before baking if desired.

Joni Strum
Muenster Public Sch., Muenster, Texas

## EXTRA-EASY MEAT LOAF

1 1/2 lb. ground chuck
1 pkg. dry onion soup mix
1/2 c. bread crumbs
2 tbsp. catsup
1 egg

**Combine** .... all ingredients in bowl, mixing well.
**Press** ....... into round glass casserole.
**Insert** ...... microwave probe.
**Microwave** .. to desired degree of doneness.

Linda Tole
R. L. Turner H. S., Carrollton, Texas

## MEAT LOAF AND STUFFING

1 1/2 lb. ground beef
1/2 lb. pork sausage
1 sm. onion, chopped
1 c. quick-cooking oats
3/4 c. milk
2 eggs
1 tsp. each salt, monosodium glutamate
1 1/2 c. herb-seasoned stuffing mix
1  4-oz. can mushroom pieces, drained

**Combine** .... first 8 ingredients in large bowl, mixing well.
**Press** ....... half the ground beef mixture into 5 x 9-inch glass baking dish.
**Sprinkle** .... with stuffing mix and mushrooms.
**Press** ....... remaining ground beef mixture over stuffing, mounding in center.
**Microwave** .. loosely covered, for 18 to 22 minutes or until set in the center, turning several times.
**Let** ........ stand, covered, for 10 minutes before slicing.
**Yields** ...... 4-6 servings.

Linda Panter
Heppner Sr. H. S., Heppner, Oregon

## MINI MEAT LOAF FLORENTINES

1 lb. ground beef
1 egg, beaten
2 tbsp. milk
1 tbsp. Worcestershire sauce

1/2 tsp. garlic salt
Dry bread crumbs
Salt
Pepper
1 pkg. frozen chopped spinach, thawed, drained
3/4 c. grated Swiss cheese
Kitchen Bouquet

**Combine** .... first 5 ingredients with 1/4 cup bread crumbs, 1/2 teaspoon salt and 1/4 teaspoon pepper in bowl, mixing well; set aside.
**Mix** ........ spinach, cheese, 1/3 to 1/2 cup bread crumbs and salt and pepper to taste in bowl.
**Divide** ...... ground beef into 4 equal portions, indenting centers.
**Fill** ........ with spinach mixture.
**Reshape** .... into loaves covering filled area.
**Place** ....... loaves in glass baking dish.
**Brush** ...... lightly with Kitchen Bouquet.
**Microwave** .. covered, on Roast for 15 minutes.
**Yields** ...... 4 servings.

Judy Touby
Scottsdale H. S., Scottsdale, Arizona

## MICROWAVE BURRITO CASSEROLE

1 lb. ground beef, crumbled
1 med. onion, chopped
1 clove of garlic, minced
1 tbsp. butter
1 tsp. salt
1/4 tsp. pepper
1 tbsp. chili powder
1  8-oz. can tomato sauce
6 lg. tortillas, buttered
2 c. shredded Cheddar cheese

**Microwave** .. ground beef, onion and garlic in butter in glass baking dish on High for 6 minutes or until cooked through; drain.
**Add** ....... next 4 ingredients, mixing well.
**Alternate** ... layers of tortillas, ground beef mixture and 1 1/2 cups cheese in 2-quart glass casserole.
**Top** ........ with remaining 1/2 cup cheese.
**Pour** ....... 1/2 cup water around inside edge of casserole.

**Microwave** .. covered, on High for 8 to 10 minutes or until heated through.
**Yields** ...... 4-6 servings.

Betty Carman
Northwest H. S., Justin, Texas

## CHARLES CARLOS' EL PASO

1 lb. lean ground beef, crumbled
Seasoned salt to taste
1 can tomato soup
4 flour tortillas
Oil for deep frying
3 to 4 c. chili
1 c. chopped lettuce
1 c. chopped tomatoes
1 c. grated Colby cheese
Chopped green onions (opt.)
Chopped ripe olives (opt.)

**Microwave** .. ground beef in glass baking dish until cooked through; drain.
**Add** ....... seasoned salt and soup, mixing well.
**Deep-fry** .... tortillas in oil in skillet until crisp; drain.
**Layer** ...... ground beef mixture and chili on tortillas on ovenproof plates.
**Microwave** .. on High for 30 seconds.
**Top** ........ with remaining ingredients.
**Yields** ...... 4 servings.

Nancy J. Evans-Freed
Reynoldsburg Jr. H. S., Reynoldsburg, Ohio

## MEXICAN HOMINY SKILLET

1  16-oz. can yellow hominy
1 lb. ground beef, crumbled
1/4 c. chopped green pepper
2 to 3 tbsp. chili seasoning mix
2 tbsp. dry onion soup mix
1 c. grated cheese

**Drain** ...... hominy, reserving liquid.
**Add** ....... enough water to reserved liquid to measure 1/2 cup.
**Microwave** .. ground beef and green pepper in glass casserole on Medium for 6 to 8 minutes or until ground beef is cooked through; drain.

**Mix** ........ in hominy, reserved liquid and next 2 ingredients.
**Microwave** .. for 4 minutes longer.
**Top** ........ with cheese.
**Microwave** .. for 1 minute longer or until cheese melts.
**Yields** ...... 6 servings.

Anita Stubblefield
Rivercrest H. S., Bogata, Texas

## MICROWAVE MEXICAN CASSEROLE

1 lb. ground beef, crumbled
1 can Ro-Tel
1 can cream of chicken soup
1 bag tortilla chips, crumbled
4 oz. shredded Cheddar cheese

**Brown** ...... ground beef in glass baking dish in microwave on High for 5 minutes, stirring until crumbly; drain.
**Add** ....... Ro-Tel and soup, mixing well.
**Layer** ...... half the chips, half the ground beef mixture and half the cheese in glass casserole.
**Repeat** ..... layers with remaining ingredients.
**Microwave** .. on High for 10 to 12 minutes.
**Yields** ...... 6 servings.

Dianna Roller
Mountain Home Sr. H. S., Mountain Home, Arkansas

## TACO CASSEROLE

1 lb. hamburger
1 onion, chopped
8 oz. cheese, shredded
1 can mushroom soup
1 can enchilada sauce
1 pkg. corn chips, crushed

**Brown** ...... hamburger with onion in skillet, stirring until crumbly; drain.
**Add** ....... cheese, soup and sauce, mixing well.
**Place** ....... corn chips in glass baking dish.
**Pour** ....... hamburger mixture over chips.
**Microwave** .. on High until cheese is melted.
**Yields** ...... 5-6 servings.

Mary Ann McGovern
Truman H. S., Independence, Missouri

## MICROWAVE TACO BEEF SOUP

3/4 lb. ground beef
1/2 c. chopped onion
1  16-oz. can stewed tomatoes, chopped
1  16-oz. can kidney beans
1  8-oz. can tomato sauce
2 tbsp. taco seasoning mix
1 sm. avocado, peeled, chopped
Shredded Cheddar cheese
Corn chips
Sour cream

Brown ...... ground beef with onion in large glass casserole in microwave on High for 3 to 4 minutes; drain.
Add ....... 1 1/4 cups water and next 4 ingredients, mixing well.
Microwave .. on High for 5 minutes.
Microwave .. covered, on Medium for 10 minutes.
Stir ........ in avocado.
Top ........ each serving with cheese, corn chips and sour cream.
Yields ...... 6 servings.

Marilyn Jean Mancewicz
Ottawa Hills H. S., Grand Rapids, Michigan

## MICROWAVE TAMALE PIE

1 c. cornmeal
2 tbsp. chili powder
1 tsp. salt
1 lb. ground beef, crumbled
1/2 c. chopped onion
1/3 c. chopped green pepper
1 lg. clove of garlic, minced
1 can chili-beef soup
1  16-oz. can tomatoes, chopped
1/3 c. sliced ripe olives
1 c. shredded sharp Cheddar cheese

Combine .... cornmeal, 2 teaspoons chili powder, 1/2 teaspoon salt and 3 cups water in 8 x 12-inch glass baking dish, mixing well.
Microwave .. for 7 minutes or until thick, stirring 3 times.
Mix ........ remaining 4 teaspoons chili powder and 1/2 teaspoon salt with next 4 ingredients in 1 1/2-quart glass casserole.

Microwave .. for 6 minutes, stirring 3 times; drain.
Add ....... soup, tomatoes and olives, mixing well.
Spoon ...... over cornmeal mixture.
Microwave .. for 12 minutes or until heated through, turning every 5 minutes.
Top ........ with cheese.
Microwave .. for 1 minute or until cheese is melted.
Yields ...... 6 servings.

Dorothy Tipping
Yantis H. S., Yantis, Texas

## ONE-STEP LASAGNA

1 lb. ground beef, crumbled
32 oz. spaghetti sauce
1 tsp. salt
8 oz. lasagna noodles
2 c. cottage cheese
3 c. shredded mozzarella cheese
1/2 c. Parmesan cheese

Microwave .. ground beef on High in 2-quart glass casserole for 5 to 6 minutes; drain.
Stir ........ in spaghetti sauce, 1/2 cup water and salt.
Microwave .. covered, on High for 5 to 6 minutes or until heated through.
Layer ...... 1/3 of the sauce, half the noodles, 1 cup cottage cheese and half the mozzarella cheese in 9 x 13-inch casserole.
Repeat ..... layers, ending with sauce.
Sprinkle .... with Parmesan cheese.
Microwave .. tightly covered, on High for 30 to 35 minutes or until bubbly.
Let ........ stand for 5 minutes before serving.
Yields ...... 6-8 servings.

Brenda Brandt
Logan Middle Sch., LaCrosse, Wisconsin

## SUPER SUPPER CASSEROLE

1 lb. hamburger, crumbled
1 sm. onion, chopped
1  8-oz. can each peas, corn, drained

1 can each chicken noodle, cream of
   chicken soup
Salt and pepper to taste
1/2 c. cashews (opt.)
1 6-oz. package noodles, cooked
6 slices cheese
1 c. crushed potato chips

**Microwave** .. hamburger and onion in
   2 1/2-quart covered glass casse-
   role; drain.
**Stir** ........ in vegetables, soups, salt, pepper,
   cashews and noodles.
**Arrange** ..... cheese slices over mixture.
**Sprinkle** .... potato chips over top.
**Microwave** .. on High for 20 minutes, turning
   twice.
**Yields** ...... 12 servings.

Carolyn Van Arnberg
Maurice-Orange City Community Sch.
Orange City, Iowa

## PIZZA ON A BISCUIT CRUST

1 lb. ground beef
1/4 c. chopped onion
3 c. biscuit mix
1 15-oz. jar spaghetti sauce
Sliced olives (opt.)
Sliced mushrooms (opt.)
Sliced green pepper (opt.)
1 c. each shredded Cheddar cheese,
   mozzarella cheese

**Brown** ...... ground beef with onion in skillet, stirring until crumbly; drain.
**Mix** ........ biscuit mix and 1 1/2 cups water
   in bowl.
**Spread** ..... in 10 x 15-inch glass baking pan.
**Top** ........ with spaghetti sauce, ground
   beef and remaining ingredients
   ending with cheeses.
**Microwave** .. on High for 15 to 17 minutes or
   to desired doneness.
**Yields** ...... 12 servings.

Mrs. Jack Criswell
Alliance Christian Sch., Birmingham, Alabama

## BEEF CRUST PIZZA PIE

1 lb. ground beef
1 tsp. salt

1/4 tsp. pepper
1 tsp. each Worcestershire sauce,
   Dijon mustard
1 16-oz. can tomatoes, drained
2 tbsp. minced onion
1 c. grated cheese
2 tbsp. minced parsley
1/2 tsp. basil
1/4 tsp. oregano

**Combine** .... first 5 ingredients in bowl, mix-
   ing well.
**Press** ....... over bottom and side of 9-inch
   glass pie plate.
**Layer** ...... tomatoes, onion and cheese over
   ground beef mixture.
**Sprinkle** .... with remaining 3 seasonings.
**Microwave** .. on High for 15 minutes, draining
   halfway through cooking cycle.
**Yields** ...... 4 servings.

Lois Cynewski
Portsmouth Jr. H. S., Portsmouth, New Hampshire

## PIZZA FONDUE

1 lb. ground beef, crumbled
2/3 c. chopped onion
3 8-oz. cans pizza sauce with cheese
1 tbsp. cornstarch
3/4 tsp. oregano
1/4 tsp. garlic powder
1 c. shredded mozzarella cheese
2 5-oz. jars process cheese spread

**Combine** .... ground beef with onion in 2-
   quart glass casserole.
**Microwave** .. on High for 5 to 6 minutes or
   until cooked through; drain.
**Mix** ........ next 4 ingredients in bowl.
**Add** ....... to ground beef mixture, mixing
   well.
**Microwave** .. on Roast for 13 to 15 minutes
   or until heated through.
**Add** ....... cheeses 1/3 at a time, mixing
   well after each addition.
**Microwave** .. on Roast for 6 to 7 minutes or
   until cheeses are melted.
**Serve** ....... with chips or French bread
   cubes.

Karen Olson
North Platte Sr. H. S., North Platte, Nebraska

## PATRICIA'S BEEFBURGER STROGANOFF

*1 lb. ground beef, crumbled*
*1/2 c. finely chopped onion*
*1 clove of garlic, minced*
*1  8-oz. can mushrooms*
*1 can cream of mushroom soup*
*3 tbsp. flour*
*1 tsp. salt*
*1/4 tsp. pepper*
*1  8-oz. carton sour cream*
*1/2 tsp. Kitchen Bouquet*

**Combine** .... first 8 ingredients in 2-quart glass casserole, mixing well.
**Microwave** .. covered, on High for 13 to 15 minutes, or until cooked through.
**Stir** ........ in sour cream and Kitchen Bouquet, mixing well.
**Serve** ....... over rice, noodles or chow mein noodles.
**Yields** ...... 6 servings.

Patricia A. Marcotte
Newburyport H. S., Newburyport, Massachusetts

## FAVORITE STROGANOFF

*1 lb. ground beef, crumbled*
*1/2 c. finely chopped onion*
*1  4-oz. can mushrooms, drained*
*2 tbsp. flour*
*1 tsp. salt*
*1/2 tsp. paprika*
*1 can cream of chicken soup*
*1 c. sour cream*

**Place** ....... ground beef and onion in 2-- quart glass casserole, mixing well.
**Microwave** .. on High for 6 minutes, stirring once.
**Add** ....... next 5 ingredients, mixing well.
**Microwave** .. on Medium for 7 minutes.
**Stir** ........ in sour cream.
**Microwave** .. on Medium for 4 minutes.
**Serve** ....... over noodles.
**Yields** ...... 4 servings.

Martha Ann Andrews Horn
Rosenwald Jr. H. S., Panama City, Florida

## HAMBURGER-BROCCOLI CREAM

*1 pkg. frozen broccoli*
*4 eggs*
*1 lb. hamburger*
*1 tbsp. margarine, melted*
*3 tbsp. flour*
*1/2 tsp. each dry mustard, salt, pepper, garlic*
*2 c. milk*
*6 oz. process cheese spread*

**Microwave** .. broccoli in package on High for 6 minutes; drain and set aside.
**Beat** ....... eggs in glass bowl.
**Microwave** .. on High for 4 minutes, stirring twice.
**Brown** ...... hamburger in browning dish for 2 minutes, stirring once.
**Microwave** .. on High for 5 minutes longer; drain.
**Blend** ...... margarine and flour in glass baking dish.
**Microwave** .. on High for 2 minutes.
**Stir** ........ in seasonings and milk.
**Microwave** .. on High for 5 minutes or until thick, stirring twice.
**Add** ....... hamburger, eggs, broccoli and cheese, mixing well.
**Microwave** .. on Medium-High for 5 minutes or until cheese is melted, stirring twice.
**Serve** ....... over English muffins.
**Yields** ...... 8 servings.

Linda J. Dobbins
Indian River H. S., Chesapeake, Virginia

## CURRIED BEEF AND PINEAPPLE

*1 lb. ground beef, crumbled*
*1 med. onion, cut into halves lengthwise and sliced*
*2 tsp. cornstarch*
*1 1/2 tsp. salt*
*1 to 2 tsp. curry*
*1/8 tsp. ginger*
*1  8-oz. can juice-pack pineapple chunks*
*2 c. hot cooked rice*

**Place** ....... ground beef and onion in glass baking dish.
**Cover** ...... with plastic wrap, vented at one end.

**Microwave** .. on High for 4 minutes, stirring after 2 minutes; drain.

**Combine** .... next 4 ingredients in small bowl, mixing well.

**Sprinkle** .... over meat; stir.

**Add** ....... pineapple.

**Microwave** .. covered, on High for 5 minutes.

**Stir** ........ in rice.

**Microwave** .. for 2 minutes longer, stirring after 1 minute.

Photograph for this recipe above.

## STUFFED WHOLE CABBAGE

1  2-lb. head cabbage
1 lb. lean ground beef
1  8-oz. can tomato sauce
1/3 c. minute rice
1 egg
1 env. dry onion soup mix
1/4 tsp. thyme

**Remove** .... core from cabbage; hollow out center.

**Combine** .... remaining ingredients in bowl, mixing well.

**Spoon** ...... into cabbage shell.

**Place** ....... in 1 1/2-quart glass baking dish.

**Microwave** .. tightly covered, on High for 17 minutes, turning after 9 minutes.

**Let** ........ stand for 10 minutes before serving.

**Yields** ...... 6 servings.

Audrey P. Fisher
I. C. Norcom H. S., Portsmouth, Virginia

## SEVENTEEN-MINUTE SUPPER

1 lb. ground beef
1 sm. onion, chopped
1 pkg. frozen chopped broccoli
1 can cream of mushroom soup
1 sm. jar cheese

**Microwave** .. ground beef and onion in glass baking dish for 4 minutes or until cooked through; drain.

**Thaw** ...... broccoli in package in microwave on Defrost for 3 1/2 minutes.

**Mix** ........ ground beef, broccoli and remaining ingredients with 1 soup can water in glass casserole.

**Microwave** .. on Medium for 8 to 10 minutes, stirring once.

Jan McAninch
Wes-Del H. S., Gaston, Indiana

## SPEEDY SHEPHERD'S PIE

1 lb. lean ground beef
2 slices white bread, torn into
    small pieces
2/3 c. milk
1 egg, slightly beaten
1/4 c. finely chopped onion
1 tbsp. Worcestershire sauce
1 tsp. salt
3 c. hot mashed potatoes
1 c. grated sharp Cheddar cheese

**Combine** .... first 7 ingredients in medium bowl, mixing well.

**Spread** ..... in 9-inch glass pie plate.

**Microwave** .. on Medium-High for 7 minutes.

**Spread** ..... mashed potatoes over ground beef mixture.

**Sprinkle** .... with cheese.

**Microwave** .. on Medium-High for 5 minutes or until cheese is melted.

**Let** ........ stand for 3 minutes.

Mary Jane Laing
Canutillo Jr. H. S., Canutillo, Texas

## LAYERED BEEF CASSEROLE

*1 lb. ground beef, crumbled*
*1 tsp. salt*
*1/4 tsp. pepper*
*2 med. potatoes, thinly sliced*
*1/4 c. chopped green pepper*
*1 med. onion, thinly sliced*
*1 can soup*

**Brown** . . . . . . ground beef in covered 2-quart glass casserole in microwave on High for 5 minutes; drain.
**Stir** . . . . . . . . in salt and pepper.
**Layer** . . . . . . half the potato slices, green pepper and onion over ground beef mixture.
**Top** . . . . . . . . with remaining potato slices.
**Pour** . . . . . . . soup over top.
**Microwave** . . covered, on High for 15 to 20 minutes or until potatoes are tender.
**Let** . . . . . . . . stand covered, for 5 minutes before serving.
**Yields** . . . . . . 4-6 servings.

Susan West
Martins Ferry H. S., Martins Ferry, Ohio

## BEEF AND TATER TOTS CASSEROLE

*1 lb. ground beef, crumbled*
*2 tsp. instant minced onion*
*1 lb. frozen Tater Tots*
*1 can each cream of chicken, cream of celery soup*
*Paprika*

**Place** . . . . . . . ground beef in 2-quart glass casserole.
**Microwave** . . covered with paper towel, on High for 5 minutes; drain and separate into small pieces.
**Top** . . . . . . . . with minced onion and Tater Tots.
**Pour** . . . . . . . soups over all.
**Microwave** . . on High for 15 minutes.
**Sprinkle** . . . . paprika on top.
**Yields** . . . . . . 4-6 servings.

Judy Queen
Braman H. S., Braman, Oklahoma

## BEEF-POTATO AND CARROT CASSEROLE

*1 1/2 to 2 lb. ground chuck*
*1 to 2 tbsp. Worcestershire sauce*
*1 onion, sliced*
*2 or 3 sm. potatoes, peeled, quartered*
*3 or 4 carrots, sliced 1/2 in. thick*
*Salt and pepper to taste*

**Shape** . . . . . . ground chuck into ring around custard cup in center of 3-quart glass casserole.
**Sprinkle** . . . . Worcestershire sauce over ground chuck, puncturing with fork.
**Arrange** . . . . . onion and potatoes in center of ring and carrots around outer edge.
**Season** . . . . . with salt and pepper.
**Microwave** . . covered, on Medium-High for 25 minutes.
**Let** . . . . . . . . stand for 5 minutes.
**Yields** . . . . . . 4-5 servings.

Winn Williams
Lake Hamilton H. S., Pearcy, Arkansas

## BETTY'S SPINACH FLANDANGO

*1/2 lb. hamburger*
*1/2 onion, chopped*
*1 clove of garlic, minced*
*1 pkg. frozen chopped spinach, cooked, drained*
*Dash of hot sauce*
*1/2 tsp. each salt, oregano*
*Dash of pepper*
*1 can mushrooms*
*1/2 c. sour cream*
*1 c. grated mozzarella cheese*

**Brown** . . . . . . hamburger with onion and garlic in skillet, stirring until crumbly; drain.
**Combine** . . . . spinach, hamburger mixture and next 6 ingredients in glass casserole, mixing well.
**Top** . . . . . . . . with cheese.
**Microwave** . . on High for 6 minutes.

Grace Hemingway
North Jr. H. S., Joplin, Missouri

# Casseroles

## CATCH-ALL CASSEROLE

1 lb. ground beef
1 onion, chopped
6 tbsp. margarine
1 tsp. salt
1/2 tsp. celery salt
1 c. canned corn
2 c. canned tomatoes
1 c. prepared stuffing

Brown . . . . . . ground beef with onion in 2
tablespoons margarine in skillet,
stirring until crumbly.
Combine . . . . with salt, celery salt, corn and
tomatoes in 2-quart casserole.
Mix . . . . . . . . stuffing with remaining 1/4 cup
melted margarine and 1/4 cup
water in bowl, mixing well.
Spread . . . . . over top of casserole.
Bake . . . . . . . at 350 degrees for 30 minutes.
Yields . . . . . . 6-8 servings.

Murriel Riedesel
Wauconda H. S., Wauconda, Illinois

## CHILI CASSEROLE

1 lb. ground beef
1 lg. can chili
1 lg. bag tortilla chips, crushed
1 6-oz. package grated cheese

Brown . . . . . . ground beef in skillet, stirring
until crumbly; drain.
Add . . . . . . . chili.
Cook . . . . . . . until heated through, stirring
occasionally.
Layer . . . . . . tortilla chips and chili mixture in
casserole.
Top . . . . . . . . with cheese.
Bake . . . . . . . at 400 degrees until cheese is
melted.
Yields . . . . . . 4-6 servings.

Betty C. Nutt
Lewis County H. S., Hohenwald, Tennessee

## TACO CASSEROLE

2 lb. hamburger
2 sm. onions, chopped
1 can cream of chicken soup
1 can cream of mushroom soup

1 sm. can taco sauce
1 can mild enchilada sauce
1 lg. package tortilla chips
Grated cheese

Brown . . . . . hamburger with onions in skillet,
stirring until crumbly; drain.
Stir . . . . . . . . in remaining ingredients except
chips and cheese, mixing well.
Spoon . . . . . . over tortilla chips in baking dish.
Bake . . . . . . . at 350 degrees for 30 minutes.
Sprinkle . . . . cheese over top.
Bake . . . . . . . for 5 minutes longer.
Yields . . . . . . 4-6 servings.

Peggy Haynes
El Reno H. S., El Reno, Oklahoma

## CHOW MEIN CASSEROLE

1 lb. ground beef
1/4 tsp. pepper
1/2 tsp. oregano
1 tbsp. Worcestershire sauce
1 20-oz. can chow mein noodles
1 can each cream of celery, cream of
mushroom soup

Brown . . . . . . ground beef in skillet, stirring
until crumbly.
Add . . . . . . . next 3 ingredients, mixing well.
Place . . . . . . . 1/4 of the noodles in greased
1-quart baking dish.
Layer . . . . . . half the ground beef, half the
soups and half the remaining
noodles in casserole.
Repeat . . . . . layers, ending with noodles.
Bake . . . . . . . at 350 degrees for 45 minutes.
Yields . . . . . . 6 servings.

Judy Swinny
Crittendon County H. S., Marion, Kentucky

## LAYERED CHEESEBURGER CASSEROLE

1 lb. ground beef
1/2 c. chopped celery
1/4 c. chopped onion
1 tsp. seasoned salt
1/4 tsp. pepper
1 pkg. Hamburger Helper for
Cheeseburger-Macaroni
2 1/2 c. milk

**Brown** . . . . . . ground beef in skillet, stirring
until crumbly.

**Mix** . . . . . . . . with next 6 ingredients in 2-
quart casserole, reserving 1 cup
corn chips and 1/2 cup cheese.

**Bake** . . . . . . . at 375 degrees for 20 to 25 minutes or until heated through.

**Top** . . . . . . . . with sour cream and reserved
cheese.

**Place** . . . . . . . reserved corn chips around edge
of casserole.

**Bake** . . . . . . . for 3 to 4 minutes longer or
until cheese is melted.

**Yields** . . . . . . 6 servings.

Photograph for this recipe on this page.

---

4 eggs
1 tsp. dry mustard

**Brown** . . . . . . ground beef with celery and
onion in skillet, stirring until
crumbly.

**Add** . . . . . . . seasoned salt and pepper, mixing
well.

**Cook** . . . . . . . macaroni from Hamburger
Helper, using package directions.

**Layer** . . . . . . macaroni and ground beef mixture in greased baking dish.

**Beat** . . . . . . . Hamburger Helper sauce mix
with remaining 3 ingredients in
bowl.

**Pour** . . . . . . . over ground beef mixture.

**Bake** . . . . . . . at 350 degrees for 40 to 50 minutes or until knife inserted in
center comes out clean.

**Let** . . . . . . . . stand for 5 minutes before
serving.

**Garnish** . . . . . with chopped parsley.

**Yields** . . . . . . 6-8 servings.

Dolly Rose Holley
Daingerfield Lone Star H. S., Daingerfield, Texas

## MEXI-CHILI CASSEROLE

1 lb. ground beef
1 16-oz. can kidney beans, drained
1 15-oz. can mild enchilada sauce
1 8-oz. can tomato sauce
1 tbsp. instant minced onion
1 6-oz. package corn chips
2 c. shredded Cheddar cheese
1 1/2 c. sour cream

## LASAGNA WITH SPINACH

1 1/2 lb. ground beef
1/2 lb. pork sausage
1/2 tsp. salt
1/4 tsp. pepper
3/4 tsp. oregano
1 tsp. Worcestershire sauce
2 cans chopped spinach, drained
2 cans cream of mushroom soup
1 1/4 c. milk
1 lg. box lasagna noodles, cooked
8 oz. mozzarella cheese, grated
1 sm. can tomato sauce
1/4 c. Parmesan cheese

**Brown** . . . . . . ground beef and sausage in skillet, stirring until crumbly; drain.

**Stir** . . . . . . . . in salt, pepper, oregano and
Worcestershire sauce.

**Simmer** . . . . . for 5 minutes.

**Add** . . . . . . . spinach, mixing well.

**Cook** . . . . . . . soup and milk in saucepan, stirring until well blended.

**Layer** . . . . . . noodles, ground beef mixture
and mozzarella cheese alter-
nately in baking dish until all ingredients are used.

**Pour** . . . . . . . soup mixture and tomato sauce
over top.

**Sprinkle** . . . . with Parmesan cheese.

**Bake** . . . . . . . at 350 degrees for 1 hour.

**Yields** . . . . . . 10-12 servings.

Jane Markham
Spring Oaks Jr. H. S., Houston, Texas

## CAROL'S LASAGNA

1 lb. ground beef
1 tbsp. basil
1  16-oz. can tomatoes, chopped
1 clove of garlic, minced
1  12-oz. can tomato paste
2 tsp. salt
2 1/2 c. cottage cheese
2 tbsp. parsley flakes
1/2 c. Parmesan cheese
2 eggs, beaten
1  10-oz. package lasagna noodles,
   cooked, drained
1 lb. mozzarella cheese, grated

**Brown** ...... ground beef in skillet, stirring until crumbly.
**Add** ....... next 4 ingredients with 1 1/2 teaspoons salt.
**Simmer** ..... for 30 minutes, stirring occasionally.
**Combine** .... cottage cheese with next 3 ingredients and 1/2 teaspoon salt in bowl, mixing well.
**Layer** ...... noodles, cottage cheese mixture, mozzarella cheese and ground beef mixture alternately in 9 x 13-inch baking dish until all ingredients are used.
**Bake** ....... at 375 degrees for 30 minutes.
**Yields** ...... 12-16 servings.

Carol Winter
Millcreek Jr. H. S., Bountiful, Utah

## CHEESEBURGER CASSEROLE WITH BISCUITS

1 can refrigerator biscuits
1 lb. ground beef
1/4 c. each chopped onion, green pepper
1  8-oz. can tomato sauce
1/4 c. catsup
1/8 tsp. pepper
1/2 lb. sliced cheese

**Bake** ....... biscuits according to package directions for several minutes; set aside.
**Brown** ...... ground beef with onion and green pepper in skillet, stirring until crumbly; drain.
**Add** ....... tomato sauce, catsup and pepper, mixing well.

**Alternate** ... layers of ground beef mixture and cheese in casserole.
**Arrange** ..... biscuits around edge of casserole.
**Bake** ....... at 400 degrees for 20 to 25 minutes.
**Yields** ...... 4-6 servings.

Vivian C. Pike
Bunker Hill H. S., Claremont, North Carolina

## DOUBLE CHEESEBURGER CASSEROLE

1 lb. ground beef
1 lg. onion, chopped
Oil
1  8-oz. can tomato sauce
1/4 c. catsup
Salt and pepper to taste
6 slices American cheese
1 can refrigerator biscuits
Parmesan cheese

**Brown** ...... ground beef with onion in a small amount of oil in skillet, stirring until crumbly; drain.
**Stir** ........ in next 4 ingredients.
**Cook** ....... until heated through.
**Layer** ...... ground beef mixture and American cheese slices alternately in casserole until all ingredients are used.
**Arrange** ..... biscuits on top.
**Sprinkle** .... with Parmesan cheese.
**Bake** ....... at 400 degrees for 20 to 25 minutes or until biscuits are golden brown.
**Yields** ...... 6 servings.

Dianne C. Merritt
Westview H. S., Martin, Tennessee

## ALL-AMERICAN MACARONI CASSEROLE

1 1/2 lb. ground beef
2 med. onions, chopped
1 med. green pepper, chopped
1  6-oz. can tomato paste
2  8-oz. cans tomato sauce
1 1/2 tsp. salt

1 can mushroom soup
1 sm. jar jalapeno Cheez Whiz
3 c. cooked elbow macaroni
1/4 c. grated Cheddar cheese

Brown . . . . . . ground beef with onion in skillet, stirring until crumbly; drain.
Mix . . . . . . . . soup, Cheez Whiz and 1/2 soup can water in small bowl.
Pour . . . . . . . over ground beef.
Stir . . . . . . . . in macaroni.
Pour . . . . . . . into greased casserole.
Sprinkle . . . . with grated cheese.
Bake . . . . . . . at 375 degrees until cheese is melted.
Yields . . . . . . 6-8 servings.

JoAnn R. Sicking
Forestburg H. S., Forestburg, Texas

## UNCLE MIKE'S JOHNNY MARZETTI

6 med. onions, chopped
Butter
2 lb. lean ground beef
1 clove of garlic, crushed
2 8-oz. cans tomato sauce
1 sm. can chopped mushrooms
4 c. grated sharp Cheddar cheese
1 lb. shell macaroni, cooked, drained
1/4 c. Burgundy

Saute . . . . . . onions in a small amount of butter in skillet for several minutes.
Add . . . . . . . ground beef and garlic.
Saute . . . . . . until ground beef is brown and crumbly.
Add . . . . . . . 1 can tomato sauce and mushrooms, mixing well.
Cook . . . . . . . until heated through; remove from heat.
Mix . . . . . . . . in 2 2/3 cups cheese.
Combine . . . . macaroni and 1/2 stick butter in casserole, tossing to mix.
Add . . . . . . . ground beef mixture, mixing well.
Top . . . . . . . . with remaining tomato sauce and cheese.
Bake . . . . . . . at 325 degrees for 1 hour.
Pour . . . . . . . Burgundy over top.
Yields . . . . . . 10-12 servings.

Jeanne B. Reed
Horn Lake Jr. H. S., Horn Lake, Mississippi

3/4 tsp. oregano
1/4 tsp. red pepper
2 c. elbow macaroni, cooked
1 c. cream-style cottage cheese
1 c. grated Cheddar cheese

Brown . . . . . . ground beef in skillet, stirring until crumbly; drain.
Add . . . . . . . onions and green pepper, mixing well.
Cook . . . . . . . for 1 minute.
Stir . . . . . . . . in next 5 ingredients.
Simmer . . . . . covered, for 45 minutes.
Layer . . . . . . half the macaroni and ground beef mixture, all the cottage cheese and 1/4 cup Cheddar cheese in 2 1/2-quart casserole.
Top . . . . . . . . with remaining macaroni, ground beef mixture and Cheddar cheese.
Bake . . . . . . . at 375 degrees for 15 minutes.
Bake . . . . . . . loosely covered, for 15 minutes longer.

Photograph for this recipe above.

## AUNT MILDRED'S CHEESY BEEF

1 lb. ground beef
1 sm. onion, chopped

## PASTA SHELLS WITH TOMATO MEAT SAUCE

*1/2 lb. ground round*
*1/2 c. each finely chopped onion, celery*
*1 clove of garlic, minced*
*1   35-oz. can Italian plum tomatoes, chopped*
*3/4 tsp. crumbled bay leaves*
*3/4 tsp. salt*
*Pepper*
*1 1/2 c. finely chopped broccoli*
*1   15-oz. container ricotta cheese*
*1 tbsp. grated onion*
*2 egg whites*
*24 jumbo macaroni shells, cooked*

Brown . . . . . . ground round in skillet, stirring until crumbly.
Add . . . . . . . onion, celery and garlic.
Cook . . . . . . . for 5 minutes or until tender, stirring frequently; drain.
Add . . . . . . . tomatoes, bay leaves, 1/2 teaspoon salt and 1/4 teaspoon pepper.
Simmer . . . . . covered, for 30 minutes, stirring occasionally.
Cook . . . . . . . uncovered, for 10 to 20 minutes longer or until thick, stirring occasionally.

Combine . . . . broccoli, ricotta cheese, onion, remaining 1/4 teaspoon salt and 1/8 teaspoon pepper in bowl, mixing well.
Beat . . . . . . . egg whites until stiff peaks form.
Fold . . . . . . . into broccoli mixture.
Spoon . . . . . . into shells.
Spread . . . . . 3 cups tomato sauce in lightly oiled 9 x 13-inch baking dish.
Arrange . . . . . shells, open side up, in single layer in sauce.
Drizzle . . . . . with remaining tomato sauce; cover with foil.
Bake . . . . . . . at 350 degrees for 45 minutes or until bubbly.

Photograph for this recipe on this page.

## CHEESE AND PASTA IN A POT

*2 lb. ground beef*
*1 onion, chopped*
*1 tsp. garlic salt*
*1   4-oz. can mushrooms*
*1   16-oz. can stewed tomatoes*
*1   16-oz. jar spaghetti sauce*
*1   8-oz. package large shell macaroni, cooked*
*1   16-oz. carton sour cream*
*1   8-oz. package grated mozzarella cheese*

Brown . . . . . . ground beef with onion and garlic salt in skillet, stirring until crumbly.
Add . . . . . . . next 3 ingredients, mixing well.
Layer . . . . . . half the macaroni, half the ground beef mixture, half the sour cream and half the cheese in baking dish.
Repeat . . . . . layers, ending with cheese.
Bake . . . . . . . covered, at 350 degrees for 35 to 40 minutes or until bubbly.
Bake . . . . . . . uncovered, until cheese is lightly browned.
Yields . . . . . . 6-8 servings.

Wanda A. Gerard
Superior Sr. H. S., Superior, Wisconsin

## CREAMY BEEF-MACARONI CASSEROLE

*1 lb. ground beef*
*1 c. chopped onion*

1 clove of garlic, minced
1 tbsp. paprika
1 1/2 tsp. salt
Pinch of cayenne pepper
1  15-oz. can tomato sauce
2 c. elbow macaroni, cooked
1 c. sour cream

**Brown** . . . . . . ground beef with onion and gar-
lic in skillet, stirring until
crumbly.
**Add** . . . . . . . remaining ingredients, mixing
well.
**Spoon** . . . . . . into 2-quart casserole.
**Bake** . . . . . . . at 350 degrees for 30 minutes.
**Yields** . . . . . . 4-5 servings.

Marjorie Grantham
Dolan Middle Sch., Stamford, Connecticut

## SOUPY HAMBURGER CASSEROLE

1 lb. hamburger
1 can each chili-beef, tomato soup
1 c. macaroni, cooked
Cheese slices

**Brown** . . . . . . hamburger in skillet, stirring
until crumbly; drain.
**Add** . . . . . . . soups and macaroni, mixing
well.
**Spoon** . . . . . . into 2-quart casserole.
**Top** . . . . . . . . with cheese.
**Bake** . . . . . . . at 350 degrees until cheese is
melted.
**Yields** . . . . . . 6 servings.

Karen Thompson
Screven County H. S., Sylvania, Georgia

## INFLATION CASSEROLE

1 lb. ground beef
2 c. shredded cabbage
1 c. shredded carrots
1  14-oz. can tomatoes
1 can cream of celery soup
1 tsp. onion flakes
1 tsp. pepper
2 c. broken noodles

**Brown** . . . . . . ground beef in skillet, stirring
until crumbly; drain.
**Add** . . . . . . . remaining ingredients, mixing
well.

**Spoon** . . . . . into casserole.
**Bake** . . . . . . . at 350 degrees for 1 1/2 hours or
until noodles are tender.
**Yields** . . . . . . 6 servings.

Shirley J. Dickey
Justin F. Kimball H. S., Dallas, Texas

## BEEF-NOODLE CASSEROLE

1 lb. ground beef
1 can mushroom soup
1  8-oz. can tomato sauce
1  6-oz. package noodles, cooked
1/2 lb. Cheddar cheese, grated

**Brown** . . . . . . ground beef in skillet, stirring
until crumbly.
**Add** . . . . . . . soup and tomato sauce, mixing
well.
**Simmer** . . . . . until heated through.
**Layer** . . . . . . noodles and ground beef mixture alternately in greased 9 x
13-inch baking dish until all ingredients are used.
**Top** . . . . . . . . with cheese.
**Bake** . . . . . . . at 350 degrees for 15 to 20 minutes or until cheese is melted.
**Yields** . . . . . . 4-6 servings.

Brenda Deadman
Coffee County Jr. H. S., Manchester, Tennessee

## DELUXE BEEF CASSEROLE

1 lb. ground beef
2  8-oz. cans tomato sauce
2 c. each sour cream, cottage cheese
1/3 c. chopped green onion
1/4 c. chopped green pepper
1  8-oz. package noodles, cooked, drained

**Brown** . . . . . . ground beef in skillet, stirring
until crumbly.
**Stir** . . . . . . . . in tomato sauce.
**Combine** . . . . next 4 ingredients in bowl, mix-
ing well.
**Layer** . . . . . . noodles and cottage cheese mix-
ture alternately in casserole until
all ingredients are used.
**Top** . . . . . . . . with ground beef mixture.
**Bake** . . . . . . . at 350 degrees for 30 minutes.
**Yields** . . . . . . 6-8 servings.

Relda Epperson Blythe
Olive Vista Jr. H. S., Sylmar, California

## EASY GROUND BEEF CASSEROLE

1 lb. lean ground beef
1 sm. onion, chopped
1 sm. green pepper, chopped
1 tbsp. oil
1 tsp. oregano
Salt and pepper to taste
1 can tomato soup
1  16-oz. can pork and beans
1  10-oz. package noodles, cooked
1 c. grated Cheddar cheese
1 bag corn chips

**Brown** . . . . . . ground beef with onion and green pepper in oil in skillet, stirring until crumbly; drain.
**Stir** . . . . . . . . in seasonings.
**Mix** . . . . . . . tomato soup, 1/2 soup can water and pork and beans in casserole.
**Add** . . . . . . . noodles and ground beef mixture.
**Sprinkle** . . . . with cheese.
**Bake** . . . . . . . at 350 degrees until cheese is melted.
**Serve** . . . . . . . over corn chips.
**Yields** . . . . . . 8 servings.

Carolyn Sue Merritt
Bethel Sch., Shawnee, Oklahoma

## GROUND BEEF-CORN BAKE

1 1/2 lb. ground beef
1 c. chopped onion
1  12-oz. can whole kernel corn, drained
1 can cream of chicken soup
1 can cream of mushroom soup
1 c. sour cream
1/4 c. chopped pimento
3/4 tsp. salt
1/4 tsp. pepper
1/2 tsp. monosodium glutamate
3 c. medium noodles, cooked, drained
1 c. soft bread crumbs
2 tbsp. butter, melted

**Brown** . . . . . . ground beef with onion in large skillet, stirring until crumbly.
**Add** . . . . . . . next 8 ingredients, mixing well.
**Stir** . . . . . . . . in noodles.
**Spoon** . . . . . . into 2 1/2-quart casserole.
**Mix** . . . . . . . . bread crumbs and butter in small bowl.

**Sprinkle** . . . . over casserole.
**Bake** . . . . . . . at 350 degrees for 45 minutes.
**Yields** . . . . . . 8-10 servings.

Linda Roeder
R. L. Turner H. S., Carrollton, Texas

## HUSBAND'S DELIGHT

1 lb. ground beef
2 cans tomato sauce
1 1/2 tsp. each salt, pepper, garlic salt
1 med. onion, finely chopped
1 sm. package cream cheese, softened
1  8-oz. carton sour cream
1  8-oz. package noodles, cooked
Grated cheese

**Brown** . . . . . . ground beef in skillet, stirring until crumbly; drain.
**Add** . . . . . . . tomato sauce and seasonings, mixing well.
**Combine** . . . . onion, cream cheese and sour cream in bowl, mixing well.
**Layer** . . . . . . noodles, ground beef mixture and sour cream mixture alternately in lightly greased baking dish until all ingredients are used.
**Top** . . . . . . . . with grated cheese.
**Bake** . . . . . . . at 350 degrees for 20 minutes.

Judy Gebhardt
J. L. Williams Jr. H. S., Copperas Cove, Texas

## DELICIOUS BEEF AND RICE

1 lb. ground beef
1 c. rice
1 sm. onion, chopped
2 tbsp. oil
1 tsp. each salt, paprika
1/2 tsp. pepper
1 sm. bottle of olives, sliced
2 c. tomato juice
1/2 c. grated cheese

**Brown** . . . . . . ground beef with rice and onion in oil in skillet, stirring until crumbly.
**Add** . . . . . . . remaining ingredients except cheese with 1 1/2 cups boiling water, mixing well.
**Pour** . . . . . . . into 1 1/2-quart casserole.

Bake ....... covered, at 300 degrees for 1 hour.
Top ........ with cheese.
Bake ....... uncovered, for 10 minutes longer or until cheese is melted.
Yields ...... 6 servings.

Hassie Hunter Rodgers
Goshen H. S., Goshen, Alabama

## CHEROKEE CASSEROLE

*1 1/2 lb. ground beef*
*1 lg. onion, chopped*
*1/2 tsp. each garlic salt, oregano, pepper*
*1 tsp. salt*
*1  16-oz. can whole tomatoes*
*1 c. cooked rice*
*1 can mushroom soup*
*1 1/4 c. shredded cheese*

Brown ...... ground beef with onion and seasonings in large skillet, stirring until crumbly.
Add ....... tomatoes, mixing well.
Simmer ..... for 5 minutes.
Stir ........ in rice and soup.
Spoon ...... into casserole.
Sprinkle .... with cheese.
Bake ....... at 350 degrees until cheese is melted.

Elsie Jo LaFever
Eakly H. S., Eakly, Oklahoma

## SPECIAL RICE CASSEROLE

*1 c. each chopped celery, onion*
*1 tbsp. butter*
*1 c. tomato juice*
*1/2 c. tomato paste*
*1 lb. ground beef*
*1 tsp. salt*
*1/2 tsp. Italian seasoning*
*1/4 tsp. pepper*
*1 c. brown rice, cooked*
*1/4 c. Parmesan cheese*
*1/2 c. grated Cheddar cheese*

Saute ...... celery and onion in butter in small skillet until golden brown.
Cook ....... covered, until tender.
Stir ........ in tomato juice and tomato paste.

Simmer ..... for 10 minutes.
Brown ...... ground beef with seasonings in skillet, stirring until crumbly.
Stir ........ in vegetable mixture.
Layer ...... hot rice and ground beef mixture in casserole.
Sprinkle .... cheeses over top.
Bake ....... at 350 degrees for 10 to 15 minutes or until cheeses are melted.
Yields ...... 8 servings.

Delores Carriere
Irvine Sch., Irvine, Alberta, Canada

## SPANISH RICE

*2 c. minute rice, cooked*
*1 qt. tomatoes*
*1/2 c. chopped onion*
*1/2 c. green pepper, chopped*
*3/4 lb. ground beef, browned*

Combine .... all ingredients in bowl, mixing well.
Place ....... in casserole.
Bake ....... at 350 degrees for 45 minutes.

Jeanne M. Lamb
North East H. S., North East, Pennsylvania

## TEXAS HASH

*1/2 c. each chopped onion, green pepper*
*2 tbsp. shortening*
*1 lb. ground beef*
*2 tsp. each salt, chili powder*
*1/4 tsp. pepper*
*1 c. rice*
*1  20-oz. can tomatoes*
*1 sm. can tomato juice*

Saute ...... onion and green pepper in shortening in skillet.
Brown ...... ground beef with sauteed vegetables, stirring until crumbly.
Add ....... remaining ingredients, mixing well.
Pour ....... into casserole.
Bake ....... covered, at 350 degrees for 35 to 45 minutes or until rice is tender.
Yields ...... 6 servings.

Mary Ann Hoffman
Clear Lake H. S. Annex, Houston, Texas

## SHANGHAI CASSEROLE

1 1/2 lb. ground beef
1 c. chopped onions
1 clove of garlic, minced
2 c. sliced celery
1 can cream of mushroom soup
1  10-oz. package frozen mixed
   vegetables, thawed
2 c. cooked rice
2 tbsp. soy sauce
2 tsp. salt
1/2 tsp. pepper
1  3-oz. can Chinese noodles

Brown . . . . . . ground beef with onions and gar-
lic in skillet, stirring until
crumbly.
Stir . . . . . . . . in remaining ingredients except
noodles.
Spoon . . . . . . into greased 2 1/2-quart
casserole.
Bake . . . . . . . covered, at 350 degrees for 25
minutes.
Top . . . . . . . . with noodles.
Bake . . . . . . . uncovered, for 5 minutes longer.
Yields . . . . . . 6-8 servings.

Photograph for this recipe on page 70.

## PIZZA-STYLE SPAGHETTI

1 lb. spaghetti
2 eggs
1 c. milk
1  32-oz. jar spaghetti sauce
1 1/2 lb. ground beef, crumbled
Chopped onion, green pepper
1/4 tsp. garlic salt
1/2 tsp. oregano
1 c. sliced pepperoni
2 c. grated mozzarella cheese

Break . . . . . . spaghetti into thirds.
Cook . . . . . . . using package directions.
Beat . . . . . . . eggs and milk together in large
bowl.
Add . . . . . . . spaghetti, tossing to mix.
Pour . . . . . . . into 9 x 13-inch baking dish.
Layer . . . . . . next 4 ingredients over spaghetti
in order listed.
Sprinkle . . . . with garlic salt and oregano.
Top . . . . . . . . with pepperoni and cheese.
Bake . . . . . . . at 350 degrees for 40 minutes.

Let . . . . . . . . stand for 5 minutes before
serving.
Yields . . . . . . 10-12 servings.

Ground beef may be cooked before assembling
casserole.

Mary Lois Larr
West Ottawa H. S., Holland, Michigan

## CHEESY SPAGHETTI

1 lb. ground beef
1/2 med. onion, chopped
1/2 tsp. salt
1/4 tsp. pepper
1 tbsp. olive oil
1 med. jar Ragu Sauce
1 small pkg. spaghetti, cooked
8 oz. mozzarella cheese, grated

Saute . . . . . . ground beef with onion, salt and
pepper in oil in skillet until
brown; drain.
Add . . . . . . . Ragu Sauce, simmering for 10 to
15 minutes.
Layer . . . . . . 1/2 of the spaghetti, ground beef
sauce and cheese into 8 x 8-inch
casserole, repeating layers.
Bake . . . . . . . at 350 degrees for 20 minutes or
until cheese melts.

Sister Julie Budai
Providence H. S., San Antonio, Texas

## KATHERINE'S SPAGHETTI

1 lb. hamburger
1 med. onion, chopped
1 box spaghetti, cooked
1 can mushrooms
1 sm. can evaporated milk
1 can tomato soup
1 pkg. grated Cheddar cheese
Salt and pepper to taste

Brown . . . . . . hamburger with onion in skillet,
stirring until crumbly; drain.
Stir . . . . . . . . in remaining ingredients.
Pour . . . . . . . into casserole.
Bake . . . . . . . at 350 degrees for 30 minutes.
Yields . . . . . . 6 servings.

Linda Halterman
Winfield-Mt. Union Jr.-Sr. H. S., Winfield, Iowa

## CABBAGE HOT DISH

*1 lb. hamburger*
*1/2 c. chopped onion*
*Salt and pepper to taste*
*1 sm. head cabbage, shredded*
*1 can tomato soup*

**Brown** . . . . . . hamburger with onion, salt and pepper in skillet, stirring until crumbly.

**Layer** . . . . . . cabbage and hamburger mixture alternately in buttered 1-quart casserole until all ingredients are used.

**Top** . . . . . . . . with soup, mixing gently with fork.

**Bake** . . . . . . . covered, at 350 degrees for 1 hour.

**Yields** . . . . . . 4-6 servings.

Jenney L. Kubal
Eisenhower H. S., Houston, Texas

## GOLDEN BEEF CASSEROLE

*1 lb. ground beef*
*1/2 c. chopped onion*
*1/4 c. chopped green pepper*
*1 tsp. salt (opt.)*
*1 can mushroom soup*
*1  16-oz. can whole kernel corn*
*1 c. grated Cheddar cheese*

**Brown** . . . . . . ground beef in skillet, stirring until crumbly.

**Add** . . . . . . . next 2 ingredients.

**Cook** . . . . . . . until vegetables are tender; drain.

**Combine** . . . . with remaining ingredients in greased 1 1/2-quart casserole, mixing well.

**Bake** . . . . . . . at 350 degrees for 45 minutes.

Delinda McCormick
Caldwell County H. S., Princeton, Kentucky

## GROUND BEEF AND BROCCOLI CASSEROLE

*1 lb. ground beef*
*1/2 c. chopped onion*
*6 tbsp. shortening, melted*
*1/2 c. flour*

*1 tsp. salt*
*3 1/2 c. milk*
*1/3 c. Parmesan cheese*
*2 pkg. frozen broccoli spears, cooked*
*1 pkg. refrigerator biscuits, quartered*

**Brown** . . . . . . ground beef in skillet, stirring until crumbly; drain.

**Saute** . . . . . . onion in shortening in large saucepan.

**Mix** . . . . . . . . in flour and salt, stirring until smooth.

**Add** . . . . . . . milk and cheese.

**Cook** . . . . . . . until thickened, stirring constantly.

**Stir** . . . . . . . . in broccoli and ground beef.

**Pour** . . . . . . . into 2-quart casserole.

**Bake** . . . . . . . at 375 degrees for 30 minutes.

**Arrange** . . . . . biscuits around edge of casserole.

**Bake** . . . . . . . for 15 minutes longer.

**Yields** . . . . . . 8 servings.

Karlene Gullberg
Cahokia H. S., Cahokia, Illinois

## HAMBURGER CORN BREAD-TOPPED CASSEROLE

*1 lb. lean hamburger*
*1 lg. onion, chopped*
*1 can ranch-style beans*
*1 can whole kernel corn, drained*
*1  16-oz. can tomato sauce*
*3 to 5 tsp. chili powder*
*Garlic powder, salt and pepper to taste*
*1 or 2 sm. boxes corn bread mix*

**Brown** . . . . . . hamburger with onion in skillet, stirring until crumbly; drain.

**Add** . . . . . . . next 3 ingredients and seasonings, mixing well.

**Simmer** . . . . . for 10 minutes, adding water if necessary.

**Spoon** . . . . . . into 9 x 11-inch baking pan.

**Prepare** . . . . . corn bread, using package directions.

**Spoon** . . . . . . over hamburger mixture.

**Bake** . . . . . . . at 375 degrees for 25 to 35 minutes or until corn bread tests done.

**Yields** . . . . . . 6-8 servings.

Deborah Jacoway
Central Jr. H. S., Putnam City, Oklahoma

## CAULIFLOWER-BEEF CASSEROLE

1 med. cauliflower, cut into pieces
1 1/2 lb. ground beef
1 onion, chopped
1/2 tsp. salt
1/2 tsp. Tabasco sauce
1 tbsp. flour
1 tbsp. oil
1 c. milk
1/2 lb. cheese, grated
1 c. bread crumbs

Cook ....... cauliflower in a small amount of water in saucepan until tender.
Brown ...... ground beef with onion in skillet, stirring until crumbly.
Stir ........ in salt and Tabasco sauce.
Blend ...... flour and oil in saucepan.
Add ....... milk, stirring well.
Cook ....... over low heat until thickened, stirring constantly.
Add ....... cheese.
Cook ....... until cheese melts, stirring constantly.
Layer ...... ground beef mixture, bread crumbs and cauliflower in 2-quart casserole.
Pour ....... cheese sauce over top.
Bake ....... at 375 degrees for 30 minutes.
Yields ...... 6 servings.

Beverly H. Kish
Seabreeze Jr. H. S., Daytona Beach, Florida

## BEEF-EGGPLANT STACKS

6  1/2-in. slices eggplant
6 thin slices onion
6 thick slices tomato
Salt and pepper
1 lb. ground beef
1 1/2 c. crushed corn flakes
1 c. milk
1/4 tsp. Worcestershire sauce
1/2 tsp. garlic salt

Arrange ..... eggplant, onion and tomato slices in 6 stacks in greased baking dish.
Sprinkle .... with salt and pepper.
Combine .... remaining ingredients with 1/4 teaspoon pepper in bowl, mixing well.
Shape ...... into 6 patties.

Place ....... on top of tomatoes.
Bake ....... at 350 degrees for 1 hour.

Louise B. Howell
Stewart County H. S., Dover, Tennessee

## GROUND BEEF-MIXED VEGETABLE CASSEROLE

1 1/2 lb. ground beef
1/2 c. chopped onion
3 beef bouillon cubes
1 c. each chopped carrots, celery
1 pkg. frozen peas, thawed
1 c. rice
1 can cream of mushroom soup
1 c. shredded American cheese

Brown ...... ground beef with onion in skillet, stirring until crumbly.
Dissolve .... bouillon cubes in 3 cups boiling water.
Combine .... with ground beef mixture and remaining ingredients in casserole, mixing well.
Bake ....... at 350 degrees for 1 1/2 hours.
Yields ...... 8-10 servings.

Cynthia Kalberg
Fairfield Jr.-Sr. H. S., Goshen, Indiana

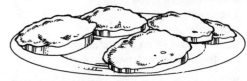

## MEAL-IN-A-BUNDLE

2 lb. lean ground beef
6 med. potatoes, chopped
6 tbsp. chopped onion
6 carrots, sliced 1/4 in. thick
2 cans golden mushroom soup
Tabasco sauce
Salt and pepper to taste

Layer ...... first 5 ingredients equally onto six 18-inch squares of heavy-duty foil.
Add ....... 1 tablespoon water with Tabasco sauce, salt and pepper to taste to each.
Fold ....... foil to enclose filling; seal.
Grill ....... over hot coals for 1 hour.
Yields ...... 6 servings.

Mary Jean Earl
Meritt Hutton Jr. H. S., Thornton, Colorado

## LYD'S HAMBURGER CASSEROLE

1   16-oz. can green beans
1 lb. ground beef
1 med. onion, chopped
3 med. potatoes, sliced
1/4 tsp. garlic salt
1 can cream of celery soup
1 c. grated cheese

**Drain** ...... green beans, reserving 1/2 cup juice.
**Brown** ...... ground beef with onion in skillet, stirring until crumbly.
**Place** ...... potatoes in greased 6 x 10-inch baking dish.
**Spoon** ...... ground beef mixture over potatoes.
**Combine** .... beans and garlic salt in bowl.
**Spoon** ...... over ground beef mixture.
**Mix** ........ reserved bean liquid with soup in bowl.
**Spread** ..... over beans.
**Sprinkle** .... with cheese.
**Bake** ....... at 350 degrees for 45 minutes.
**Yields** ...... 5-6 servings.

Virginia E. Grafe
Bertrand Community Sch., Bertrand, Nebraska

## SHIPWRECK

6 med. potatoes, chopped
1 onion, chopped
2 lb. ground beef, crumbled
1 lg. can chili with beans
3/4 c. minute rice
1 beef bouillon cube
1 can tomato soup
1 tsp. salt
1/4 tsp. pepper
1/4 tsp. Worcestershire sauce

**Place** ....... potatoes and onion in large baking dish.
**Layer** ...... next 3 ingredients on top.
**Dissolve** .... bouillon cube in 1 1/2 cups hot water in bowl.
**Add** ....... soup, salt, pepper and Worcestershire sauce, mixing well.
**Pour** ....... over rice. Do not stir.
**Bake** ....... at 325 degrees for 1 1/2 hours.
**Yields** ...... 12 servings.

Frances Stewart
Congress Jr. H. S., Denton, Texas

## EASY GROUND BEEF AND POTATO CASSEROLE

1 lb. ground beef
Salt and pepper to taste
1 sm. onion, sliced
4 med. potatoes, sliced
1 green pepper, sliced (opt.)
1 can cream of mushroom soup

**Brown** ...... ground beef with salt and pepper in skillet, stirring until crumbly; drain.
**Place** ....... in 1-quart casserole.
**Layer** ...... next 3 ingredients over ground beef.
**Top** ........ with soup.
**Bake** ....... covered, at 350 degrees for 1 hour or until potatoes are tender.
**Yields** ...... 4-6 servings.

Betty Lewis
Princess Anne Jr. H. S., Virginia Beach, Virginia

## SNO-CAPPED MEAT CASSEROLE

1 lb. ground steak
1 med. onion, chopped
2 cloves of garlic, minced
Shortening
1 can corn, drained
1 can peas, drained
1 tsp. salt
1/8 tsp. pepper
1 can mushroom sauce
4 med. potatoes, cooked
1 egg
Butter, melted

**Brown** ...... ground steak with onion and garlic in a small amount of shortening, in skillet, stirring until crumbly.
**Layer** ...... ground steak, corn, peas, salt and pepper in casserole.
**Pour** ....... mushroom sauce over top.
**Mash** ....... potatoes with egg and butter to taste in bowl.
**Spoon** ...... over casserole.
**Garnish** ..... with paprika.
**Bake** ....... at 350 degrees for 30 minutes.
**Yields** ...... 6-8 servings.

Grace Edwards
Robert E. Lee H. S., Baytown, Texas

## TATER TOT CASSEROLE

1 lb. ground beef
1/4 c. chopped onion (opt.)
1 can cream of chicken soup
1 16-oz. box Tater Tots

Brown . . . . . . ground beef with onion in skil-
let, stirring until crumbly.
Place . . . . . . . in 2-quart casserole.
Top . . . . . . . . with soup and Tater Tots.
Bake . . . . . . . at 350 degrees for 45 minutes.
Yields . . . . . . 4-6 servings.

Nora V. Sweat
West Hardin H. S., Stephensburg, Kentucky

## ZUCCHINI HOT DISH

1 lb. hamburger
1 sm. onion, chopped
Salt and pepper to taste
4 or 5 6-in. zucchini, sliced
1 can cream of mushroom soup
1 to 2 c. shredded Cheddar cheese

Brown . . . . . . hamburger with onion, salt and
pepper in skillet, stirring until
crumbly; drain.
Layer . . . . . . zucchini and hamburger mixture
alternately in 1 1/2-quart
casserole.
Top . . . . . . . . with soup and cheese.
Bake . . . . . . . at 300 degrees for 1 hour.
Yields . . . . . . 4 servings.

Shirley J. Kanne
Central Middle Sch., Eden Prairie, Minnesota

## GRATED ZUCCHINI CASSEROLE

7 c. grated zucchini
1 c. grated carrots
1/2 c. finely chopped onion
1 1/2 c. ground beef
3 env. Stove Top Stuffing mix
1 can cream of chicken soup
1 c. sour cream
1/2 c. melted butter

Steam . . . . . . vegetables in salted water for 5
minutes; drain.
Brown . . . . . . ground beef in skillet, stirring
until crumbly.

Prepare . . . . . stuffing mix, using package
directions.
Spread . . . . . half the stuffing in 9 x 13-inch
baking pan.
Layer . . . . . . vegetables and beef over top.
Combine . . . . soup and sour cream in small
bowl, mixing well.
Spread . . . . . over ground beef layer.
Top . . . . . . . . with remaining stuffing mix.
Drizzle . . . . . butter over top.
Bake . . . . . . . covered, at 350 degrees for 30
minutes.
Bake . . . . . . . uncovered, for 10 minutes
longer.
Yields . . . . . . 15 servings.

Kathryn Jensen
Box Elder H. S., Brigham City, Utah

## CASSEROLE ITALIANO

1 1/2 lb. zucchini, sliced 1/4 in. thick
1 c. minced onion
1 sm. clove of garlic, minced
2 tbsp. butter
1 lb. ground beef
1 c. minute rice
1 tsp. basil
1 can tomato soup
1 16-oz. container cream-style cottage
cheese
1 c. shredded sharp American cheese

Cook . . . . . . . zucchini in a small amount of
boiling salted water in saucepan
until tender-crisp; drain.
Saute . . . . . . onion with garlic in butter in
skillet until tender.
Add . . . . . . . ground beef.
Cook . . . . . . . until brown and crumbly, stirring frequently.
Mix . . . . . . . . in rice and basil.
Blend . . . . . . soup with 2/3 cup water in
bowl.
Layer . . . . . . half the zucchini, all of the
ground beef mixture and cottage
cheese in buttered 2 1/2-quart
casserole.
Top . . . . . . . . with remaining zucchini, soup
mixture and American cheese.
Bake . . . . . . . at 350 degrees for 35 to 40 minutes or until lightly browned.
Yields . . . . . . 6-8 servings.

Photograph for this recipe on page 125.

# Foreign Favorites

## BELGIAN MEATBALLS

3 slices bread
1 1/2 lb. ground beef
1 egg, beaten
1 1/2 tsp. salt
1/4 tsp. pepper
1/2 tsp. allspice
2 tsp. grated onion
1/3 c. melted butter
Flour
4 onions, chopped
1/4 c. margarine

**Place** ....... bread in bowl in water to cover; drain and squeeze to remove excess moisture.
**Add** ....... next 6 ingredients, mixing well.
**Stir** ........ in butter and 3 tablespoons water.
**Shape** ...... into balls.
**Coat** ....... with flour.
**Saute** ...... onions in margarine in skillet until lightly browned; remove onions.
**Brown** ...... meatballs in pan drippings.
**Add** ....... sauteed onions and 1/2 cup water.
**Simmer** ..... covered, for 1 1/2 hours.
**Yields** ...... 4-6 servings.

Theresa M. Fox
Campbell Memorial H. S., Campbell, Ohio

## FOURTIERE

2 lb. ground pork, crumbled
1 lb. ground beef, crumbled
1 sm. onion, ground
1/2 tsp. each salt, cinnamon
1/4 tsp. each pepper, celery salt, cloves
1 sm. clove of garlic, minced
3 lg. potatoes, cooked, mashed
Pastry for 2  2-crust pies

**Place** ....... first 9 ingredients in saucepan, mixing well.
**Cook** ....... over medium heat for 20 minutes, stirring frequently; drain.
**Let** ........ stand for 10 minutes.
**Add** ....... potatoes, mixing well; cool.
**Line** ....... 2 pie plates with pastry.
**Spoon** ...... half the ground beef mixture into each prepared pie plate.

**Cover** ...... with remaining pastry, sealing edges.
**Bake** ....... at 400 degrees for about 30 minutes or until golden brown.
**Yields** ...... 2 pies.

Elsie Klassen
G. P. Vanier Sch., Donnelly AB, Canada

## CANADIAN GROUND BEEF DISH

2 c. chopped potatoes
1 c. chopped celery
2 lb. ground beef
1 c. each chopped onion, green pepper
2 cans chicken vegetable soup
1 c. tomato juice
Salt, pepper, parsley flakes, oregano to taste

**Layer** ...... first 7 ingredients in order given in baking dish.
**Sprinkle** .... with seasonings.
**Bake** ....... at 350 degrees for 1 1/2 hours or until potatoes are tender.

Lorraine French
Terryville H. S., Terryville, Connecticut

## RIPE OLIVE BRIDIES

1 lb. lean ground beef
1 tbsp. bacon drippings
1 med. chopped onion
1/4 tsp. thyme
1 1/4 tsp. salt
1/8 tsp. pepper
1 tsp. Worcestershire sauce
1 tbsp. flour
1/3 c. beef broth
1 c. pitted ripe olives
1/4 c. finely chopped parsley
2 sticks pastry mix
1 egg, beaten

**Brown** ...... ground beef in bacon drippings in skillet.
**Add** ....... onion.
**Saute** ...... until onion is tender.
**Stir** ........ in next 6 ingredients.
**Cook** ....... for 10 minutes, stirring occasionally.

**Cook** . . . . . . . carrots in boiling salted water in saucepan for 20 minutes; drain.

**Brown** . . . . . . hamburger with onions in skillet, stirring until crumbly.

**Add** . . . . . . . garlic, 2 cups boiling water, bouillon cubes, Worcestershire sauce and carrots, mixing well.

**Simmer** . . . . . covered, for 20 minutes.

**Mix** . . . . . . . flour and a small amount of water in bowl to make paste.

**Add** . . . . . . . to hamburger mixture.

**Season** . . . . . with salt and pepper.

**Serve** . . . . . . with mashed potatoes.

**Yields** . . . . . . 6-8 servings.

Priscilla Erat Goldner
Norwalk H. S., Norwalk, Connecticut

**Add** . . . . . . . olives and parsley; cool slightly.

**Prepare** . . . . . pastry mix, using package directions.

**Roll** . . . . . . . into six 5 x 8-inch rectangles on floured surface.

**Spoon** . . . . . . ground beef mixture onto half of each pastry.

**Fold** . . . . . . . pastry to enclose filling.

**Moisten** . . . . . edges with egg mixed with 1 tablespoon water; seal with fork.

**Cut** . . . . . . . . 1-inch circle in top of each; brush with remaining egg wash.

**Bake** . . . . . . . at 425 degrees for 20 minutes or until golden brown.

**Yields** . . . . . . 6 servings.

Photograph for this recipe above.

## SCOTCH HAMBURG

1 lb. carrots, peeled, cut into
    2 1/2-in. pieces
2 lb. hamburger
2 med. onions, chopped
1 clove of garlic, minced
3 beef bouillon cubes
3 tsp. Worcestershire sauce
2 or 3 tbsp. flour
Salt and pepper to taste

## YORKSHIRE CASSEROLE

1 lb. lean ground chuck
Dry onion soup mix to taste
Parsley, chopped
1/8 tsp. pepper
2 tbsp. chili sauce
4 eggs
1 c. milk
2 tbsp. butter, melted
1 c. flour
1/2 tsp. salt
1 tsp. baking powder
1 can brown gravy

**Combine** . . . . first 5 ingredients and 1 egg in bowl, mixing lightly.

**Shape** . . . . . . into 16 balls.

**Place** . . . . . . . in greased 9 x 9-inch baking pan.

**Beat** . . . . . . . remaining 3 eggs until foamy in small bowl.

**Add** . . . . . . . milk and butter, mixing well.

**Sift** . . . . . . . . in dry ingredients, beating until smooth.

**Pour** . . . . . . . over meatballs.

**Bake** . . . . . . . at 350 degrees for 50 to 60 minutes or until puffed and browned.

**Heat** . . . . . . . brown gravy to serving temperature in saucepan.

**Serve** . . . . . . over casserole.

**Yields** . . . . . . 4 servings.

Betty Lute
Avon Lake H. S., Avon Lake, Ohio

## EASY CHINESE CASSEROLE

1 1/2 lb. ground beef
1 can sliced water chestnuts, drained
1 sm. package frozen peas, thawed
2 c. chopped celery
1 sm. onion, chopped
1 can cream of mushroom soup
6 tbsp. milk
Salt and pepper to taste
Chow mein noodles

**Combine** .... all ingredients except noodles in bowl, mixing well.
**Spoon** ...... into 2-quart casserole.
**Top** ....... with noodles.
**Bake** ...... at 350 degrees for 30 minutes.
**Yields** ...... 6 servings.

Peggy Sumner
Bishop Ward H. S., Kansas City, Kansas

## CHOW MEIN CASSEROLE

2 lb. ground beef
1 lg. onion, chopped
1 1/2 c. chopped celery
1/2 tsp. salt
2 c. cooked unsalted rice
1 can each chicken gumbo soup,
cream of chicken soup, golden cream
of mushroom soup
1 tsp. Worcestershire sauce
1 can bean sprouts, drained (opt.)
1 sm. can sliced water chestnuts,
drained (opt.)
1 tbsp. soy sauce (opt.)
1 can chow mein noodles

**Brown** ...... ground beef with onion and celery in large skillet, stirring until crumbly.
**Add** ....... remaining ingredients except noodles with 1 1/2 cups water, mixing well.
**Spoon** ...... into buttered casserole.
**Top** ....... with noodles.
**Bake** ...... at 350 degrees for 25 to 30 minutes or until bubbly.
**Yields** ...... 12 servings.

Ruby J. Dunagan
Bixby Jr. H. S., Bixby, Oklahoma

## PARTY BIEROCKS

2 pkg. dry yeast
6 tbsp. sugar
3 tbsp. oil
1 tsp. salt
Flour
1 1/2 lb. ground beef
1 sm. head cabbage, chopped
1/4 c. chopped onion

**Dissolve** .... yeast and 2 tablespoons sugar in 1 cup warm water in large bowl.
**Add** ....... remaining 4 tablespoons sugar, oil, salt, 1 cup warm water and 4 1/2 cups flour, mixing until dough clings together.
**Knead** ...... on floured surface.
**Let** ........ rise in warm place for 1 hour.
**Brown** ...... ground beef in skillet, stirring until tender; drain.
**Add** ....... cabbage and onion.
**Cook** ....... over medium heat until vegetables are tender.
**Mix** ........ in 2 tablespoons flour.
**Roll** ....... out dough on floured surface.
**Cut** ........ into 4-inch squares.
**Place** ....... large spoonful ground beef mixture on each square.
**Fold** ....... over to enclose filling; seal seams.
**Place** ....... on baking sheet.
**Let** ........ rise, covered, for 1 hour.
**Bake** ....... at 350 degrees for 15 minutes or until golden brown.

Debbie Hart
Emerson Jr. H. S., Enid, Oklahoma

## GERMAN SPAGHETTI

1 lb. spaghetti
2 med. onions, chopped
Oil
1 lb. ground beef
1 lb. sharp cheese, grated
1 16-oz. can each English peas,
cream-style corn
1 8-oz. can tomato paste
1 16-oz. can tomatoes, chopped

**Cook** ....... spaghetti, using package directions for half the given time; drain, reserving water.
**Saute** ...... onions in a small amount of oil in skillet until tender.

**Brown** . . . . . . ground beef in skillet, stirring until crumbly.

**Add** . . . . . . . spaghetti, sauteed onions, half the cheese and remaining ingredients, mixing well.

**Pour** . . . . . . . into 9 x 13-inch baking dish.

**Bake** . . . . . . . at 350 degrees for 1 hour, adding reserved spaghetti water if necessary.

**Top** . . . . . . . . with remaining cheese.

**Yields** . . . . . . 10-12 servings.

Glynda Hooper
Marlow H. S., Marlow, Oklahoma

## EASY BIEROCKS

*1 pkg. hot roll mix*
*1 lb. hamburger*
*2 tbsp. bacon drippings*
*1 med. head cabbage, shredded*
*2 med. onions, chopped*
*Salt and pepper to taste*

**Mix** . . . . . . . . hot roll mix, using package directions.

**Let** . . . . . . . . rise in warm place until doubled in bulk.

**Brown** . . . . . . hamburger in bacon drippings in skillet, stirring until crumbly.

**Add** . . . . . . . remaining ingredients.

**Simmer** . . . . . until vegetables are tender, stirring frequently; cool.

**Roll** . . . . . . . dough into 1/4-inch thick rectangle on floured surface.

**Cut** . . . . . . . . into squares.

**Place** . . . . . . . spoonful hamburger mixture in center of square.

**Fold** . . . . . . . over to enclose filling; seal seams.

**Place** . . . . . . . seam side down on greased baking sheet.

**Bake** . . . . . . . using hot roll package directions until golden brown.

Dana Ray Owens
Schleicher County H. S., Eldorado, Texas

## FLEISCHKUECHLE

*1 1/2 c. evaporated milk*
*1 1/2 c. milk*
*4 1/2 c. flour*
*1 stick margarine, softened*
*1 tsp. sugar*
*3/4 tsp. baking powder*
*3 tsp. salt*
*1 1/2 lb. each ground beef, pork*
*Pepper to taste*
*1 onion, chopped*
*Oil for deep frying*

**Combine** . . . . first 6 ingredients and 1 1/4 teaspoons salt in large bowl, stirring until dough leaves side.

**Roll** . . . . . . . on floured surface.

**Cut** . . . . . . . . into 6-inch circles.

**Mix** . . . . . . . . ground beef, pork, pepper, onion, 1 3/4 teaspoon salt and 1/2 cup water in bowl.

**Place** . . . . . . . 2 tablespoons ground beef mixture on half of each circle, folding and sealing as for turnovers.

**Fry** . . . . . . . . in hot deep oil until brown.

Donnette Vachal
Scobey H. S., Scobey, Montana

## STUFFED CABBAGE

*1 head cabbage*
*1 lb. ground beef*
*1/4 c. cooked rice*
*1 egg*
*1 onion, chopped*
*1 tsp. salt*
*1/2 tsp. pepper*
*1  16-oz. can sauerkraut, drained*
*1  16-oz. can tomatoes*
*1 or 2 bay leaves (opt.)*

**Steam** . . . . . . cabbage over boiling water until softened.

**Remove** . . . . and trim leaves.

**Combine** . . . . next 6 ingredients in bowl, mixing well.

**Shape** . . . . . . into 2-inch balls.

**Place** . . . . . . . on cabbage leaves, rolling to enclose filling.

**Spread** . . . . . sauerkraut in 9 x 9-inch baking dish.

**Place** . . . . . . . cabbage rolls seam side down on sauerkraut.

**Cover** . . . . . . with tomatoes.

**Place** . . . . . . . bay leaves on top.

**Bake** . . . . . . . covered, at 250 degrees for 2 to 3 hours or to desired degree of doneness.

Ann Litten Bost
Fred T. Foard H. S., Newton, North Carolina

## MOUSSAKA

1 lb. lean ground beef
1 c. chopped onion
1 clove of garlic, crushed
Butter
1 1/2 tsp. salt
1/2 tsp. each oregano, cinnamon
1/8 tsp. pepper
1 tsp. basil
2  8-oz. cans tomato sauce
2 tbsp. flour
1 tsp. grated onion
1 c. milk
1 c. light cream
2 eggs, beaten
2 eggplant, sliced
1/2 c. seasoned bread crumbs
1 c. shredded Cheddar cheese
1/4 c. grated Parmesan cheese

Saute ...... ground beef, chopped onion and garlic in 2 tablespoons butter in skillet, stirring until ground beef is crumbly; drain.
Add ....... 1 teaspoon salt, oregano, cinnamon, pepper, basil and tomato sauce.
Simmer ..... for 1/2 hour, stirring occasionally.
Stir ........ flour, grated onion and 1/2 teaspoon salt into 2 tablespoons butter in saucepan.
Cook ....... until smooth, stirring constantly; remove from heat.
Add ....... milk and cream gradually.
Simmer ..... for 1 minute, stirring constantly.
Stir ........ a small amount of hot sauce into eggs.

Stir ........ eggs into hot sauce; set aside.
Saute ...... eggplant in 1/3 cup butter in skillet until lightly browned.
Layer ...... 2 tablespoons bread crumbs, half the eggplant; all the meat sauce and half the Cheddar cheese in shallow 2-quart baking dish.
Top ........ with remaining crumbs and eggplant.
Layer ...... white sauce, remaining 1/2 cup Cheddar cheese and Parmesan cheese over eggplant.
Bake ....... in 350-degree oven for 1/2 hour.
Let ........ stand for 10 minutes before serving.
Yields ...... 6-8 servings.

Photograph for this recipe on this page.

## GREEK MEATBALLS

1 lb. hamburger
2 med. onions, chopped
1 c. light brown bread crumbs
2 tbsp. finely chopped mint
Salt and pepper to taste
1 c. flour
1 1/2 c. olive oil
Juice of 1 lemon

Combine .... first 6 ingredients with 2 1/2 cups water in bowl, mixing well.
Shape ...... by tablespoonfuls into meatballs.
Roll ....... in flour.
Brown ...... over medium heat in olive oil in skillet.
Remove .... to heated serving platter.
Sprinkle .... with lemon juice.
Yields ...... 5-6 servings.
May serve hot or cold.

Hazel C. Tassis
Imperial Unified H. S., Imperial, California

## FAVORITE PASTICHIO

4 tbsp. flour
Butter
4 c. milk
Salt
1/2 lb. each Romano cheese, Cheddar
     cheese, grated

4 eggs, beaten
1 med. onion, chopped
1 lb. ground beef
3 tbsp. tomato paste
Dash each of cloves, cinnamon
Pepper to taste
3 c. thick macaroni, cooked
2 c. buttered bread crumbs

**Stir** . . . . . . . flour into 1/2 cup melted butter in saucepan, mixing until smooth.

**Add** . . . . . . . milk gradually, stirring constantly.

**Mix** . . . . . . . in 2 teaspoons salt.

**Boil** . . . . . . . for 1 to 2 minutes or until thick, stirring constantly; remove from heat.

**Add** . . . . . . . cheeses, stirring until melted.

**Stir** . . . . . . . . a small amount of hot mixture into eggs; stir eggs into hot mixture.

**Saute** . . . . . . onion in a small amount of butter in skillet until golden.

**Add** . . . . . . . ground beef, tomato paste, spices, salt to taste and pepper.

**Cook** . . . . . . . until ground beef is brown, stirring constantly.

**Place** . . . . . . . half the macaroni in buttered 9 x 13-inch baking pan.

**Layer** . . . . . . ground beef mixture, remaining macaroni, cheese sauce and bread crumbs over top.

**Bake** . . . . . . . at 350 degrees for 45 minutes or until bubbly.

**Yields** . . . . . . 8-10 servings.

Constance Lebel
Mascenic Regional Sch., New Ipswich, New Hampshire

## CANNELONI ROMA

1/2 lb. ground beef
1/4 c. chopped onion
1/2 c. Parmesan cheese
1 egg, beaten
1/2 tsp. each oregano, garlic salt
8 manicotti shells
1  8-oz. can tomato sauce
1  16-oz. can tomatoes
4 oz. shredded mozzarella cheese

**Brown** . . . . . . ground beef in skillet, stirring until crumbly; drain.

**Add** . . . . . . . onion.

**Cook** . . . . . . until tender.

**Stir** . . . . . . . . in 1/4 cup Parmesan cheese and next 3 ingredients.

**Stuff** . . . . . . . shells with ground beef mixture.

**Place** . . . . . . . in 6 x 10-inch baking dish.

**Mix** . . . . . . . . tomato sauce, tomatoes and 1/4 cup water in bowl.

**Pour** . . . . . . . tomato sauce over shells.

**Sprinkle** . . . . with remaining 1/4 cup Parmesan cheese.

**Bake** . . . . . . . covered, at 350 degrees for 1 hour.

**Top** . . . . . . . . with mozzarella cheese.

**Bake** . . . . . . . until cheese is melted.

**Yields** . . . . . . 4 servings.

Jani Haraldson
Turtle Lake-Mercer H. S., Turtle Lake, North Dakota

## TOMATO-SAUCED ITALIAN MEAT LOAF

1 med. onion, chopped
2 tbsp. butter
1 egg, slightly beaten
1/2 c. milk
1/2 c. herb-seasoned stuffing mix
1 lb. ground beef
2 tbsp. chopped parsley
1 tsp. salt
1/4 tsp. pepper
1  6-oz. can tomato sauce
1/4 tsp. oregano

**Saute** . . . . . . onion in butter in saucepan until golden brown.

**Mix** . . . . . . . . egg, milk and stuffing mix in large bowl.

**Let** . . . . . . . . stand for 5 minutes.

**Add** . . . . . . . sauteed onion, ground beef, parsley, salt and pepper, mixing lightly.

**Shape** . . . . . . into loaf in shallow baking dish.

**Bake** . . . . . . . at 375 degrees for 30 minutes.

**Pour** . . . . . . . tomato sauce over loaf.

**Sprinkle** . . . . with oregano.

**Bake** . . . . . . . for 20 minutes longer.

**Yields** . . . . . . 4-6 servings.

Peggy O. Munter
Moore Sr. H. S., Moore, Oklahoma
Arlene Maisel
Highland Park H. S., Highland Park, New Jersey

## BEEF-STUFFED RIGATONI

1  12-oz. package rigatoni
1/3 c. each chopped onion, green pepper
1 clove of garlic, minced
1 tbsp. oil
1 1/2 lb. ground chuck
Salt
1 tsp. mixed Italian herbs
1 pkg. frozen chopped spinach, cooked,
   drained thoroughly
3/4 c. shredded Parmesan cheese
1  14 1/2-oz. can Italian tomatoes
1  8-oz. can tomato sauce
1  3-oz. can mushrooms
1  8-oz. package mozzarella cheese

**Cook** ....... rigatoni in 4 quarts boiling salted water in large saucepan for 8 minutes; do not overcook.
**Drain** ...... and rinse with cold water.
**Saute** ...... onion, green pepper and garlic in oil in skillet until tender.
**Add** ....... ground chuck, 1 1/2 teaspoons salt and herbs.
**Cook** ....... until beef is browned, stirring frequently.
**Combine** .... 2/3 of the ground beef mixture with spinach and 1/4 cup Parmesan cheese in bowl, mixing well.
**Add** ....... tomatoes, tomato sauce and mushrooms to remaining ground beef in skillet.
**Cook** ....... over low heat until thickened, stirring occasionally.
**Stuff** ...... rigatoni with spinach mixture.
**Layer** ...... half the sauce and all the rigatoni in greased casserole.
**Top** ........ with remaining sauce, mozzarella cheese and remaining Parmesan cheese.
**Bake** ....... at 350 degrees for 30 to 40 minutes or until bubbly.
**Yields** ...... 8 servings.

Photograph for this recipe on this page.

## ITALIAN NOODLE CASSEROLE

1 lb. ground beef
1/2 lb. sausage
1 c. chopped onion
1 green pepper, chopped
1  12-oz. can whole kernel corn
1 can tomato soup
1  8-oz. can tomato sauce
1/2 c. sliced stuffed olives
1 clove of garlic, minced
1 tsp. salt
1  8-oz. package wide noodles, cooked
8 oz. Cheddar cheese, shredded

**Brown** ...... ground beef and sausage in skillet, stirring until crumbly; drain.
**Add** ....... next 9 ingredients and half the cheese, mixing well.
**Spoon** ...... into 3-quart casserole.
**Top** ........ with remaining cheese.
**Bake** ....... covered, at 350 degrees for 45 minutes.
**Bake** ....... uncovered, for 10 minutes longer.
**Yields** ...... 6 servings.

Dorothy Scott
Ponca City Sr. H. S., Ponca City, Oklahoma

## BEST MANICOTTI

1/2 lb. ground beef
1 clove of garlic, crushed
1 c. cream-style cottage cheese
4 oz. mozzarella cheese, shredded

1/2 tsp. salt
1/2 c. mayonnaise
8 manicotti, cooked, drained
1  16-oz. jar spaghetti sauce
1/2 tsp. oregano
Parmesan cheese

Brown . . . . . . ground beef with garlic in skillet, stirring until crumbly; drain.
Combine . . . . cottage cheese with next 3 ingredients in bowl, mixing well.
Stir . . . . . . . . in ground beef.
Fill . . . . . . . . each manicotti with 1/4 cup ground beef mixture.
Place . . . . . . . in single layer in baking dish.
Top . . . . . . . . with remaining ground beef mixture, and remaining ingredients.
Bake . . . . . . . covered, at 350 degrees for 15 minutes.
Bake . . . . . . . uncovered, for 10 minutes longer.
Yields . . . . . . 4 servings.

Photograph for this recipe on page 103.

## TAGLIARINI

1 lb. ground beef
1 onion, chopped
2 tbsp. chopped green pepper
Salt and pepper to taste
1 sm. can mushrooms
1 can niblet corn
2 c. tomato juice
1 med. package noodles, cooked
1/2 lb. Cheddar cheese, grated

Brown . . . . . . ground beef with onion and green pepper in skillet, stirring until crumbly.
Stir . . . . . . . . in remaining ingredients except cheese.
Pour . . . . . . . into casserole.
Top . . . . . . . . with cheese.
Bake . . . . . . . covered, at 350 degrees for 45 minutes.

Mary Jane Nash
Bay Sch., Bay, Arkansas

## ITALIAN MEAT PIE

1 lb. ground beef
2/3 c. oats

1/2 c. catsup
1/2 c. chopped onion
1 egg
3/4 tsp. salt
1/4 tsp. each pepper, garlic powder
2 med. zucchini sliced, cooked, drained
1/2 c. tomato sauce
1/2 c. chopped olives
1/2 tsp. each oregano, basil
Dash of Tabasco sauce
2 tbsp. Parmesan cheese
1 c. grated mozzarella cheese

Combine . . . . first 8 ingredients in bowl, mixing well.
Press . . . . . . . into 9-inch pie plate, thinner on bottom than side.
Bake . . . . . . . at 400 degrees for 20 minutes; drain.
Combine . . . . zucchini and next 5 ingredients in bowl, mixing well.
Spoon . . . . . . into prepared pie plate.
Top . . . . . . . . with cheeses.
Bake . . . . . . . at 350 degrees for 20 to 25 minutes or until cooked through.
Yields . . . . . . 5 servings.

Bonnie Roelofs
Evangelical Christian Sch., Cordova, Tennessee

## MEAT LOAF FLORENTINE

1 1/2 lb. ground beef
1  10-oz. package frozen chopped spinach, thawed
1 egg, slightly beaten
1/2 c. fine dry bread crumbs
1/2 c. chopped onion
1/2 c. milk
1 tbsp. brown mustard
1 1/4 tsp. salt
1/2 tsp. pepper
1/4 tsp. garlic powder

Combine . . . . all ingredients in large bowl, mixing well.
Shape . . . . . . into loaf.
Place . . . . . . . in shallow 8 x 12-inch baking dish.
Bake . . . . . . . at 350 degrees for 1 1/4 hours.
Let . . . . . . . . stand for 10 minutes before cutting.

Sybil B. Murphy
Northwood H. S., Pittsboro, North Carolina

## ITALIAN SPAGHETTI SAUCE WITH MEATBALLS

1 1/2 lb. ground beef
2 tbsp. olive oil
1 med. onion, chopped
4 oz. button mushrooms
3 cloves of garlic, minced
2 tbsp. (or more) minced parsley
1/8 tsp. oregano
1 tsp. sugar
3/4 tsp. pepper
Salt
1  29-oz. can plum tomatoes
1 green pepper, chopped
2 oz. red wine
1  6-oz. can tomato paste
2 slices bread
2 eggs
1 tbsp. flour
2 tbsp. cracker meal, Parmesan cheese

**Cook** . . . . . . . 1/2 pound ground beef in skillet until lightly browned, stirring constantly.
**Add** . . . . . . . olive oil, onion, mushrooms, 2/3 of the garlic, 1 tablespoon parsley, oregano, sugar, 1/2 teaspoon pepper and 1 tablespoon or less salt, mixing well.
**Cook** . . . . . . . for 10 minutes, stirring frequently.
**Place** . . . . . . . in blender container with tomatoes and green pepper; process for several seconds.
**Combine** . . . . with wine, tomato paste and 2 cups water in skillet, mixing well.
**Cook** . . . . . . . for 20 minutes.
**Soak** . . . . . . . bread in water in bowl; squeeze out excess moisture.
**Combine** . . . . with remaining 1 pound ground beef, minced garlic, 1 tablespoon parsley, 1/4 teaspoon pepper, 1 teaspoon salt and remaining ingredients in bowl, mixing well.
**Shape** . . . . . . into balls.
**Drop** . . . . . . . into sauce.
**Cook** . . . . . . . for 20 minutes.
**Let** . . . . . . . . stand for 10 minutes.
**Serve** . . . . . . over spaghetti.

Betty Jeanne Callaway Schuchmann
Hughes-Quinn Jr. H. S., E. St. Louis, Illinois

## CLASSIC LASAGNA

1 med. onion, chopped
2 cloves of garlic, crushed
4 tbsp. olive oil
1  28-oz. can tomatoes
2  6-oz. cans tomato paste
1 tsp. salt
1/2 tsp. basil
1/2 tsp. oregano
1/8 tsp. crushed red pepper
1 lb. ground chuck
1/2 lb. ground lean pork
1/4 c. chopped parsley
2 eggs
1/2 c. fine dry bread crumbs
Parmesan cheese
1/8 tsp. pepper
1 lb. curly edge lasagna noodles, cooked
1 lb. ricotta or cream-style cottage cheese
1/2 lb. mozzarella cheese, sliced

**Saute** . . . . . . onion and garlic in 2 tablespoons oil in saucepan until lightly browned.
**Add** . . . . . . . tomatoes, tomato paste, 1/2 cup water, 1/2 teaspoon salt, herbs and red pepper.
**Simmer** . . . . . covered, 1 hour, stirring occasionally.
**Combine** . . . . ground chuck and pork, parsley, eggs, bread crumbs, 2 tablespoons Parmesan cheese, pepper and remaining 1/2 teaspoon salt in bowl, mixing well.
**Shape** . . . . . . into 1/2-inch meatballs.
**Saute** . . . . . . in remaining 2 tablespoons oil in skillet until brown.
**Add** . . . . . . . to sauce and simmer 15 minutes.
**Layer** . . . . . . sauce with meatballs, lasagna noodles, Parmesan cheese and dollops of ricotta cheese alternately into casserole, repeating until all ingredients are used.
**Top** . . . . . . . . with mozzarella cheese.
**Bake** . . . . . . . at 375 degrees for 25 minutes or until bubbly.

Photograph for this recipe on page 139.

## JAMAICAN MEAT PATTIES

2/3 c. finely chopped scallions
3 tbsp. oil

1 lb. lean ground beef
1 c. finely chopped fresh tomatoes
1 1/2 tsp. each salt, garlic powder,
   dry mustard
1/2 tsp. pepper
1/4 tsp. red pepper
1 tsp. hot sauce
2 eggs, slightly beaten
1 box pastry mix

**Saute** ...... scallions in oil in skillet until tender.
**Add** ....... ground beef.
**Cook** ....... until lightly browned, stirring constantly.
**Add** ....... next 7 ingredients.
**Cook** ....... for 5 minutes or until tomatoes are tender, stirring frequently; remove from heat.
**Mix** ........ in eggs.
**Cook** ....... over low heat for 1 to 2 minutes or until thick, stirring constantly; cool.
**Prepare** ..... pastry mix, using package directions.
**Roll** ....... out 1/16 inch thick on floured surface.
**Cut** ........ into 6-inch circles.
**Spoon** ...... 1/2 cup ground beef mixture onto each circle.
**Fold** ....... over, enclosing filling; seal edges.
**Place** ....... on baking sheet; prick tops with fork.
**Bake** ....... at 425 degrees for 20 minutes.
**Yields** ...... 10 servings.

Lucille H. Wiggins
I. C. Norcom H. S., Portsmouth, Virginia

## CHILI CON CARNE PIE

1 1/2 lb. ground beef
1/2 c. chopped onion
1 clove of garlic, minced
1  8-oz. can tomato sauce
1  16-oz. can whole tomatoes
1  20-oz. can kidney beans
1 1/2 tsp. salt
1 tbsp. chili powder
1/4 c. Parmesan cheese
3/4 c. cornmeal
1/4 c. flour
1 1/2 tsp. baking powder
1 egg

1/4 c. shortening, melted
1/2 c. milk
1 tbsp. parsley

**Brown** ...... ground beef with onion and garlic in skillet, stirring until crumbly.
**Add** ....... tomato sauce, tomatoes, beans, 1 teaspoon salt, chili powder and cheese, mixing well.
**Pour** ....... into casserole.
**Mix** ........ cornmeal, flour, baking powder and 1/2 teaspoon salt in bowl.
**Add** ....... egg and shortening, mixing well.
**Stir** ........ in milk and parsley gradually.
**Drop** ....... by spoonfuls onto ground beef mixture.
**Bake** ....... at 425 degrees for 15 to 20 minutes or until topping is golden brown.
**Yields** ...... 6-8 servings.

Mary Louise Hedrick
Doddridge County H. S., West Union, West Virginia

## MEXICORN CORN BREAD

1 lb. ground beef
2 lg. onions, chopped
1 c. cornmeal
1 c. milk
1/2 tsp. soda
1 tsp. salt
2 eggs
1/2 c. oil
2 jalapeno peppers, chopped
1 can Mexicorn
1 lb. mild Cheddar cheese, grated

**Brown** ...... ground beef with half the onions in skillet, stirring until crumbly.
**Combine** .... next 6 ingredients in bowl, mixing well.
**Pour** ....... half the cornmeal batter into baking dish.
**Layer** ...... ground beef mixture, remaining onions, jalapeno peppers, Mexicorn and cheese over batter.
**Cover** ...... with remaining batter.
**Bake** ....... at 375 degrees for 45 minutes or until golden brown.
**Yields** ...... 8-10 servings.

Becky Raney
Central Heights Sch., Nacogdoches, Texas

## BEEFY BAKED BURRITOS

*1 lb. ground beef*
*1 env. taco seasoning mix*
*1  16-oz. can refried beans*
*1  8-oz. can enchilada sauce*
*1 head lettuce, chopped*
*1 pkg. 12-in. flour tortillas*
*1 lb. Colby cheese, shredded*
*1 pt. sour cream*
*1 med. onion, chopped*

**Brown** ...... ground beef in skillet, stirring until crumbly; drain.
**Stir** ........ in taco seasoning mix and 1/2 cup water.
**Simmer** ..... for 15 minutes.
**Combine** .... beans and sauce in saucepan, mixing well.
**Cook** ....... until heated through.
**Place** ....... spoonful ground beef and lettuce on each tortilla, rolling to enclose filling.
**Place** ....... seam side down in greased 9 x 13-inch baking dish.
**Pour** ....... bean mixture over top.
**Sprinkle** .... with cheese.
**Bake** ....... at 400 degrees for 15 to 20 minutes or until heated through.
**Garnish** ..... with sour cream and onion.

Glenda Muller
Ballard H. S., Huxley, Iowa

## CHEESY MEXICAN CASSEROLE

*1 1/2 lb. ground beef*
*1/2 c. chopped onion*
*1 tsp. salt*
*2 tsp. chili powder*
*12 corn tortillas*
*1 can cream of chicken soup*
*1 can Mexican tomatoes*
*2 med. cans Mexican beans*
*1 lb. Velveeta cheese, shredded*

**Brown** ...... ground beef with onion in skillet, stirring until crumbly.
**Add** ....... salt and chili powder, mixing well.
**Place** ....... 6 tortillas in 6 x 10-inch baking dish.
**Mix** ........ soup and tomatoes in bowl.
**Layer** ...... ground beef mixture, beans and cheese over tortillas.

**Cover** ...... with remaining tortillas.
**Pour** ....... soup mixture over all.
**Bake** ....... covered, at 350 degrees for 45 minutes.
**Yields** ...... 8 servings.

Joanne M. Wooley
F. D. Roosevelt H. S., Hyde Park, New York

## EL DORADO BEEF CASSEROLE

*1 lb. ground beef*
*1 tsp. minced onion*
*1/2 tsp. garlic salt*
*1/2 c. tomato sauce*
*1 c. sliced ripe olives*
*1 c. sour cream*
*1 c. small curd cottage cheese*
*3 or 4 green chilies, chopped*
*1 pkg. tortilla chips*
*2 c. grated Monterey Jack cheese*

**Brown** ...... ground beef in skillet, stirring until crumbly; drain.
**Add** ....... onion, garlic salt, tomato sauce and olives, mixing well.
**Simmer** ..... until heated through.
**Mix** ........ next 3 ingredients in bowl.
**Crush** ...... tortilla chips slightly, reserving a few whole chips for garnish.
**Layer** ...... half the chips, ground beef mixture, sour cream mixture and grated cheese alternately until all ingredients are used.
**Bake** ....... at 350 degrees for 30 to 35 minutes or until bubbly.
**Garnish** ..... with whole tortilla chips.
**Yields** ...... 8-10 servings.

Karen L. Rhodes
England H. S., England, Arkansas

## EL GANDO

*2 lb. ground beef*
*4 c. tomatoes*
*1 pkg. chili mix*
*Salt to taste*
*1 can Cheddar cheese soup*
*1/3 c. milk*
*1 box yellow rice mix, cooked*
*1/2 c. each chopped onion, olives*
*1/2 c. grated cheese*
*2 c. crushed corn chips*

**Brown** . . . . . . ground beef in skillet, stirring until crumbly; drain.
**Add** . . . . . . . next 3 ingredients, mixing well.
**Simmer** . . . . . until liquid is reduced.
**Cook** . . . . . . . soup and milk in saucepan until heated through.
**Layer** . . . . . . half the ground beef mixture, rice and remaining ground beef mixture in casserole.
**Pour** . . . . . . . soup mixture over all.
**Sprinkle** . . . . with onion, olives and cheese.
**Top** . . . . . . . . with corn chips.
**Bake** . . . . . . . at 350 degrees until bubbly.
**Yields** . . . . . . 8-10 servings.

Lynne Otwell
Beauregard H. S., Opelika, Alabama

## TEXAS ENCHILADA CASSEROLE

*1 1/2 lb. ground beef*
*Chopped onion to taste*
*1 can ranch-style beans*
*12 flour tortillas*
*8 oz. Velveeta cheese, sliced*
*1 can cream of chicken soup*
*1 can Ro-Tel*

**Brown** . . . . . . ground beef with onion in skillet, stirring until crumbly; drain.
**Add** . . . . . . . beans, mixing well.
**Place** . . . . . . . 6 tortillas in casserole.
**Layer** . . . . . . ground beef mixture, cheese and remaining tortillas in casserole.
**Mix** . . . . . . . . soup and Ro-Tel in bowl.
**Pour** . . . . . . . over tortillas.
**Bake** . . . . . . . at 350 degrees for 45 minutes.

Amanda Goodson
Cedar Hill H. S., Cedar Hill, Texas

## BEEF AND BEAN ENCHILADAS

*1 1/2 lb. ground beef*
*1 med. onion, chopped*
*1 16-oz. can refried beans*
*1 tsp. salt*
*1/8 tsp. garlic powder*
*1/3 c. red taco sauce*
*1 c. chopped ripe olives*
*12 corn tortillas*
*Oil*
*2 10-oz. cans enchilada sauce*
*Grated cheese to taste*

**Brown** . . . . . . ground beef with onion in skillet, stirring until crumbly; drain.
**Add** . . . . . . . next 5 ingredients, mixing well.
**Cook** . . . . . . . until bubbly.
**Soften** . . . . . tortillas in oil in skillet; drain.
**Cook** . . . . . . . enchilada sauce in saucepan until heated through.
**Pour** . . . . . . . half the sauce into shallow 3-quart baking dish.
**Spoon** . . . . . . 1/3 cup ground beef mixture onto each tortilla, rolling to enclose filling.
**Place** . . . . . . . seam side down in sauce in baking dish.
**Pour** . . . . . . . remaining enchilada sauce over all.
**Top** . . . . . . . . with cheese.
**Bake** . . . . . . . at 350 degrees for 15 minutes or until heated through.
**Garnish** . . . . . with sour cream and green chile salsa.

Nancy Blue
Mount Vernon H. S., Mount Vernon, Washington

## RO-TEL ENCHILADAS

*2 lb. hamburger*
*1 can Ro-Tel*
*2 sm. cans tomato juice*
*2 tsp. chili powder*
*Garlic powder and seasoned salt to taste*
*1 pkg. tortillas*
*1 can kidney beans, drained*
*1 med. onion, minced*
*2 to 3 c. shredded cheese*
*1 can mushroom soup*

**Brown** . . . . . . hamburger in skillet, stirring until crumbly; drain.
**Add** . . . . . . . Ro-Tel, tomato juice, chili powder, garlic powder and seasoned salt to taste.
**Simmer** . . . . . for 10 to 15 minutes.
**Layer** . . . . . . tortillas, half the hamburger mixture, all the kidney beans, onion and cheese in large casserole.
**Top** . . . . . . . . with remaining hamburger mixture and soup.
**Bake** . . . . . . . at 350 degrees for 20 minutes or until bubbly.
**Garnish** . . . . . with additional cheese.

Sandra Whitman
Porum H. S., Porum, Oklahoma

## MEXICAN CORN CHIP PIE

1 lg. bag corn chips
1 lg. can chili
1 lg. onion, chopped
2 c. grated cheese

Layer ...... half the chips, chili and onion and 3/4 cup cheese in casserole.
Repeat ..... layers with remaining ingredients, ending with cheese.
Bake ....... at 350 degrees for 15 minutes or until heated through.
Yields ...... 8 servings.

Doris S. Hartman
Mexia H. S., Mexia, Texas

## MEXICAN MEAT LOAF

2 lb. ground beef
1 sm. onion, chopped
1   4-oz. can chopped green chilies
1 clove of garlic, minced
1 can chicken with rice soup
1/2 can mushroom soup
4 oz. tomato paste
2   8-oz. cans taco sauce
Salt and pepper to taste
12 corn tortillas
1 c. grated cheese

Brown ...... ground beef in skillet, stirring until crumbly; drain.
Add ....... next 9 ingredients, mixing well.
Simmer ..... for 5 minutes.
Layer ...... half the tortillas and ground beef mixture in 9 x 13-inch baking pan.
Top ........ with remaining tortillas, ground beef mixture and cheese.
Bake ....... covered, at 350 degrees for 35 minutes.
Yields ...... 18 servings.

Helen Boren
Ponca City H. S., Ponca City, Oklahoma

## MEXICAN PUFF

1 lb. lean ground beef
1   4-oz. can green chilies, chopped
1/2 c. finely chopped onion
Salt and pepper to taste
3 eggs, separated

1/8 tsp. cream of tartar
2 c. shredded longhorn cheese

Brown ...... ground beef in skillet, stirring until crumbly; drain.
Add ....... chilies, onion, salt and pepper, mixing well.
Cook ....... until onion is tender, stirring frequently.
Spoon ...... into 1 1/2-quart souffle dish.
Beat ....... egg whites and cream of tartar in bowl until stiff peaks form. Do not overbeat.
Beat ....... egg yolks in bowl until thick and lemon colored.
Stir ........ in cheese.
Fold ....... into egg white mixture.
Spoon ...... over ground beef mixture.
Bake ....... at 400 degrees for 20 to 25 minutes or until center is set.
Serve ...... immediately.
Yields ...... 4 servings.

Joy L. Manson
Miami H. S., Miami, Arizona

## COMBINATION NACHOS

1 lb. hamburger
1 pkg. taco seasoning mix
1/2 can refried beans
1 pkg. tortilla chips
Cheddar cheese, grated
Monterey Jack cheese, grated
Jalapeno peppers, chopped

Brown ...... hamburger in skillet, stirring until crumbly; drain.
Add ....... taco seasoning mix with water according to package directions, and refried beans, mixing well.
Layer ...... chips, hamburger mixture, Cheddar cheese and Monterey Jack cheese in baking pan.
Top ........ with jalapeno peppers.
Bake ....... at 425 degrees until cheese is melted.

Annie Rust
Blanchard H. S., Blanchard, Oklahoma

## SHOOTING STARS

1 lb. hamburger
1 lg. green pepper, chopped

1 med. onion, chopped
1 pkg. dry onion soup mix
1 can enchilada sauce
1 can cream of chicken soup
1 can green chilies, chopped
1 can Ro-Tel
12 tortillas, cut into pieces
1 jar green olives, sliced
1 can ripe olives, sliced
12 oz. Cheddar cheese, grated
1 c. chopped pecans

**Brown** . . . . . . hamburger with green pepper and onion, stirring until crumbly; drain.
**Stir** . . . . . . . . in onion soup mix and 1/2 cup water.
**Simmer** . . . . . for 5 minutes; remove from heat.
**Combine** . . . . next 4 ingredients in bowl, mixing well.
**Layer** . . . . . . tortillas, hamburger mixture, enchilada sauce mixture, olives, cheese and pecans alternately in large casserole until all ingredients are used, ending with pecans.
**Bake** . . . . . . . at 350 degrees for 1 hour.
**Yields** . . . . . . 8 servings.

Ann Knopfel
Waukomis Sch., Waukomis, Oklahoma

## SOUTH-OF-THE-BORDER HASH

1 lb. ground beef
2 onions, chopped
2 green peppers, chopped
2 16-oz. cans tomatoes
1 tsp. chili powder
1/2 tsp. red pepper
1 c. rice
Salt and pepper to taste

**Brown** . . . . . . ground beef with onions and green peppers in skillet, stirring until crumbly.
**Add** . . . . . . . remaining ingredients, mixing well.
**Spoon** . . . . . . into 2 1/2-quart baking dish.
**Bake** . . . . . . . at 350 degrees for 45 minutes.
**Yields** . . . . . . 6-8 servings.

Ellon Ramey
Gate City H. S., Gate City, Virginia

## MEXICAN LASAGNA

1 1/2 lb. hamburger
1 onion, chopped
2 8-oz. cans tomato sauce
2 tbsp. chili powder
2 c. shredded Cheddar cheese
1 c. shredded Monterey Jack cheese
1 pkg. tortillas
Sour cream

**Brown** . . . . . . hamburger with onion in skillet, stirring until crumbly.
**Add** . . . . . . . next 2 ingredients with 1 1/2 cups water, mixing well.
**Simmer** . . . . . for 20 minutes.
**Combine** . . . . both cheeses in bowl.
**Spread** . . . . . tortillas with sour cream.
**Layer** . . . . . . tortillas, hamburger mixture and combined cheeses in 9 x 13-inch baking pan.
**Garnish** . . . . . with ripe olives.
**Bake** . . . . . . . at 350 degrees for 20 minutes.
**Yields** . . . . . . 6 servings.

Kristi Speaker
Washington Sr. H. S., Sioux Falls, South Dakota

## GOOD-TO-EAT TACO CASSEROLE

1 lb. ground beef
2 pkg. taco seasoning mix
1 tsp. each salt, pepper
3 8-oz. cans tomato sauce
2 cans ranch-style beans
1 10-oz. package corn chips
1 lb. Cheddar cheese, shredded

**Brown** . . . . . . ground beef in skillet, stirring until crumbly; drain.
**Add** . . . . . . . next 5 ingredients and 1/2 cup water, mixing well.
**Cook** . . . . . . . for 5 to 10 minutes or until blended.
**Layer** . . . . . . corn chips, ground beef mixture and cheese, alternately in 9 x 13-inch baking dish until all ingredients are used, ending with cheese.
**Bake** . . . . . . . at 350 degrees for 30 minutes.
**Yields** . . . . . . 8 servings.

Judy Meek
Marshall Jr. H. S., Wichita, Kansas

## NORWEGIAN MEATBALLS

*6 tbsp. finely chopped onion*
*2 tbsp. butter*
*1 lb. ground beef*
*1/2 lb. ground pork*
*1 slice bread, crumbled*
*1/2 c. milk*
*1 egg, beaten*
*1/2 tsp. nutmeg*
*1/4 tsp. allspice*
*1 3/4 tsp. salt*
*3 tsp. sugar*
*3 tbsp. flour*
*1 c. cream*

**Saute** ...... onion in butter in skillet until tender; remove onion.
**Combine** .... sauteed onion, next 7 ingredients, 1 1/4 teaspoons salt and 2 teaspoons sugar in bowl, mixing well.
**Shape** ...... into 1-inch balls.
**Brown** ...... in pan drippings; remove to warm platter.
**Add** ....... remaining teaspoon sugar, 1/2 teaspoon salt and flour to pan drippings.
**Cook** ....... until thick, stirring constantly; remove from heat.
**Stir** ........ in 1 cup water and cream.
**Cook** ....... until thick, stirring constantly. Do not boil.
**Yields** ...... 40 meatballs.

Audrey Starkey
Keene H. S., Keene, New Hampshire

## POLYNESIAN PARTY DISH

*2 lb. ground beef*
*1 lg. onion, chopped*
*1 lg. green pepper, chopped*
*1 c. chopped celery*
*1 c. rice, cooked*

*1 can cream of mushroom soup*
*2 cans cream of chicken soup*
*1/4 c. soy sauce*
*2 tbsp. brown sugar*
*1  4-oz. can mushrooms*
*1/2 c. slivered onion*
*2 cans water chestnuts, sliced*
*1 sm. can Chinese noodles*

**Brown** ...... ground beef with chopped onion, green pepper and celery in skillet, stirring until crumbly.
**Combine** .... with next 8 ingredients in 9 x 13-inch baking dish, mixing well.
**Top** ........ with noodles.
**Bake** ....... at 350 degrees for 1 hour.
**Yields** ...... 12-15 servings.

Linsae Snider
Robert E. Lee H. S., Baytown, Texas

## SWEDISH MEATBALLS IN SAUCE

*1 lb. ground beef*
*2 tbsp. finely chopped onion*
*1/2 c. fine dry bread crumbs*
*1 egg, beaten*
*1 tbsp. brown sugar*
*1/8 tsp. allspice*
*1/4 tsp. nutmeg*
*Salt and pepper*
*Milk*
*Flour*
*4 tbsp. oil*

**Combine** .... first 7 ingredients, 1 teaspoon salt, 1/8 teaspoon pepper and 2/3 cup milk in bowl, mixing well.
**Shape** ...... into 16 balls.
**Coat** ....... with flour.
**Brown** ...... in oil in skillet; remove meatballs.
**Add** ....... 2/3 cup milk to pan drippings, mixing well.
**Stir** ........ in 2 tablespoons flour mixed with 1/3 cup water.
**Cook** ....... until thick, stirring constantly.
**Season** ..... with salt and pepper.
**Add** ....... meatballs.
**Simmer** ..... covered, for 15 minutes.
**Yields** ...... 4 servings.

Fleda Lambert
Duncanville H. S., Duncanville, Texas

# Nutrition Chart

This chart details the nutrients provided by ground beef and the ways in which the body uses them.

| NUTRIENT | HOW USED IN THE BODY |
|---|---|
| **Iron** | Helps make hemoglobin (the red pigment in blood) and carry oxygen to issues. |
| **Phosphorus** | Forms bones and teeth. |
| **Copper** | Forms hemoglobin. |
| **Sodium, Potassium** | Helps regulate bodily functions. |
| **Vitamin A** | Promotes growth and repair of body tissues, builds good health, maintains normal vision and healthy eyes, keeps skin soft and mucous membranes healthy. |
| **Vitamin $B_1$ (thiamine)** | Important in the transformation of carbohydrates to energy forms the body can use and in the normal functioning of heart, nerves, and muscles. |
| **Vitamin $B_2$ (riboflavin)** | Maintains good vision, builds healthy skin and mouth tissues, aids in the conversion of carbohydrates to energy forms. |
| **Niacin** | Builds and maintains healthy skin and mucous membranes, aids in the use of carbohydrates and in the healthy functioning of the nervous system. |
| **Vitamin $B_6$ (pyridoxine)** | Helps the body use amino and fatty acids. |
| **Vitamin $B_{12}$** | Necessary for the formation of red blood cells and the proper functioning of the brain. |

# Grilling Suggestions

For an outdoor party or picnic, grilled hamburgers are perfect. Here are a few rules to remember on outdoor cooking.

1. For an easy-to-clean grill, line the bowl with heavy aluminum foil.

2. A gravel base is needed if the fire bowl doesn't have openings in the sides and bottom. This basic will allow the fire to breathe. A gravel base can be formed by arranging small stones (about 1/2 to 1 inch in diameter) in the bottom of the bowl.

3. Charcoal should be arranged over the gravel base. If the bowl has openings in the sides and bottom, you will not need the gravel base.

4. Start your fire about 45 minutes before you plan to cook. Be sure to have a good bed of glowing coals.

5. Coals should glow but not flame. Tap each coal with fire tongs to rid it of the gray ash. You will get better heat results.

6. Meat is best when cooked at a low or moderate temperature. So check the coals for the best time to begin cooking. A very large pile of coals can give too much heat for the meat; do not build too large a fire.

7. Spread coals so they are about an inch apart. They will provide a more even heat.

8. Keep the rack far enough from the coals so that the flames from the fat drippings will not burn the meat. Three inches is a good distance to remember.

9. The rack on which you place the patties should be lightly greased.

10. Allow 5 minutes on each side for hamburgers to cook.

11. Choose the sauce you wish to serve and have it prepared as soon as the hamburgers are ready.

# Equivalent Chart

| | WHEN RECIPE CALLS FOR: | YOU NEED: |
|---|---|---|
| **BREAD & CEREAL** | 1 c. soft bread crumbs | 2 slices |
| | 1 c. fine dry bread crumbs | 4-5 slices |
| | 1 c. small bread cubes | 2 slices |
| | 1 c. fine cracker crumbs | 24 saltines |
| | 1 c. fine graham cracker crumbs | 14 crackers |
| | 1 c. vanilla wafer crumbs | 22 wafers |
| | 1 c. crushed corn flakes | 3 c. uncrushed |
| | 4 c. cooked macaroni | 1 8-oz. package |
| | 3 1/2 c. cooked rice | 1 c. uncooked |
| **DAIRY** | 1 c. freshly grated cheese | 1/4 lb. |
| | 1 c. cottage cheese or sour cream | 1 8-oz. carton |
| | 2/3 c. evaporated milk | 1 sm. can |
| | 1 2/3 c. evaporated milk | 1 tall can |
| | 1 c. whipped cream | 1/2 c. heavy cream |
| **SWEET** | 1 c. semisweet chocolate pieces | 1 6-oz. package |
| | 2 c. granulated sugar | 1 lb. |
| | 4 c. sifted confectioners' sugar | 1 lb. |
| | 2 1/4 c. packed brown sugar | 1 lb. |
| **MEAT** | 3 c. diced cooked meat | 1 lb., cooked |
| | 2 c. ground cooked meat | 1 lb., cooked |
| | 4 c. diced cooked chicken | 1 5-lb. chicken |
| **NUTS** | 1 c. chopped nuts | 4 oz. shelled |
| | | 1 lb. unshelled |
| **VEGETABLES** | 4 c. sliced or diced raw potatoes | 4 medium |
| | 2 c. cooked green beans | 1/2 lb. fresh or 1 16-oz. can |
| | 1 c. chopped onion | 1 large |
| | 4 c. shredded cabbage | 1 lb. |
| | 2 c. canned tomatoes | 1 16-oz. can |
| | 1 c. grated carrot | 1 large |
| | 2 1/2 c. lima beans or red beans | 1 c. dried, cooked |
| | 1 4-oz. can mushrooms | 1/2 lb. fresh |
| **FRUIT** | 4 c. sliced or chopped apples | 4 medium |
| | 2 c. pitted cherries | 4 c. unpitted |
| | 3 to 4 tbsp. lemon juice plus 1 tsp. grated peel | 1 lemon |
| | 1/3 c. orange juice plus 2 tsp. grated peel | 1 orange |
| | 1 c. mashed banana | 3 medium |
| | 4 c. cranberries | 1 lb. |
| | 3 c. shredded coconut | 1/2 lb. |
| | 4 c. sliced peaches | 8 medium |
| | 1 c. pitted dates or candied fruit | 1 8-oz. package |
| | 2 c. pitted prunes | 1 12-oz. package |
| | 3 c. raisins | 1 15-oz. package |

## COMMON EQUIVALENTS

| | |
|---|---|
| 1 tbsp. = 3 tsp. | 4 qt. = 1 gal. |
| 2 tbsp. = 1 oz. | 6 1/2 to 8-oz. can = 1 c. |
| 4 tbsp. = 1/4 oz. | 10 1/2 to 12-oz. can = 1 1/4 c. |
| 5 tbsp. + 1 tsp. = 1/3 c. | 14 to 16-oz. can (No. 300) = 1 3/4 c. |
| 8 tbsp. = 1/2 c. | 16 to 17-oz. can (No. 303) = 2 c. |
| 12 tbsp. = 3/4 c. | 1-lb. 4-oz. can or 1-pt. 2-oz. can (No. 2) = 2 1/2 c. |
| 16 tbsp. = 1 c. | 1-lb. 13-oz. can (No. 2 1/2) = 3 1/2 c. |
| 1 c. = 8 oz. or 1/2 pt. | 3-lb. 3-oz. can or 46-oz. can or 1-qt. 14-oz. can = 5 3/4 c. |
| 4 c. = 1 qt. | 6 1/2-lb. or 7-lb. 5-oz. can (No. 10) = 12 to 13 c. |

# Metric Conversion Chart

### VOLUME

| | | |
|---|---|---|
| 1 tsp. | = | 4.9 cc |
| 1 tbsp. | = | 14.7 cc |
| 1/3 c. | = | 28.9 cc |
| 1/8 c. | = | 29.5 cc |
| 1/4 c. | = | 59.1 cc |
| 1/2 c. | = | 118.3 cc |
| 3/4 c. | = | 177.5 cc |
| 1 c. | = | 236.7 cc |
| 2 c. | = | 473.4 cc |
| 1 fl. oz. | = | 29.5 cc |
| 4 oz. | = | 118.3 cc |
| 8 oz. | = | 236.7 cc |

| | | |
|---|---|---|
| 1 pt. | = | 473.4 cc |
| 1 qt. | = | .946 liters |
| 1 gal. | = | 3.7 liters |

### CONVERSION FACTORS

| | | | | |
|---|---|---|---|---|
| Liters | X | 1.056 | = | Liquid quarts |
| Quarts | X | 0.946 | = | Liters |
| Liters | X | 0.264 | = | Gallons |
| Gallons | X | 3.785 | = | Liters |
| Fluid ounces | X | 29.563 | = | Cubic centimeters |
| Cubic centimeters | X | 0.034 | = | Fluid ounces |
| Cups | X | 236.575 | = | Cubic centimeters |
| Tablespoons | X | 14.797 | = | Cubic centimeters |
| Teaspoons | X | 4.932 | = | Cubic centimeters |
| Bushels | X | 0.352 | = | Hectoliters |
| Hectoliters | X | 2.837 | = | Bushels |

### WEIGHT

| | | |
|---|---|---|
| 1 dry oz. | = | 28.3 Grams |
| 1 lb. | = | .454 Kilograms |

### CONVERSION FACTORS:

| | | | | |
|---|---|---|---|---|
| Ounces (Avoir.) | X | 28.349 | = | Grams |
| Grams | X | 0.035 | = | Ounces |
| Pounds | X | 0.454 | = | Kilograms |
| Kilograms | X | 2.205 | = | Pounds |

# Substitution Chart

| | INSTEAD OF: | USE: |
|---|---|---|
| **BAKING** | 1 tsp. baking powder<br>1 c. sifted all-purpose flour<br>1 c. sifted cake flour<br>1 tsp. cornstarch<br>(for thickening) | 1/4 tsp. soda plus 1/2 tsp. cream of tartar<br>1 c. plus 2 tbsp. sifted cake flour<br>1 c. minus 2 tbsp. sifted all-purpose flour<br>2 tbsp. flour or 1 tbsp. tapioca |
| **SWEET** | 1  1-oz. square chocolate<br>1 2/3 oz. semisweet<br>chocolate<br>1 c. granulated sugar<br><br>1 c. honey | 3 to 4 tbsp. cocoa plus 1 tsp. shortening<br>1 oz. unsweetened chocolate plus 4 tsp. sugar<br><br>1 c. packed brown sugar or 1 c. corn syrup,<br>molasses, honey minus 1/4 c. liquid<br>1 to 1 1/4 c. sugar plus 1/4 c. liquid or<br>1 c. molasses or corn syrup |
| **DAIRY** | 1 c. sweet milk<br>1 c. sour milk<br><br>1 c. buttermilk<br>1 c. light cream<br>1 c. heavy cream<br>1 c. sour cream | 1 c. sour milk or buttermilk plus 1/2 tsp. soda<br>1 c. sweet milk plus 1 tbsp. vinegar or<br>lemon juice of 1 c. buttermilk<br>1 c. sour milk or 1 c. yogurt<br>7/8 c. skim milk plus 3 tbsp. butter<br>3/4 c. skim milk plus 1/3 c. butter<br>7/8 c. sour milk plus 3 tbsp. butter |
| | 1 c. bread crumbs | 3/4 c. cracker crumbs |
| **SEASONINGS** | 1 c. catsup<br><br>1 tbsp. prepared mustard<br>1 tsp. Italian spice<br><br>1 tsp. allspice<br>1 medium onion<br><br>1 clove of garlic<br><br><br>1 tsp. lemon juice | 1 c. tomato sauce plus 1/2 c. sugar<br>plus 2 tbsp. vinegar<br>1 tsp. dry mustard<br>1/4 tsp. each oregano, basil, thyme, rosemary<br>plus dash of cayenne<br>1/2 tsp. cinnamon plus 1/8 tsp. cloves<br>1 tbsp. dried minced onion or 1 tsp. onion<br>powder<br>1/8 tsp. garlic powder or 1/8 tsp. instant<br>minced garlic or 3/4 tsp. garlic salt<br>or 5 drops of liquid garlic<br>1/2 tsp. vinegar |

# Index

# PHOTOGRAPHY CREDITS

*Cover: National Live Stock and Meat Board; National Pasta Association; Ruth Lundgren, Ltd.; Mazola Corn Oil; Rice Council; Best Foods: Hellmann's Real Mayonnaise; The McIlhenny Company (Tabasco); Spanish Green Olive Commission; Pickle Packers International, Inc.; Pet, Inc.; Pineapple Growers Association; California Iceberg Lettuce Commission; National Macaroni Institute; California Raisin Advisory Board; American Dairy Association; Evaporated Milk Association; National Dairy Council; The Quaker Oats Company; Glass Packaging Institute; Diamond Walnut Kitchen; American Mushroom Institute; California Bartlett Pears; Campbell Soup Company; Cling Peach Advisory Board; United Dairy Industry Association; Olive Advisory Board; and California Beef Council.*

Library of Congress Cataloging in Publication Data
Main entry under title:
Ground beef cookbook.

(Favorite recipes of home economics teachers)
Includes index.
1. Cookery (Beef) I. Favorite Recipes Press.
II. Series.
TX749.G886  1983      641.6'62    83-8925
ISBN 0-87197-152-6

# Favorite Recipes®
## of Home Economics Teachers
# COOKBOOKS

# Add to
# Your Cookbook Collection
# Select from These ALL-TIME
# Favorites

| BOOK TITLE | ITEM NUMBER |
|---|---|
| Foods From Foreign Nations (1977) 200 Pages | 01279 |
| Desserts — Revised Edition (1979) 304 Pages | 01422 |
| Breads (1981) 128 Pages | 15032 |
| Holiday Season Cookbook (1981) 168 Pages | 15040 |
| Meats (1981) 128 Pages | 14958 |
| Casseroles (1982) 128 Pages | 18295 |
| Desserts (1982) 232 Pages | 18635 |
| Outdoor Cookbook (1982) 128 Pages | 23000 |
| Today's All-Purpose Cookbook (1982) 168 Pages | 15717 |
| Cook Lite & Eat Right (1983) 128 Pages | 25372 |
| Ground Beef (1983) 168 Pages | 25380 |

# FOR ORDERING INFORMATION
## Write to:
Favorite Recipes Press
P. O. Box 77
Nashville, Tennessee 37202

BOOKS OFFERED SUBJECT TO AVAILABILITY.